# JUAN GOYTISOLO

# JUAN GOYTISOLO

## *The Case for Chaos*

ABIGAIL LEE SIX

*Yale University Press*
*New Haven and London · 1990*

*For my husband, Jean-Louis*

Set in Linotron Bembo by Best-set Typesetter Ltd., Hong Kong and
printed in Great Britain by The St. Edmundsbury Press

Library of Congress Catalog Card No: 90-70102
ISBN 0-300-04792-4

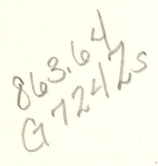

# Contents

# Acknowledgements

Thanks, first and foremost, to Dr Alison Sinclair of Clare College, Cambridge, my stimulating and ever helpful supervisor for the doctoral thesis on which this book is based. My thanks also go to the Master and Fellows of Sidney Sussex College, Cambridge, for their support throughout my studies and for the Research Fellowship which enabled me to finish my Ph.D. I am grateful to my colleagues in the Spanish Departments both at Cambridge and Queen Mary College, London, for their constructive criticism and moral support; and especially to my former examiners and now my colleagues, Dr David Henn of University College London and Ms Jo Labanyi of Birkbeck College, London, for their continuing interest and faith in my work.

I am indebted to the staff at the Computer Centre of Westfield College, London, for their help in the preparation of the revised manuscript and to Goytisolo's English publishers, Serpent's Tail, who were kind enough to lend me copies of American translations now out of print.

Finally, I thank Juan Goytisolo himself for being good enough to meet me and for the fruitful interchange of ideas that ensued.

# Editions and Abbreviations

For the trilogy, I have used recent Seix Barral editions, as these are the most easily available, though pagination is almost identical to the original Joaquín Mortiz ones. In the case of *Señas de identidad*, the first edition differs greatly from all subsequent ones; I follow the author and most critics in accepting the later version as definitive, though where a variant is of interest, I have indicated this in a note.

The translations are the British editions where these exist at the time of going to press, and the American ones where they do not. I am informed by Goytisolo's UK publishers, Serpent's Tail, however, that when *John the Landless* comes out in the United Kingdom, the pagination will match that of the American edition. I have had to alter the translated versions in quotations from time to time, where the rendering causes the specific point being illustrated to be lost. I have indicated this by adding 'adapted' to the page reference. I should like to make it clear that this is not intended to imply criticism of the translation.

All quotations from the Bible are taken from the King James Authorized Version.

*Señas de identidad* (1966), Biblioteca Universal Formentor (Barcelona: Seix Barral, 1980).

*Reivindicación del conde don Julián* (1970), Biblioteca Breve, second edition (Barcelona: Seix Barral, 1982).

*Juan sin tierra* (1975), Biblioteca Breve, third edition (Barcelona: Seix Barral, 1982).

*Makbara* (1980), Biblioteca Breve, fourth edition (Barcelona: Seix Barral, 1983).

*Paisajes después de la batalla*, Visio Tundali/Contemporáneos (Barcelona: Montesinos, 1982).

*Las virtudes del pájaro solitario*, Biblioteca Breve (Barcelona: Seix Barral, 1988).

*Marks of Identity* (1969–Grove, New York), translated by Gregory Rabassa (London: Serpent's Tail, 1988).

*Count Julian*, translated by Helen Lane (London: Serpent's Tail, 1989).

*Juan the Landless*, translated by Helen R. Lane (New York: Richard Seaver/Viking, 1977).

*Makbara*, translated by Helen R. Lane (New York: Seaver, 1981).

*Landscapes After the Battle* (1987–Seaver, New York), translated by Helen Lane (London: Serpent's Tail, 1987).

| | |
|---|---|
| DJ | *Reivindicación del conde don Julián* |
| JT | *Juan sin tierra* |
| Ma | *Makbara* (Spanish) |
| PB | *Paisajes después de la batalla* |
| SI | *Señas de identidad* |
| VPS | *Las virtudes del pájaro solitario* |
| | |
| CJ | *Count Julian* |
| JL | *Juan the Landless* |
| LB | *Landscapes After the Battle* |
| Mb | *Makbara* |
| MI | *Marks of Identity* |

# Introduction

This book is written with two rather different types of reader in mind: the professional Hispanist or student of Spanish on the one hand, and on the other, the person interested in modern fiction generally, who may very well read exclusively in English, but who likes to be aware of foreign literature through translations. For the sake of the latter, all Spanish quotations have been translated, using professional versions where these are available and my own where they are not. In the pages that follow, I attempt to provide some background for the curious newcomer to Goytisolo – although his works stand up dazzlingly enough on their own – and to elucidate certain elements that are likely to puzzle readers without his traditional Spanish, Roman Catholic upbringing. But at the same time, this book offers specialists and amateur enthusiasts alike a new reading of Goytisolo's recent fiction, one that takes account of, but extends beyond the work of distinguished critics like Linda Gould Levine, Michael Ugarte, and Genaro Pérez. My reading shifts the emphasis away from the well-trodden socio-historical paths and focuses instead on deeper, timeless, and universal patterns of narrative tradition which the texts exploit.

I shall be principally concerned with the so-called Mendiola trilogy, named after the protagonist, Alvaro Mendiola, and consisting of *Señas de identidad* (1966), *Reivindicación del conde don Julián* (1970), and *Juan sin tierra* (1975). The corresponding translations are called *Marks of Identity* (published in the United States in 1969 and in the United Kingdom in 1988), *Count Julian* (published in the United States in 1974 and about to appear in the United Kingdom), and *Juan the Landless* (published in the United States in 1977 and forthcoming in the United Kingdom).[1] However, the more recent *Makbara* (1980) and *Paisajes después de la batalla* (1982) will also be discussed and although Goytisolo's latest novel, *Las virtudes del pájaro solitario*

(1988), came out too late to be included in the main part of this book,
I have added an afterword that briefly discusses it. *Makbara* was
published in translation (with the same title) in the United States in
1981, but is not yet available in the United Kingdom; a translation of
*Paisajes*, called *Landscapes after the Battle*, was published in the United
States in 1983 and in Britain in 1987.

Much of the critical spadework has already been done: unattributed quotations and allusions that Goytisolo inserts into his texts
have been unearthed and identified in large measure. In the case of
*Don Julián*, an excellent annotated edition has been compiled by
Linda Gould Levine and published in the Cátedra series.[2] Examples
of other helpful illumination include Carlos-Peregrín Otero's reference to the influence of Sterne's *Tristram Shandy* on *Juan sin tierra*,
together with Genaro Pérez's similar observation in his Russian
Formalist study of Goytisolo's works.[3] Pérez also traces the term
*carpetovetónico* (translated as 'Hispano' or 'Hispano male' and roughly
meaning archetypically Spanish or an archetypal Spaniard), to Camilo José Cela's collection of quaint vignettes of national life and
personalities, *El gallego y su cuadrilla y otros apuntes carpetovetónicos*. He
notes too an echo of Azorín's cuckoo in D. Alvaro Peranzules's last
stuttering sounds and further reveals that there was a real Alvaro
Peranzules, a Count of León and uncle of the Infantes de Carrión.
Perhaps more useful than these incidental facts, though, are his
translations of many of the Latin section headings of *Juan sin tierra*,
which he also attributes and glosses.[4]

Severo Sarduy identifies Changó, featured in *Juan sin tierra* and
briefly in *Señas de identidad* too, as a Yoruba deity and Guillermo
Cabrera Infante adds that Changó became a goddess in Cuba.[5] In
addition, Sarduy provides information about the Ibn Turmeda mentioned in *Juan sin tierra*, as does Michael Ugarte, who also uncovers a
volume of poetry called *Jean sans Terre*, by the Alsatian poet Ivan
Goll and elaborates on parallels between Goytisolo's John Lackland
and Goll's.[6] Pérez, on the other hand, associates the title *Juan sin tierra*
with King John of England's nickname and, perhaps most significantly of all, Gould Levine reveals that it was one of the pseudo-
nyms used by José María Blanco White, an eighteenth-century
critic of the Spanish establishment and especially of the Catholic
Church in Spain, who exiled himself to England and whose English
writings have been translated into Spanish by Goytisolo. In a lengthy
introduction Goytisolo talks of his feelings of empathy and affinity
with Blanco White, arising from their common condition of living

as self-exiles, disillusioned with their country and branded a traitor by their compatriots.[7] A final example of helpful information comes from Claudia Schaefer-Rodríguez, who explains the term *halaiquí nesraní*, used to describe the story-teller of *Makbara*; evidently, it means a Christian in Muslim lands.[8]

As the above – a small sample – illustrates, it would be superfluous to concentrate on this aspect of commentary and glossing of the texts. However, where the significance of Goytisolo's sources has not been fully recognized or where a quotation or allusion's origin may be interpreted in a new way that has some bearing on my argument, it will be elucidated. Thus, for example, the implications of Goytisolo's reproductions of whole passages from the extreme right-winger Manuel García Morente's works, although noted by other critics such as Gould Levine and Jesús Lázaro,[9] have been underestimated, in my view; furthermore, the consequences for Goytisolo's discourse of such extensive borrowing from this author merit critical consideration and therefore this particular source will be analysed at some length in chapter 2.

My approach is not based on the chronological development of Goytisolo's ideas, although this is considered in chapter 1, as a preliminary foundation from which to start constructing the new reading I propose; nor does it spring from a series of specific themes, though various ones are examined for their illustrative value. The argument is structured around antique patterns, embedded more deeply in the texts than the motifs and themes that betray their presence. The direction I shall take is inward or downward, in search of the heart or bedrock of their ideology, a quest for the source from which the texts gush so powerfully.

Thus, chapter 2 opens the argument near the surface, with an examination of the numerous pairs of opposites in the texts: black and white, vice and virtue, sinner and saint, to name but a few. Many critics have noted these oppositions, but have not studied them beyond observing their presence in the discourse and discussing their relationship with other themes, such as the rebellion against Spain. Some have sought to identify one principal polarity, to which all the others would then be subjugated: Jerome Bernstein, for example, studies this in *Juan sin tierra* and deems *cara-culo* ('face-arse') to be the basic pair: 'En torno a cada uno de éstos [cara y culo] se agrupan varias ideas asociadas, de las que las principales son: limpio/sucio, "ojo de Dios"/"ojo del diablo", blancura/negrura-oscuridad, . . . la Parejita Reproductora-heterosexualidad/narradorhomsexualidad'; ('Around each of these [face and arse] are grouped various associated ideas, of which the main ones are: clean/dirty, "God's eye"/"the devil's eye" [anus], whiteness/blackness-darkness, ... the Reproductive Couple-heterosexuality/narrator-homosexuality'). But the last pair in Bernstein's list undermines his own assertion that *cara-culo* is the basic concept, for in the contrast between the heterosexual Parejita Reproductora (Reproductive Couple) and the homosexual narrator, it is surely vaginal sex, not the face, that is juxtaposed with the *culo* image of anal sex, not to mention impotence with virility and frustration with fulfilment, which cannot be grouped around the *cara-culo* concept either. In the same article, Bernstein further undermines his own argument by defining both the Parejita and the narrator in terms of anal symbolism: 'La modalidad psicológica del estreñimiento caracteriza el mundo justo de la Parejita Reproductora, y la "Cópula bárbara" (contacto anal) de la homosexualidad es el emblema del mundo "gay" del narrador'; ('The psychological mode of constipation characterizes the just world of the Reproductive Couple, and the "barbarous copulation" (anal contact) of homosexuality is the emblem of the narrator's gay world').[10] Schaefer-Rodríguez, on the other hand, stresses the importance of East versus West and Muslim versus Christian, whilst Jesús Lázaro is an example of those critics who simply list many oppositions of this type.[11] I shall argue, however, that the source of these contrasts is the fundamental opposition between good and evil and that Goytisolo's treatment of the subject effects a reversal of the traditional correspondences, so that blackness, vice, and so on, take on a positive value whilst their opposites, whiteness and virtue, for example, become associated with negative qualities like intolerance, constraint, coldness, artificiality, and stagnation. The pariah motif, to which chapter 3 is devoted, illustrates this revaluation.

Chapter 3 also acts as a stepping-stone to the next stage of the argument, contained in chapter 4. Pariahs, after all, stand both as one-half of the touchable-untouchable dualism, and as the lowliest creatures in the much more complex hierarchy of society. It is Goytisolo's attack on the concept of ordered hierarchy that is examined in chapter 4. This reveals that the identification of order with good and chaos with evil is vehemently rejected in the texts, notably by means of a response to the literary genre of utopianism. Chapter 5, therefore, addresses itself to the question of what is to be understood by this favoured concept of chaos and how it relates to the notion of fluidity, especially fluidity of form and its contingent phenomenon, metamorphosis.

Chapter 6 is a study of the recurrent motif of blood in the fiction. It demonstrates that the argument of the previous chapters may be traced through a single thread of the symbolic fabric of the texts, and in this way, provides both a synthesis and confirmation of the reading I propose.

\* \* \*

In 1985 and 1986, Goytisolo published two volumes of memoirs, called *Coto vedado* ('Forbidden Territory') and *En los reinos de Taifa* ('In the Realms of the Moorish Kings'), respectively.[12] Both are vivid, detailed, unpretentious, and provide fascinating insight not only into the author's own life and personality, but also into the varied environments in which he has lived: Spain during and after the Civil War; Paris from the late 1950s onwards; the Maghreb, Cuba, America. The following brief biographical sketch is largely culled from these works.

Juan Goytisolo was born in 1931 in Barcelona, though his surname indicates Basque ancestry. His maternal family is Catalonian, but he was brought up speaking Castilian at home. His paternal forebears were wealthy slave-owning sugar planters in colonial Cuba, a feature of family history that would both inspire and haunt the fiction he was to write. His childhood, along with that of his two brothers, Luis (also to become a novelist) and José Agustín (a poet), and of his sister Marta, was traumatized not only by the Civil War as an environmental upheaval, but also by the personal tragedy of their mother's death in 1938, when a bus on which she was travelling was struck by a bomb.

His relationship with the conservative but somewhat eccentric father was distant at best and certainly not helped by the long-standing antagonism between the widower and his father-in-law, Juan's grandfather. The latter was particularly execrated for his homosexual attraction to boys, including Juan himself, a fact that was discovered by the father and increased the antipathy to an extreme.

Juan was educated in the standard middle-class fashion, sent to Roman Catholic schools and finally enrolled at Barcelona University to read law. He was soon disenchanted with his studies and univer-

sity teaching, which at the time was strictly controlled by the Franco
regime, so that only the most stalwart supporters held academic
posts. Neglecting his work, Goytisolo turned instead to reading
banned literature obtained on the black market and to writing fiction
himself.

The first taste of freedom came when he went to Madrid, thus
escaping from the burdensome pretence of being the model son for
his father's sake. Finally, in 1957, he left for Paris, where he worked
for the publishers, Gallimard. There he met and fell in love with
Monique Lange, with whom he still spends much of the year, but as
he tells in his memoirs, he discovered his own homosexual feelings
in the course of their involvement, feelings that he faced honestly
with Monique; their relationship weathered the storm and survived. He also fell in love with North Africa, studied Arabic and, for
many years now, he has spent the part of the year when he is away
from Paris living with his male companion in his other home in
Marrakech.

Although Paris and Marrakech stand out in Goytisolo's life as his
two principal bases, he has travelled widely, lectured in the United
States, visited Cuba and the Soviet Union, as well as a host of other
countries East and West. In *Don Julián*, he puts the following
memorable words into the narrator's mouth: 'La patria no es la
tierra: el hombre no es el árbol: ayúdame a vivir sin suelo y sin
raíces: móvil, móvil' (*DJ*, pp. 124–5; 'one's true homeland is not the
country of one's birth: man is not a tree: help me to live without
roots: ever on the move', *CJ*, p. 104). And indeed, the author shares
this opinion with his fictional character, preferring to see his *patria*
('motherland') as his language, Spanish, rather than a geographical
location: 'para el exiliado la lengua se convierte en su patria auténtica'
('for the exiled, the language becomes the real motherland'), he
writes in an essay.[13] In the light of this opinion, another essay,
'Hemos vivido una ocupación', logically expresses particular resentment at the effect of the Franco regime on the Spanish language, seen
as a more insidious type of occupation than the territorial subjuga-
tion of Spain; the piece is reminiscent of Orwell's concept of News-
peak in *Nineteen Eighty-Four*, where the Ministry of Truth dealt with
deception, thus subverting the meaning of the word 'truth' itself.[14]
Goytisolo writes:

Años y años de posesión ilegítima y exclusiva destinada a vaciar los
vocablos de su genuino contenido—evocar la libertad humana

cuando se defendía la censura . . . – a fin de esterilizar la potencia subversiva del lenguaje y convertirlo en un instrumento dócil de un discurso voluntariamente amañado, engañoso y adormecedor.

(Years and years of illegitimate and exclusive possession aimed at emptying words of their genuine content – evoking human freedom when defending censorship . . . – in order to sterilize the subversive potential out of the language and turn it into the docile instrument of a deliberately twisted, deceptive, soporific discourse.)[15]

Politically, Goytisolo has amusingly likened himself to the 'fea del baile', the ugly wallflower at the ball, since no party has ever invited him to join it. As a young man, he was sympathetic towards communism, especially the Cuban variety in the early years of the Castro regime. Indeed, he wrote extremely enthusiastically about life there in a travelogue called *Pueblo en marcha* (1962) ('People on the Move').[16] More recently, he has explained this enthusiasm as the 'exorcismo de tus contradicciones y culpabilidad ancestral' (the 'exorcism of your contradictions and ancestral guilt').[17] However, the authoritarian corollaries of a communist system, whether in Eastern Europe, Cuba, or indeed within the Party in Paris, put him off and he has kept his distance from party politics ever since. Nevertheless, his writing – both fictional and essayistic – is anything but apolitical; he holds strong opinions on political issues and does not shrink from expressing them, but they remain individual rather than aligned to a single party's manifesto. He made no secret, for example, of his approval of Spain's joining the EEC, or of his dislike of separatism within the country, this last a controversial stance, distancing him from the conventionally sympathetic position on regional autonomy of the political left in Spain.[18]

Goytisolo is as impossible to pigeon-hole in his attitudes to literature and critical theory as he is politically. Despite his extraordinary and undisputed originality and the experimentalism of his fiction since *Señas de identidad*, he sees himself diachronically as descending from medieval and Golden Age Spanish writers (not to mention Sterne in England, the Marquis de Sade in France, Faulkner in America, to name but a few of the international literary forebears he is fond of citing), rather than synchronically as a contemporary of, say, the French *nouveau roman* writers or Latin Americans such as Carlos Fuentes. In a recent interview, for example, he said this: 'Lo que a mí me interesa ... es ... tener antepasados: forjarme un linaje de abuelos y bisabuelos ilustres, y por eso miro hacia Cervantes, hacia Fernando de Rojas, hacia San Juan de la Cruz' ('What interests me ... is ... to have ancestors: to forge myself a lineage of illustrious grandparents and great-grandparents, and that is why I look to Cervantes, Fernando de Rojas, Saint John of the Cross'). But in the same interview, he also stated: 'Me parece tan obvio que toda escritura auténtica es experimental que no hay por qué señalarlo' ('It seems so obvious to me that any authentic writing is experimental, that there is no reason to point it out'), and quoting Genet, he endorsed the latter's opinion that 'si sabes de dónde sales y adónde llegas, esto no es una aventura literaria sino un trayecto en autobús' ('if you know where you're leaving from and where you'll be arriving, that isn't a literary adventure but a bus-ride').[19]

He also finds it important to stay abreast of modern critical theory and to react to it in his writing, though he is quick to point out that this is not a twentieth-century innovation:

> Cervantes conocía perfectamente el arte literario de su tiempo y todos los códigos literarios de entonces y el *Quijote* es una demostración clara de que era un magnífico crítico y un magnífico profesor de literatura. Pero, volviendo a la época actual, el perfeccionamiento, el desarrollo de la poética y la lingüística en los últimos años pone al escritor en una situación de o bien conocer el mecanismo del lenguaje que emplea o bien adoptar una actitud acientífica y artesanal lo cual me parece, hasta cierto punto, suicida.

> (Cervantes had a perfect acquaintance with the literary art of his time and all the literary codes then, and the *Quixote* is a clear demonstration that he was a magnificent critic and a magnificent teacher of literature. But, to come back to the present era, the perfecting, the development of poetics and linguistics in recent years places the writer in the situation of either knowing the mechanism of the language he uses or adopting an ascientific, craftsman-like attitude, which seems to me, to a certain extent, suicidal.)[20]

Goytisolo then, is a curious mixture who cannot be stereotyped aesthetically – descending from and loving many (but not all) of the classics of Spanish and world literature, and yet in some senses an iconoclastic, experimental writer – nor politically – taking an individual position on each issue whether this happens to coincide with left or right or neither – nor even personally, with his dual residence in Europe and Africa and with his wife Monique but openly homosexual too.

And yet, this resistance to classification of the man, which might seem to add to the difficulty of coping with his writing, is on the contrary a very helpful way in. In the pages that follow, I shall be arguing that central to Goytisolo's mature fiction is a rejection of the principle, ordinarily taken as beyond argument, that order is a fundamentally good thing, irrespective of quibbles about which types of order may be preferable. And when one stops to ponder over exactly what *order* means, it becomes clear that it has a good deal to do with hierarchies – of values, of people, or whatever – and that hierarchies can exist only where there is differentiation: it cannot mean anything to say, for example, that mammals are a superior life-form to insects unless one can distinguish between them. In his life and lifestyle, one might even venture, Goytisolo is practising what his fiction preaches, for he will not be fitted in to any orderly categories, but remains a free and fluid combination – a Spaniard but also a Parisian and a Moroccan; a writer and a critic; a traditionalist and an iconoclast – which, as we shall see, is the ideal posited in the fiction he writes.

\* \* \*

Before ending an introduction to a book about Goytisolo's fiction, the subject of myth requires some preliminary comment. The chapters that follow deal with his extensive and complex use of mythical figures and patterns, yet he regards himself and is regarded by many if not most critics as a destroyer of myths. Clearly some solution to these apparently contradictory factors must be sought. Owing to the complexity of scholarly debate concerning the meaning of the word *myth* and given that this matter is not central to the reading offered in this book, a lengthy discussion would be out of place. However, it would be useful briefly to consider certain aspects of the controversy in order to clarify my usage of the terminology. For the interested reader, Karl Ruthven's *Myth* provides concise and balanced background material.[21]

Much of the argument concerns disagreement over suitable criteria to distinguish myth from other types of traditional narrative, such as legend, saga, and folktale. However, as Mircea Eliade explains, 'in societies where myth is still alive the natives carefully distinguish myths – "true stories" – from fables or tales, which they call false stories . . . [But] the same archetypes – that is, the same exemplary figures and situations – appear alike in myths, sagas, and tales . . . . What has the prestige of myth in one tribe will be merely a tale in the neighbouring tribe'.[22] In other words, it is the status of a given story in a given community, rather than its essential content, that is the criterion; as it is content that I shall be studying, these distinctions may seem to be of secondary importance. However, the concept of true as opposed to false status of a story could be adapted to apply to Goytisolo's unusual stance of mythoclast on the one hand and user of archetypal patterns on the other. The myths that he smashes, such as those pertaining to Spanishness and Roman Catholicism, are the beliefs and narratives held to be true and sacred in the contemporary world of his novels, whereas classical mythology has amalgamated with folklore and other types of traditional tale to form the corpus of 'false stories' of modern society.

In short, the distinction between myths and stories unconnected with reality is of fundamental importance to an understanding of Goytisolo's works, but not in its conventional application. The adventures of the Greek and Roman deities are no longer functioning myth (because nobody believes in them any more), but have joined the ranks of traditional tales like 'Little Red Riding Hood'. These stories may be magnificent and awe-inspiring or charming and quaint; they may express fundamental truths about human nature and psychology or be of great interest to social historians; for all these reasons they retain immense value, but in this day and age they are not myths in the pure sense of that which is believed to be 'a sacred history . . . [which] relates an event that took place'.[23] On the other hand, the damage done to Spain by the Moorish invasion caused by Count Julian; the necessity and virtue of the Inquisition; the beauty of the bullfight as art-form; all Roman Catholic dogma and tradition; the importance of productivity and consumerism, of procreation, hygiene, and the American Dream: these are some of the modern myths, Spanish and international, that Goytisolo brings tumbling down.

Thus, a simple distinction suffices to resolve the apparent paradox of the writer labelled a mythoclast, but plainly indebted to, and respectful of, the antique patterns of myth. Two basic meanings of the word must be established as separate elements of the texts: 1) part of the corpus of Greek and Roman (or other, such as Sumerian or Norse) mythology; and 2) something false, which is nevertheless held by the populus to be true, sacrosanct, of fundamental value that may not be challenged. These categories, based on the usage of myth vocabulary by the author and critics, together with the argument I shall propose, reveal that the contradiction is illusory, for it is at once apparent that Goytisolo shatters only those myths that are held to be true and sacred by the masses, but which in his view are neither. For the sake of clarity, therefore, the term *mythology* will be applied to the first category and *myth* will be reserved for the more modern meaning of 'popularly believed and revered falsehood', the second group.[24] Indeed, the evidence that underpins the assertion that popular faith in a myth is required before it becomes worth smashing, lies in the author's use of what is to be termed mythology. The figure of Proteus, for example, or Virgil's works, are recurrently employed and never is there any *desmitificación* ('demythification') here. This is surely because classical mythology today is recognized by all to be unrelated to literal, physical truth.

The use of mythology in the texts and the abuse hurled at myths (the first and second, respectively, of the categories established above), are not unconnected components of the fiction, but often complement one another. By revealing similarities in the basic figures of myths and mythology, Goytisolo forces readers to confront their own inconsistencies and ask themselves why, for example, they take the fictional standing of Little Red Riding Hood for granted, yet accept as reality the concept of the virtuous child, as exemplified by Alvarito in the trilogy.

Lastly, the psychological dimension of myth and mythology must be addressed in order to appreciate Goytisolo's stance, for this aspect is of primary importance to the texts and my reading of them. Carl Jung identifies the crucial link between dream and myth/mythology in the form of the archetypes, which he defines as 'forms or images of a collective nature which occur practically all over the earth as constituents of myths and at the same time as autochthonous, individual products of unconscious origin. The archetypal motives presumably start from the archetypal patterns of the human mind which are transmitted by tradition and migration but also by heredity'.[25] Reflecting Jung's theories, Jane Harrison links fantasy with myth/mythology in these terms: 'Myth is a fragment of the soul-life, the dream-thinking of the people, as the dream is the myth

of the individual'.[26] It is important for a critic of Goytisolo to bear
this personal, psychological dimension of myth in mind, for it is the
imagination of his protagonists that fabricates the discourse of each
text. Therefore it is presumably their own personalities that have
determined their selection of, and obsession with, certain archetypes
and their exclusion of others. Thus, if the protagonist of *Don Julián*
dwells, for example, on 'Little Red Riding Hood', out of all the
stories he is bound to have been told as a child, this must surely be
because he feels some particular affinity between his own dream-
thinking (to borrow Harrison's phrase) and that specific tale. This
bridge between dream and myth/mythology is therefore valuable to
the student of Goytisolo, for it introduces the idea, vitally important
to the texts, of subjective captivation, fascination, and of personal
participation in what otherwise might be viewed as a distant—
because lofty and ancient—art-form.

   Finally, for the sake of Anglo-Saxon readers of Goytisolo, something must be said about the use of the words *cristiano/Christian*
where 'Roman Catholic' would be more accurate. In the trilogy,
Alvaro's experience of Christianity is the Spanish post-Civil War
Roman Catholic establishment and—wrongly or rightly—he takes
this extremely conservative manifestation of Christianity as representative of the tenets of the religion as a whole. That this is the case
is borne out by his use of *cristiano*, when the context makes it clear
that 'Roman Catholic' is what is meant. When, to cite just one
example of a great many, the voices of the establishment are criticizing the rebellious younger generation in *Señas de identidad*, they say
that these youths had nevertheless been given a *Christian* education
and then go on to elaborate, clearly showing that, more precisely, it
was Roman Catholic: 'educados todos cristianamente en colegios de
pago algunos de ellos especialmente consagrados al Inmaculado
Corazón de María y beneficiarios de la divina promesa respecto a la
práctica de los primeros viernes del mes' (*SI*, p. 283; 'all having had a
Christian education in private schools some of them especially
dedicated to the Immaculate Heart of Mary and beneficiaries of the
divine promise in respect to the practice of the first Friday of the
Month', *MI*, p. 234). The first Friday is a Roman Catholic belief that
taking communion on the first Friday of the month for nine months
entitles one to an indulgence.

   One might add, for the benefit of those unfamiliar with everyday
usage, that it is not an idiosyncrasy on Alvaro's part, but exceedingly
common amongst Spaniards, to consider *Christian* as virtually

synonymous with 'Roman Catholic', except in a context specifically dealing with the different branches of the Church. I have decided, therefore, to follow the usage of the texts themselves, since studiously to alter all the references from *Christian* to 'Roman Catholic' in commenting on them would be to narrow Alvaro's attack to a set of sectarian issues, which would not be justified by any evidence within the novels.

# 1
## The Seeds of Chaos:
## Genesis of Goytisolo's Ideology

### The Post-Civil War Novel

The Spanish Civil War created a devastating rift in the country's literature as well as in its people and politics. The generation of writers who were adults when it broke out had almost all disappeared by the time it ended, whether they had been killed like García Lorca, coincidentally died a natural death like Unamuno and Machado, had left the country like Cernuda, or had reached the end of their writing career, like Baroja. The new regime imposed strict censorship of foreign and domestic literature too, heightening the sense of literary isolation in Spain. For these reasons, it is misleading to consider the twentieth century as a single period in Spanish literary history, no matter how broad one may wish to make one's brush-strokes. As far as the novel is concerned, the post-Civil War era is generally agreed to have been initiated by Camilo José Cela with *La familia de Pascual Duarte* ('Pascual Duarte's Family') (1942). This is the fictional autobiography of a murderer and matricide, written in Death Row and transcribed by a chronicler as unreliable as the protagonist. A tale of gratuitous violence, misplaced machismo, and shocking deprivation and ignorance, with its obvious but unstated commentary on the carnage that had just ravaged the country, this work set the tone for the fiction of the 1940s, a crop of novels dwelling on brutality in unflinching detail, a trend that came to be known as *tremendismo*. The characteristic *tremendista* perspective is individual, subjective: in Cela's work, Pascual Duarte is assessing his own past; in another typical work of the decade, Carmen Laforet's *Nada* ('Nothing') (1944), a woman in later life is looking back on a year she spent as a student in Barcelona. Although social criticism arises naturally from such personal visions, these novels were at least as concerned with depicting an individual's response to the environment and the effect that this milieu had on such a person's mentality and development.

The 1950s brought a shift in perspective, away from the individual and the close examination of his or her psyche, to a technique that has been likened to that of the cinema for the dispassionate camera-lens style of the most celebrated novels of the decade. The 1940s structure of one central character tends to give way to a collective protagonist – often a group of friends as in Rafael Sánchez Ferlosio's *El Jarama* ('The Jarama') (1956) and Juan Goytisolo's own first novel, *Juegos de manos* ('The Young Assassins') (1954) – and the discourse limits itself chiefly to what is visible or audible, with a minimum of authorial comment on characters' inner feelings and motives. These emerge through speech and action or are left to the reader's imagination; even when an authorial voice does come in to describe private thoughts, the style is dead-pan reportage, rather than aesthetically elaborate or emotionally charged. Indeed, the use of the journalistic term 'reportage' is appropriate to this behaviourist fiction, as it is sometimes called, for although plots and characters were invented, the writers were concerned to give a truthful account of Spanish society at a time when the press and the news media were strictly controlled and biased for propagandistic purposes. Looking back to the 1950s, Goytisolo has talked about 'la necesidad que sentíamos los autores de suplir el silencio de la prensa y de los medios de información española sobre situaciones reales del país' ('the necessity which we authors felt to fill in for the silence of the press and the Spanish news media about real situations in the country'), adding that he saw his role as that of 'testigo de una época' ('witness to a period').[1]

The writers who made their publishing debut in the 1950s are known as the *generación de medio siglo* (the 'mid-century generation'). They had been children during the Civil War and this placed them in a peculiar position: thrust prematurely into adulthood by the violence they had witnessed and yet powerless to take a side other than that of their parents, when the time in their lives came to assume adult responsibilities – when they were mature enough to make choices – the Franco regime was at its most oppressive and they found themselves impotent in a paternalistic, stagnant society, deprived of all possibilities except conformity. Compounding their predicament was their resentment concerning the side of the conflict on which the accident of birth had placed them; when they grew up, they realized they would have wished to oppose the side with which they had automatically been aligned, for they were Republicans in spirit but from Nationalist families. Hence, the writers of the *generación de medio siglo* were not only angry young men and women in the 1950s, angry at the socially and politically oppressive nature of the regime in which they lived, angry too at their cultural isolation from their predecessors in Spain and their contemporaries abroad; they were also guilt-ridden for their former unchosen identification with the Nationalists. The different stages and aspects of developing this problematic identity are treated by Goytisolo and his contemporaries in the fiction they wrote in the 1950s, despite the alleged aim of objectivity and the lack of explicit breast-beating by an authorial narrator. As well as bearing witness to a period, they quite clearly bore witness to being their age in that period too.

However, it is only in this first decade of Goytisolo's writing career that he can be fitted usefully into a school or generation of contemporary novelists. And it is only in the 1950s that his fiction does not loom noticeably larger than that of other Spanish writers. Accomplished, and well described by the cliché 'a good read', these novels seem interesting for the student of Spanish literature only as examples of what was the fashion of a decade, or, with the benefit of hindsight, as the curiously unexceptional early works of a novelist who was to become such a unique and outstanding creator. From the vantage-point of the 1980s, though, it is worthwhile to pause, if only briefly, over these early novels, for in retrospect certain preoccupations already present then can be identified, with a double benefit for the reader: firstly, such discoveries enrich the study of the 1950s novels themselves, betraying a depth easily missed beneath their superficial conformity to the literary fashion of the times; and secondly, they elucidate some aspects of the mature works, showing the evolution of the author's ideas on certain subjects, such as the nature of childhood and growing up, the phenomenon of gratuitous cruelty, the interest in outsiders and underdogs coupled with antipathy towards those who fit unproblematically into their community.

## The Early Novels

In the following chapters, Juan Goytisolo's fiction will not be analysed in chronological order, nor will there be a detailed discussion of each work's significance relative to its chronological position in his literary output. The rest of this chapter will attempt to justify an atemporal approach at the same time as providing an introductory outline of the novels' sequential development, in order to provide an adequate framework in which to consider the concepts that form the basis of my reading of the novels from *Señas de identidad* onwards. For the sake of economy, I shall call the novels published before *Señas* the early novels and those from *Señas* to the present, the mature or later ones.

In the first chapter of her excellent study of *Señas de identidad* and *Reivindicación del conde Don Julián*, called *Juan Goytisolo: la destrucción creadora*, Linda Gould Levine looks at the evolution pre-*Señas* of the theme of betrayal, together with the interplay of the figures of executioner and victim. Her analysis is illuminating, the basic thrust being that the early fiction was as preoccupied with the interlinked concepts of betrayal and the executioner-victim relationship, as the Mendiola trilogy would be; but at first, she explains, the elements appeared embodied in separate characters, whereas later, they fused together. Thus, Goytisolo's first published novel, *Juegos de manos* ('The Young Assassins') is the story of a group of youths, longing to make their mark by rebelling against the regime and their conformist families. They decide to shoot a politician, but the plan fails dismally, when the member of the group chosen to perpetrate the crime is too afraid to carry it out. This person is David, a shy adolescent, unlike his tough, often unscrupulous companions and he has been chosen unfairly through the trickery of a character called Luis. The outcome of the flop is that Agustín, the *de facto* leader of the group and hitherto David's sponsor, feels obliged to kill him. The novel ends as Agustín is being led away by the police, grimly resigned to what the future must hold for him and actually pleased that he has committed himself to a new identity – that of murderer – and truly burnt his boats behind him. As Gould Levine points out, the roles of traitor, executioner, and victim are dramatized in clearly separate characters here, with Luis the traitor, David the sacrificial victim, and Agustín the executioner.

A similar structure can be identified in Goytisolo's second novel, *Duelo en el Paraíso* ('Children of Chaos') (1955), which is set during the Civil War.[2] The main characters are a group of savage Republican children who have been evacuated to a rural boarding-school and their Nationalist neighbours on the estate called 'Paraíso' ('Paradise'), consisting of assorted eccentric women and a boy called Abel, who has been sent there for his safety. Bored and lonely, Abel finally overcomes his shyness and snobbery and makes friends with one of the evacuees, a certain Pablo. Together they plan to run away and join the war, but Pablo betrays Abel and leaves him behind. The remaining evacuees then involve him in their war-games, but these turn nightmarishly serious when they decide to execute Abel for being on the enemy side. Again we have a betrayer – Pablo – a sacrificial victim – Abel – whose only crime is to have been born into a Nationalist family, and an implacable executioner, a child nicknamed *Arquero* ('Archer').

In both novels, the three characters seem predestined to play the role assigned to them in the betrayer-executioner-victim triangle, aware of and resigned to their part in the drama. But this is not the only prefiguration of the later novels. *Juegos* focuses on the impotence imposed on the main characters by the system: the only one who does succeed in asserting his freedom to some extent is Agustín, the executioner, and ironically, the price he will pay for it is no doubt his liberty, as the ending of the book indicates with his being led away by the police. Yet despite the pessimism of this irony, it conceals a glimmer of hope which will not return until the end of the Mendiola trilogy: by becoming a murderer, Agustín has successfully changed his identity, cast off the blue-eyed-boy shell in which his parents had enclosed him against his will, cut himself off irrevocably from his social background. Of his mother's love for him, he says, 'me envolvía como un ropaje excesivamente prieto' ('it wrapped itself around me like clothes that are too tight').[3] He feels impelled to rid himself of the constraining garment in such a way that it can never be donned again: 'Me es preciso quemar las naves' ('I must burn my bridges'), he says to David, and once he has done so, by killing him, he feels that he has killed himself too. This is true in the sense that he has killed his former self and taken on a new identity: that of a murderer.[4] All these ideas – the parental vision of oneself resembling a form of imprisonment, the need to murder this virtuous shell, the consequence of the murder expressed as a change of identity – would be reworked and incorporated into the mature fiction, not to mention certain more obvious parallels: the use of masks and play-acting to create changeable identities, the nonconformism of the protagonists, their wish to be pariahs as far as the establishment was concerned, but also to be accepted by other social outcasts whom they admired (there is a more active group of rebels in *Juegos*, that the protagonists wish to impress by murdering the politician).

*Duelo* introduces the notion, crucial to the later fiction, of a character stigmatized by the accident of birth. The transparent symbolism of the victim-to-be having the name Abel, alerts the reader to his unchosen role; indeed, an air of inexorability hangs over the whole novel, since it is constructed as a flash-back, starting with the discovery of Abel's body. Another concept that appears in this novel and will take on considerable importance in the Mendiola trilogy is the split between the individual's childhood and adult selves. In *Juegos*, it had seemed that this abyss separating the two only existed for characters like Agustín, who had fought hard to create it; in *Duelo*, we realize that it is a natural phenomenon. Abel sees a photograph of his late grand-uncle as a child and wonders 'cómo aquel niño había podido trocarse en hombre viejo' (how that little boy could have changed into an old man). He reasons that 'puesto que no había muerto entonces, debía de andar oculto en algún sitio: los cuerpos de los niños que no morían jóvenes se metamorfoseaban y habitaban sus sueños' (since he had not died then, he must be hidden away somewhere: the bodies of children who did not die young were metamorphosed and inhabited their dreams).[5]

In *Juegos*, we saw that voluntary metamorphosis was possible, as it would be again for Mendiola by the end of the trilogy; in *Duelo*, a more pessimistic vision prevails, for characters want to metamorphose but are unable to do so; Abel's aunt wants to metamorphose into a certain glamorous character called Claude, but 'comprendió la imposibilidad del cambio, el egoísmo obstinado del ser, la terca codicia de la sustancia' (she came to understand the impossibility of the change, a being's obstinate egotism, the stubborn covetousness of substance).[6] Chapter Six will be devoted to the importance of metamorphosis and fluidity of form in the later novels; let us note here how the idea was already preoccupying Goytisolo at the beginning of his literary career.

These are fleeting foretastes, appreciable only with the benefit of hindsight. In one important sense, though, the whole plot of *Duelo* prefigures one of Alvaro Mendiola's fundamental problems. Just as Abel was a middle-class child whose bourgeois identity prevented him from being fully accepted by the low-class evacuees next door, the adult Alvaro similarly comes to long to be part of an underclass from which his 'pecado de origen', the sin of his origin, his involuntary white, bourgeois birthright irremediably bars him. When asked why they had killed Abel, one of the evacuees explained that although he had done them no harm personally, 'su familia era propietaria desde hacía muchos años y él tenía dinero en la época en que nosotros pasábamos hambre' (his family had been land-owners for many years and he had money at a time when we were going hungry).[7] As in the Mendiola trilogy, *Duelo* presented this from the point of view of the frustrated member of the 'privileged' class, denied access to the ranks of the lowly. Thus, the relativity of outcast status was already treated in this early novel; the evacuees, called *desplazados*, literally those who are displaced, may have been the outcasts in the 'real' frame of reference of Spain during the Civil War, but Abel was clearly the pariah within the confines of his own self-image. As we shall see in chapter 3, Alvaro suffers the same fate exactly, of being the pariahs' pariah, rejected by the social outcasts whom he wishes to join.

After *Juegos de manos* and *Duelo en el Paraíso*, Goytisolo wrote a trilogy called 'El mañana efímero' ('Ephemeral Tomorrow'), quoting the turn-of-the-century Spanish poet, Antonio Machado, whose verse, though fiercely patriotic, was also sharply critical of national attitudes and looked to the country's future with ambivalence. The novels that constitute the trilogy, called *Fiestas* (1957), *El circo* ('The Circus') (1957), and *La resaca* ('The Ebb' or 'The Hangover') (1958), leave the bourgeois perspective behind, focusing on the Andalusian underclass of Barcelona, in the style typical of the decade, which is to say, without authorial commentary and with implicit social criticism embedded in the documentary tone. The hypocrisy of the Church, the bigotry and heartlessness of the Catalonians in their attitudes towards the Andalusians, and the pure misery of poverty and de-privation, causing various characters to retreat into a fantasy world of one kind or another, are among the themes treated. But leaving aside this *engagé* aspect of the three novels, which perhaps seems somewhat dated in the 1980s, there are other elements that merit attention. As with *Juegos* and *Duelo*, the pattern of betrayal, followed by sacrifice of a victim by an executioner continues to feature strongly, as Gould Levine observes. As with *Duelo*, again we find particular attention paid to the world of children, their games, their fantasies, their suffering. But what comes out for the first time here is the special affinity and affection the author feels for Andalusians, the same feelings that led him to visit their home territory and subsequently to write two travelogues based on the time he spent there: *Campos de Níjar* ('Fields of Níjar') (1960) and *La Chanca* (1962).[8]

Catalonians call Andalusians *africanos* ('Africans'), intending the nickname as a term of abuse, in keeping with the traditional national antipathy towards the Moors. Goytisolo also feels that the Andalusians have something in common with the people of the Maghreb, but in his case, this is a compliment rather than an insult; indeed, he talks about his love affair with North Africa being a 'prolongación natural' (a 'natural extension'), of his relationship with Andalusia.[9] And the literary progression from novels depicting Andalusians in Barcelona, to travelogues describing them at home, to North Africans in the Mendiola trilogy mirrors the author's own order of experience as he relates it in his memoirs.

Although the 'Mañana efímero' trilogy had introduced the sympathy and warmth for the Andalusians to be found in the travel books, by the time he came to write these, Goytisolo had recognized the artificiality of attempting to write with objectivity and omniscience about a society alien to him – that of poverty-stricken Andalusians – and never again would he attempt to write in this mode. The traveller is openly accepted as an enduring outsider presence in both *Campos de Níjar* and *La Chanca*, as well as in a Cuban travelogue called *Pueblo en marcha* ('People on the Move') (1962). Similarly, two collections of short fiction, *Para vivir aquí* ('To Live Here') (1960) and *Fin de fiesta* ('The Party's Over') (1962), plus a short novel originally intended as a screenplay, *La isla* ('Sands of Torremolinos') (1961) are all about the kind of people Goytisolo knew well, the bourgeoisie, even though his irritation with them had not diminished. He had simply recognized the impossibility of transmigrating his soul into the bodies of people with a radically different background from his own. This is what he said on the subject to Emir Rodríguez Monegal:

> Si me propongo describir la realidad de un barrio pobre de Barcelona o del sur de España, yo no puedo escribir como si fuese un murciano que vive en las chabolas de Barcelona, un campesino pobre de Níjar o un pescador de La Chanca. Cuando me introduzco en su mundo, para mí extraño, para mí chocante, no puedo renunciar a llevar conmigo una tradición cultural, un medio social, una educación. Si hago un análisis de este mundo, ya sea de una región pobre del sur o de Barcelona, estoy obligado a hacerlo desde mi propio enfoque, desde mi propio punto de vista . . . . A partir de *La resaca* me di cuenta que, si me proponía reflejar una serie de fenómenos propios de la sociedad española, tenía que . . . aceptar el subjetivismo.

> (If I set out to describe the reality of a poor quarter of Barcelona or of the South of Spain, I can't write as if I were a Murcian

[Andalusian] living in the shanty-dwellings of Barcelona, a poor peasant from Níjar or a fisherman from La Chanca. When I go into their world, strange to me, shocking to me, a cultural tradition, a social milieu, an upbringing which I can't renounce comes with me. If I make an analysis of that world, be it a poor region in the South, or Barcelona, I am obliged to do so with my own focus, from my own point of view . . . . From *La resaca* onwards, I realized that if I set out to reflect a series of phenomena peculiar to Spanish society, I had to . . . accept subjectivity.)[10]

In summary then, Goytisolo's early literature introduces certain preoccupations destined to come to the fore in his mature phase: betrayal and the executioner-victim relationship explored by Gould Levine; the nature of childhood and growing up seen as metamorphosis; the desire also to metamorphose at will, to take on a new identity; the plight of the pariah, especially that inverted variety which depicts a social superior rejected by the social inferiors whom he wishes to join. Alongside these issues, we find certain sentiments that will also endure, most notably, the preference for the disadvantaged in society over a smug élite and the desire to leave the native environment. Stylistically, the early novels fit into the realist documentary fashion of the times in which they were written, notwithstanding their use of symbolism and mythological patterns, but there is a marked shift away from attempted objectivity with the travel books, prefigured perhaps in the multiple points of view used in *Juegos de manos* and *Duelo en el Paraíso*, which will develop into the densely introspective, self-conscious narration of the later fiction.

## Señas de Identidad

*Señas* has been seen both by author and critics as a novel of transition, rather than a clean break with what went before: 'es a la vez una suma de mi producción juvenil y al mismo tiempo el principio de una nueva concepción de la literatura' ('it is the sum of my juvenile production and at the same time, the beginning of a new conception of literature'), Goytisolo told one interviewer.[11] Hence, the later works are not a homogeneous block of a new type of writing, but a continuing process of experiment and innovation. Especially striking is the dramatic change on passing from *Señas de identidad* to *Reivindicación del conde don Julián*; indeed, it is all too easy to confuse the stylistic gulf between the first novel of the trilogy and its successors with a thematic one. From credible and sympathetic introspective meditation by the protagonist, the discourse jumps to something verging on delirium in *Don Julián*. Moving on to *Juan sin tierra*, though the stylistic shock is far milder, a reader may still feel that new themes have been introduced with the sudden insistence on scatological and religious imagery.

On closer analysis, however, this sense of thematic novelty in the second and third novels of the trilogy proves to be deceptive, for although they may not seem significant and although the narrative skims quickly over them in *Señas*, the themes that come to the fore in *Don Julián* and *Juan sin tierra* are already present there. The seeds are sown therein (and in certain cases, earlier still, as we have just seen); it is as if Goytisolo selected some for cultivation in the succeeding novels.

It will be instructive, therefore, to unearth the important motifs of *Don Julián* and *Juan sin tierra* and take a closer look at their roots, which might otherwise remain hidden in the rich soil of *Señas*. Their origins in this novel, so different from its successors stylistically, serve to bind the trilogy together, helping to overcome the potential problem of *Señas* failing to seem sufficiently connected with *Don Julián* and *Juan sin tierra*.

Let us begin by considering the concept to which chapter 2 is devoted: *esquizofrenia colectiva* ('collective schizophrenia'), or an all-pervading dualistic mentality seen as endemic to the Occident. The term is taken from over halfway through *Juan sin tierra* (*JT*, p. 226; *JL*, p. 199) and yet, despite the novelty of the nomenclature, the concept itself may be traced back to *Señas*. It occurs there in two related contexts: first, there is the idea that Spanish Catholics see actions and people in black-and-white terms of evil and virtuous, sinful and pure; second, there is the realization by Alvaro and Antonio that in fact the world cannot be classified in this way, and the effect of this realization on them. The link between these two aspects of the theme lies in the fact that Alvaro and Antonio have both been brought up as Spanish Catholics, so their expectations of finding a world clearly divided thus derive from their *pecado de origen* ('original sin'), as Alvaro blasphemously calls his heritage.

Señorita Lourdes, the governess who is responsible to a great extent for moulding Alvarito's outlook, typifies the mentality of black-and-white classification in the assessment that she passes on to the child of the Republican fighters in the Civil War: 'te había anunciado [la señorita Lourdes] la llegada del Anti-Cristo. Los hombres mal vestidos en los camiones que circulaban bajo tu ventana eran enviados especiales del demonio, agentes empedernidos del Mal' (*SI*, p. 26; '[Señorita Lourdes] had announced to you . . . the arrival of the Anti-Christ. The poorly dressed men crowded into the trucks that were driving by beneath your window were special envoys of the devil, hardened agents of Evil', *MI*, p. 19, adapted). Another influential 'schizophrenic' in Alvaro's early years is his uncle Eulogio. He applies the dualistic division of all things into good and bad, not to the Civil War, but to the civilized West and the savage Orient: 'El tío Eulogio le había prestado ejemplares de *La decadencia de Occidente* y *El ocaso de las naciones blancas* y . . . Alvaro los había leído y releído, fascinado por el carácter ineluctable del mal . . . . El precario equilibrio de la balanza se rompía definitivamente en favor del Este. Al primer empujón los bárbaros se plantarían en el Pirineo' (*SI*, pp. 36–7; 'Uncle Eulogio had loaned him copies of *The Decline of the West* and *The Twilight of the White Nations* and . . . Alvaro had read and reread them . . . fascinated by the inevitable character of evil . . . . The precarious balance of the scales was finally being upset in favor of the East. With their first push the barbarians would be at the Pyrenees', *MI*, p. 28, adapted). In this quotation, not only is the dualism of outlook striking, with the emphasis on East versus West and the *balanza* ('scales') image, but the embodiment of the enemy in the Arabs post-*Señas* is prefigured here too, with the fear of the Orient. Of course, an us-and-them mentality was already a feature of the early novels, with the class distinctions between Abel's family and the evacuees in *Duelo en el Paraíso*, with the Catalonians versus the immigrant underclass in the 'Mañana efímero' trilogy, and with the rich holiday-makers and poor locals in *Para vivir aquí*, *Fin de fiesta*, and *La isla*, though in these works it was less a case of mutual antagonism or disapproval than of demonstrating how alien the two groups are to each other.

Later in *Señas*, Alvaro calls this dualistic mentality of his compatriots Manichæism: 'si la sociedad española es intolerante, se debe ante todo al hecho de que hay un maniqueo oculto en el corazón de todo español' (*SI*, p. 283; 'if Spanish society is intolerant, it is due above all to the fact that there is some hidden Manichee in the heart of every Spaniard', *MI*, p. 234). This concept of Manichæism unobtrusively sows the seeds of the flesh-spirit obsession which reaches its climax in *Juan sin tierra*, for the Manichees were members of a heretical sect that believed that God was infinitely good and that the principle of evil was matter. The foretaste is unobtrusive—perhaps even fortuitous – because Manichæism is commonly confused with Zoroastrianism, which preached a much more straightforward duality of the universe, whereby there were believed to be two creators, one evil and one good.[12] In María Moliner's Spanish dictionary, for example, *maniqueo* ('Manichæan') is clearly misdefined, as if it meant Zoroastrian: 'se aplica a los seguidores del hereje Maniqueo o Manes, que admitía dos principios creadores, uno para el bien y otro para el mal' ('applied to the followers of the heretic, Mani or Manichee, who accepted two creative principles, one for good and the other for evil'). Whether Goytisolo is deliberately exploiting the ambiguous potential arising from the misuse of the term *maniqueo* or simply intends it as an elegant alternative to *dualístico*, as the text stands, the introduction of the concept of Manichæism poignantly – if subtly – prefigures the flesh-spirit dichotomy of *Juan sin tierra*.

The dualistic outlook, termed *esquizofrenia colectiva* in the last novel of the trilogy and planted as Manichæism in the first, is weighted very differently in each, its treatment being unequivocally condemnatory in *Juan sin tierra*, but more nostalgic and indulgent in *Señas*. Alvaro finds it distressing to reject outright this cosy, straightforward attitude, where everything and everyone may be neatly placed in either one category or the other and he repeatedly laments the ambiguity and uncertainty of reality. When, for example, he describes his travels with Dolores, he nostalgically recalls his childhood 'schizophrenia', which had categorized Western foreign countries as wholly good, something he was forced regretfully to reject when he finally visited the lands of his boyhood dreams:

En los años de guerra y postguerra el proyecto [de viajar] parecía utópico . . . .
El rodaje del documental sobre la emigración primero y tus obligaciones profesionales después os llevaban por turno a los lugares que ambicionarais conocer en la mocedad sustituyendo así la imaginación infantil y el mito adolescente con la realidad ambigua, contradictoria y compleja.

(*SI*, pp. 316–17)

(During the war and the postwar years, the project [of travelling] seemed utopian . . . .
The filming of the documentary on emigration first and your professional obligations later, took both of you in turn to places you had been yearning to know during your youth, substituting

for childhood imagination and adolescent myth, in that way, the ambiguous, contradictory, and complex reality.)

(*MI*, pp. 262–3)

Similarly, Alvaro seems sympathetic or at least understanding when he chronicles his old friend Antonio's anguish at being let out of prison and banished to his (Antonio's) home village, where his status balances precariously and ambiguously on the fence dividing liberty from captivity: 'al arrancarle del *cómodo* maniqueísmo de la prisión, el destierro le introducía en un universo maleable y ambiguo' (*SI*, p. 176, my italics; 'by taking him away from the *comfortable* Manicheism of prison, exile was placing him in a malleable and ambiguous universe', *MI*, p. 148, adapted).

In *Juan sin tierra*, the 'schizophrenia' is seen not only to divide people and actions into good ones and bad, but also to split each individual into unnatural and psychologically detrimental components of pure spirit and tainted flesh, which are constantly fighting for supremacy. This too is prefigured in *Señas*, notably in the character of Alvaro's music mistress and landlady in Paris, Madame Heredia. She longs to see herself as a purely spiritual being, but is forced to admit her need for carnal fulfilment when she discovers her own dissatisfaction with the ethereal relationship between herself and Frédéric. At first, she proclaims his superiority over lesser mortals: 'contraponía . . . el carácter común y plebeyo del padre de Sébastien, interesado sólo por los bienes y apetitos materiales, a la nobleza y elevación de Frédéric, amante límpido de los placeres ideales e incorpóreos' (*SI*, p. 329; '[She] would . . . go on . . . about the common and plebeian character of Sébastien's father, interested only in material things and appetites, contrasting him to Frédéric's nobility and loftiness, the pure lover of ideal and bodies pleasures', *MI*, p. 273), but she is soon searching for a way to 'forzar poco a poco su pudor exquisito, para transformar imperceptiblemente aquel amor hasta entonces etéreo en una relación física' (*SI*, p. 331; 'overcome his exquisite bashfulness little by little, imperceptibly to transform that love, which up till then had been ethereal, into a physical relationship', *MI*, p. 275).

Even the imagery employed to express the internal dichotomy suffered by the victims of societies governed by the 'schizophrenic' principle may be found in *Señas*. Like the women in *Juan sin tierra* whose blood and sweat seep unstoppably through their pure white skin and garments (*JT*, pp. 44–5; *JL*, pp. 33–4), like the protagonist's child self at the end of *Don Julián*, who feels imprisoned by his shell of virtue (*DJ*, p. 224; *CJ*, p. 190), Alvaro bitterly describes in *Señas* how 'habían intentado doblegar su rebeldía y aprisionarlo en el rígido corsé de unos principios, una moral y unas reglas' (*SI*, p. 18; '[they] had tried to break his rebellious streak and bind him in the rigid corset of certain principles, morals, and rules', *MI*, p. 13). And, as in *Don Julián* and *Juan sin tierra*, not only does society actively force him into the constraining outer covering, but it also – and more insidiously – brainwashes him to impose it upon himself. Thus, when his Spanish friends arrive to visit him and Dolores, he automatically dons the shell: 'envuelto una vez más en las mallas de un diálogo que te oprimía y asfixiaba, prisionero de un personaje que no eras tú, confundido con él y por él suplantado' (*SI*, pp. 13–14; 'wrapped up once more in the mesh of a dialogue which would oppress and asphyxiate you, the prisoner of a character who was not you, mixed up with him and supplanted by him', *MI*, p. 9).[13]

Closer still to post-*Señas* imagery for internal *esquizofrenia* is the description of the Spanish expatriates in Madame Berger's café; just like the *carpetovetónico* (the archetypal Hispano) of *Don Julián*, they are seen as a cross between crustaceans and armour-clad medieval warriors. In *Señas*, Alvaro describes 'toda una extraña fauna de crustáceos amparados en sus dogmas como guerreros medievales en articulada y brillante armadura' (*SI*, p. 257; 'a whole strange breed of crustaceans, protected in their dogmas like medieval knights in their jointed and shining armor', *MI*, p. 212, adapted). Compare this with *Don Julián*, where the *carpetovetónico* 'se mueve trabajosamente, haciendo crujir las distintas piezas de su armadura ósea, mezcla híbrida de mamífero y guerrero medieval: . . . por momentos la dureza de su costra evoca el caparazón de los cangrejos' (crustaceans, of course; *DJ*, pp. 160–1; 'he has difficulty moving in his bony armor, the joints of which creak with every step he takes: a cross between a mammal and a medieval warrior: the hardness of his shell is reminiscent at times of the carapace of crabs', *CJ*, p. 135). It may seem strange to use the same imagery for Republican exiles as for the epitome of conservative Spanishness and yet, ironically, these two types have more in common than they realize perhaps, for they are equally proud of their national identity and equally convinced that they represent quintessential Spanishness.

The black-white imagery of *Juan sin tierra* is also to be found in *Señas*, and in a similarly racial context. The equation of blond hair and fair skin with virtue is stressed when Alvaro buys a copy of *Vidas de niños santos* ('Lives of Child Saints') and the cover illustration is described thus: 'un niño Jesús (rubio) abrazaba a un santito (rubio) bajo la mirada complaciente de dos angelotes (rubios)' (SI, p. 21; 'an infant Jesus (blond) embracing a child saint (blond) under the approving glance of two chubby angels (blond)', MI, p. 15). Near the end of Señas, there is also the episode of the rich Cuban relative who turns out to be black: 'no hubo efusiones ceremonias agasajos banquetes . . . /un melancólico negro cenó a solas en un restaurante de lujo de Barcelona' (SI, p. 405, Goytisolo's italics; 'there were no effusive ceremonies parties banquets . . . /a melancholy Negro dined alone in an expensive restaurant in Barcelona', MI, p. 338).

To trace each and every element of the esquizofrenia colectiva phenomenon to a prefiguration in Señas would be more lengthy than this introductory survey permits; suffice it to say that the dualistic outlook is not an innovation in Juan sin tierra, but rather that it moves into the spotlight at that point in the trilogy, having remained unobtrusively in the penumbra until then. It is because it stands in the foreground of Juan sin tierra that chapter 2 deals initially with that work. Only after having examined the concept in its most explicit and therefore most readily accessible manifestation, does it become interesting and useful to consider its roots in earlier works and outgrowths, as it were, in Goytisolo's more recent fiction.

The subject of chapter 4, the concept of ordered hierarchies in contrast to chaos is equally easy to miss in its embryonic form in Señas. This opposition, as we shall see, seems to be the key to the protagonist's preference for the Arab world over what are depicted as rigid societies in the Occident. One might think that this juxta-position of the Western ideal of perfect order with the Eastern lack of judgemental compartmentalization and hierarchy could not play a part in Señas, as the action remains almost exclusively in the Western world. Yet the motif does appear. The Western horror of disorder or chaos is scorned in Señas by means of its being expressed through unsympathetic characters. For example, Ricardo's Catalonian uncle, who refuses to take any active part in the struggle against the post-Civil War regime, preaches pompously: 'El desorden, y ésta es una lección que aprendí durante nuestra guerra, nunca es rentable' (SI, p. 101; 'Disorder, and that's a lesson I learnt during our civil war, is always unprofitable', MI, p. 83). Similarly, Alvaro's family and friends who take refuge in France during the war years are described as 'huyendo del terror y desorden de la zona republicana' (SI, p. 111; 'families who had fled from the terror and disorder of the Republican zone', MI, p. 91); in other words, it is not only bloodshed they fear, but also – and it is given equal weight in the quotation – disorder.

Balancing this fear of disorder is the desire for its opposite, order, seen by those who support the establishment as the prerequisite of peace and prosperity. Alvaro, however, sarcastically regards it more as a recipe for stagnation and lifelessness:

La vida no cambiaría nunca, la mano firme de un prudentísimo piloto ponía la nave a salvo de cualquier imprevisible contingencia. Las nodrizas, los niños, los novios, las fulanas, podían dormir tranquilos, caminar dormidos, soñar caminando, vivir en sueños, engranajes felices de una maquinaria sin fallo, inmortales como el orden que velaba la simetría exacta y repetida de sus gestos.

(*SI*, p. 279)

(Life would never change, the firm hand of a most prudent pilot was guiding the ship away from the dangers of any unforeseen contingency. The nurses, the children, the lovers, the shopgirls could sleep peacefully, walk sleepfully, dream walkfully, live in dreams, the happy cogs of a foolproof machine, as immortal as the order that watched over the exact and repeated symmetry of their gestures.)

(*MI*, p. 231, adapted)

He also expresses his negative attitude towards the social order of Spain by listing it as one of the main causes of his unsatisfactory early years: 'mediocre universo el tuyo, pensabas, de niño sano, consentido y ocioso, habitante de un mundo ordenado, sin riesgo ni posibilidad de heroísmo' (*SI*, p. 22; 'yours was a mediocre universe, you were thinking, that of a healthy, spoiled, and idle child, the inhabitant of an ordered world, without risk or the possibility of heroism', *MI*, p. 16). The ordered world to which Alvaro here refers is associated with coldness and hardness: 'Restablecida venturosamente la paz [después de la guerra] con los estratos congelados de nuevo conforme a un orden severo e inmutable ...' (*SI*, p. 51; 'Peace having been happily re-established [after the Civil War], the frozen social levels conforming once more to a severe and immutable order ...', *MI*, p. 41). This prefigures the symbolic chain later in the trilogy which links the order-lover's aspirations to purity with whiteness and loftiness, suggesting snow-capped mountain tops, and hence coldness, with an added association of hardness via the connection of snow with ice. This chain is clearly expressed in *Juan sin tierra* when the narrator imagines the white, purified sugar on his great-grandfather's plantation in Cuba, transformed into snow and the family into Russian aristocrats (*JT*, p. 39; *JL*, p. 28). The frozen immobility of hierarchized post-Civil War Spanish society is repeatedly stressed in *Señas*; the country is 'petrificada y inmóvil' (*SI*, p. 133; 'petrified and unmoving', *MI*, p. 111) and the so-called *Veinticinco Años de Paz* ('Twenty-Five Years of Peace') are characterized by the 'rígida inmovilidad de los principios' of a 'sociedad jerarquizada en categorías y clases sociales' (*SI*, p. 229; the 'rigid immobility of principles' of a 'society arranged hierarchically into categories and social classes', *MI*, p. 190, adapted).

One might suppose that since the protagonist of *Señas* has not yet discovered the joys of chaotic society with its corollary of absolute liberty in the Arab world, the praise of which he will sing so vociferously in the rest of the trilogy, no alternative to the odious order of post-Civil War Spain could be posited at this stage. However, pockets of chaos are to be found by Alvaro even in order-dominated Spain, and the pleasure their discovery affords him prefigures the fulfilment and contentment that he is later to find on the other side of the Straits of Gibraltar. When his friends Sergio and Ana show him the tumbledown old quarters of Barcelona, he declares that 'gracias a ellos habías aprendido a amar tu ciudad' (*SI*, p. 89; 'thanks to them, you had learned to love your city', *MI*, p. 73). This new-found warmth towards Barcelona is unequivocally attributed to Alvaro's delight at the lack of rational order in the areas of the city that he is visiting for the first time; previously, all he knew was the geometrical precision of the high-class neighbourhoods: 'las compactas manzanas de viviendas que cuadriculaban el plano, las calles perfectamente paralelas como un bien pautado pentagrama' (*SI*, p. 89; 'the compact blocks of houses that divided the map into neat squares, the streets perfectly parallel like a well-ruled musical staff', *MI*, p. 73, adapted). Now his love is kindled by the 'dédalo de callejuelas en las que la colada escurría entre los balcones, los gatos husmeaban los cubos de basura' (*SI*, p. 90; the 'labyrinth of narrow streets where the washing dripped between the balconies, the cats sniffed around in garbage cans', *MI*, p. 73, adapted). Impervious to spatial order then, these old quarters are equally untouched by the march of progress, the temporal order of modern times: 'tonelerías, boticas decimonónicas, tiendas de herbolarios, artículos de corcho resistían impávidos al paso del tiempo' (*SI*, p. 90; 'barrel shops, nineteenth-century apothecaries, herbalists', cork goods stores, stolidly resisted the passage of time', *MI*, p. 73). And when Alvaro takes a last, loving look at Barcelona from the vantage-point of Montjuich in the emotive final pages of the book, he refers to the 'geometría

caótica de la ciudad' (*SI*, p. 422; 'the chaotic geometry of the city',
*MI*, p. 352). In a similar vein, he rejects the tradition of admiring the
perfect order of the heavens, commenting instead on the random
pattern of the star-studded night sky: at daybreak, he says, 'las
estrellas se sustraen del caos de la noche' (*SI*, p. 149; 'the stars slip out
of the chaos of the night', *MI*, p. 124).

Although Alvaro's emigration to Paris provides him with a welcome escape from the 'orden brutal' ('brutal order') of Franco's Spain
(*SI*, p. 420; *MI*, p. 350), France is depicted as just another type of
ordered society. This is conveyed powerfully in the description of
Spanish labourers arriving there. The poor *émigrés*, accustomed to
life in the surviving chaotic pockets of Spain, such as the old quarters
of Barcelona, are shocked by the atmosphere of industrial North-
western Europe, 'países de civilización eficiente y fría' ('countries
with a cold and efficient civilization') and by the behaviour of the
natives, 'la silenciosa y disciplinada multitud, tan distinta de la
caótica y vocinglera muchedumbre española' (*SI*, p. 378; 'that silent
and disciplined multitude . . . so different from the vociferous and
chaotic Spanish crowds', *MI*, pp. 313–14). Goytisolo's subsequent
attack on the whole of Western civilization as order-bound and
therefore deplorable can thus be traced back to here.

Another prefiguration can also be discerned in this scene, and that
is the sympathy towards social underdogs, already present pre-*Señas*
as we have seen, and here continued as if in preparation for the
transfer to the figure of the Moor, the sexually heterodox, the black,
the crippled and diseased, later in the trilogy and beyond. And
although Alvaro comes to be increasingly irritated by these wretched
*émigrés*, his friend Sergio's love of all types of social pariahs – not just
victims of racial prejudice – prefigures the attitude he will adopt
himself in *Don Julián* and *Juan sin tierra*. When the two friends go to
the Barrio Chino (the red-light district) of Barcelona, it is Sergio, not
Alvaro, who says: 'La única gente interesante de Barcelona se
encuentra acá . . . . Putas, carteristas, maricones . . . . Los demás no
son personas, son moluscos' (*SI*, p. 75; 'The only place in Barcelona
you can find interesting people . . . . Whores, pickpockets, fairies.
. . . The rest aren't people, they're mollusks', *MI*, p. 60).

Sergio's image of molluscs will become Alvaro's crustaceans, but
other metaphors in *Señas* come even closer to ideas in the subsequent
fiction. Particularly noteworthy is the way in which conventions of
seniority amongst the *émigrés* at Madame Berger's café are described.
Alvaro uses a geological metaphor for the stratification of the clients:

he talks about those Spanish exiles who belong in 'la primera tanda',
'la segunda capa', and 'el tercer estrato' (*SI*, p. 247, 'the first group',
'the second layer', 'the third stratum', *MI*, pp. 204–5) and then
adds that 'el geólogo interesado hubiera podido descubrir restos de
sedimentaciones más añosas . . . y hasta un fosilizado ejemplar, único
en su género, codicia de coleccionistas, expertos e investigadores,
superviviente de la memorable Semana Trágica que ensangrentó en
1909 las calles de Barcelona' (*SI*, p. 248; 'the interested geologist
could have uncovered the remains of older sedimentations . . . and
even . . . one fossilized specimen, the only one of its kind, coveted by
collectors, experts, and researchers alike: a survivor of the memorable Tragic Week that had bloodied the streets of Barcelona in
1909', *MI*, p. 205, adapted). In *Don Julián*, too, the society of Tangier
is depicted as stratified, through the classification of its members as
solids, liquids, and gases. And in *Paisajes después de la batalla*, the
same point is made about the neighbourhood of Le Sentier in Paris,
this time via the image of a fancy layered cake. In these two cases,
the metaphors are being applied to a chaotic society, making the
point that the different types are 'juntos sí, pero no revueltos' (*DJ*,
p. 21; 'lying one atop the other without ever combining', *CJ*, p. 12);
they are societies with layers but which do not ascribe ascending
metaphysical value to each one, implying that they are not restrictive or psychologically damaging to anyone. Hence, they are treated
more as anthropological curiosities than as a serious or alarming
social issue. Exactly the same amused and amusing tone is adopted
in the description of the café society in *Señas*; indeed, any law of
ascending superiority is forcefully, if tacitly subverted in this particular choice of image, for the most senior members of the clientele correspond to the lowest geological stratum. This plants in the
reader's mind at the beginning of the trilogy that hierarchical stratification is to be ridiculed and undermined; as if in confirmation
of this, when the parallel image of solids, liquids, and gases is introduced in *Don Julián*, the earlier geological figure is explicitly
recalled, as if to stress that which way up the layers are imagined to
be here is of no consequence: 'los ingredientes se yuxtaponen sin
mezclarse jamás, como estratos geológicos superpuestos por el
poso de los siglos o líquidos de densidad diferente que sobrenadan
en la vasija experimental de científico . . .: sólidos, líquidos y gas-
eosos' (*DJ*, p. 21; 'ingredients that are juxtaposed but never mingle:
like geological strata formed by centuries of sedimentation, or

liquids of different densities that never mix in the test tube of
the scientist or the researcher . . .: solids, liquids, and gases', *CJ*,
pp. 11–12). And just the same reminder is to be found in *Paisajes*, as
if to stress that in this society, unlike Madame Berger's ridiculed
clientele, stratification is not judgemental. The cake, we are told, is
'comparable a . . . los gráficos de las eras geológicas trazados en los
libros de ciencias naturales en los que cada una de aquéllas integra un
estrato de diferente color, desde la base precámbrica a la altura
neolítica, exactamente su barrio (*PB*, p. 19; 'comparable to . . . those
charts of geological eras found in books on the natural sciences, in
which each of them is represented by a stratum of a different color,
from the Precambrian base to the Neolithic summit. Exactly the
same thing is true of his neighborhood', *LB*, p. 10). So, although it is
subversive in *Señas*, but plainly descriptive in *Don Julián* and *Paisajes*,
the concept of the stratified society divorced from an ascending
metaphysical order of superiority is born at the beginning of the
trilogy.

Up to this point, we have seen that themes that move into the
spotlight post-*Señas* are planted there, even if they are less noticeable
in that novel's dense foliage of plot and characterization, which keep
it closer to realism than its successors. The shift from *Señas* has so far
proven to be one of emphasis and style, rather than essence. However, the matter assumes greater complexity when the final stage of
my argument is reached. In brief, chapter 6 posits the theory that
the ultimate goal of Goytisolo's apologetics for chaos is a condition of
ceaseless flux or continual metamorphosis. Although there is some
evidence to suggest that Alvaro has slight inclinations in this direction in *Señas*, these momentary glimpses of an ideology to come are
outnumbered by his admissions of dismay at mutability. When, for
example, he is taken to visit his grandmother, who has lost her
reason, he is deeply distressed by the realization that seeing her so
changed triggers in him:

Fueron unos instantes dolorosos durante los cuales Alvaro había
retenido la respiración implorando a Dios que aquella sombra
errante le reconociera suyo, recobrara sus limpios y remotos
dones, retornara milagrosamente a la vida . . . .
Todo, incluido él mismo, no era definitivo y perdurable . . . sino
mudable, precario . . . todo aleatorio.

(*SI*, p. 54)

(They were painful moments, during which Alvaro had held his
breath, imploring God that the wandering shadow would recognize him as belonging to her, would recover her pure and remote
gifts, would miraculously come back to life . . . .
Everything, including himself, was not definitive and lasting . . .
but . . . changeable, precarious, . . . everything uncertain.)

                                            (*MI*, p. 43, adapted)

Later in *Señas*, using an image that in *Makbara* is to take on the
positive significance of ultimate freedom, Alvaro laments that 'tu
historia reciente se perdía en las arenas movedizas de la conjetura' (*SI*,
p. 129; 'your recent history was already being lost in the moving
sands of conjecture', *MI*, p. 107). Shifting desert sands still symbolize
ceaseless flux and formlessness in *Makbara*, even though they take on
further symbolic value therein, standing as an emblem of the Arabic,
nomadic lifestyle and in their association with heat, contrasting
sharply with the iciness of snowy purity and glacial virtue. The
delight that the narrator of the later novel takes in the very same
concept as that which haunts the Alvaro of *Señas* is striking:

> analogías entre desierto y océano: espacio ilimitado, aislamiento,
> silencio, imbricación de olas y dunas, libertad desmesurada y
> salvaje, nitidez, absoluta limpieza . . .
> movilidad, valor, incertidumbre, solidaridad ante el peligro, resis-
> tencia, moderación, hospitalidad leve, fraterna
>
>                                            (*Ma*, pp. 205–6)

> (analogies between desert and ocean: endless space, isolation,
> silence, the imbricated patterns formed by waves and dunes,
> boundless, unbridled freedom, brightness, sharp clarity, absolute
> purity . . .
> mobility, courage, uncertainty, solidarity when danger threatens,
> stamina, moderation, spontaneous and fraternal hospitality)
>
>                                            (*Mb*, pp. 245–6)

Antonio of *Señas*, a political rebel, cannot cope, as we have seen,
with blurred boundaries and is therefore driven to re-establish himself within his own self-image as a pariah, which simultaneously
re-establishes his condition of imprisonment, since his rudeness to
Don Gonzalo causes the Civil Guard to clamp down and withdraw
the privileges formerly allowed him. It is worth noting that the lack
of clear distinction in his social role is seen as disturbing, not only on
a straightforward psycho-social level, but also in terms of its effects

on language: 'se movía en un universo ambiguo en el que las palabras perdían su primitiva significación y asumían intenciones huidizas y cambiantes . . . . Libertad y prisión se mezclaban en una realidad imprecisa (*SI*, p. 221; 'he was moving about in an ambiguous universe where words had lost their primitive meaning and had assumed fleeting and changing intentions . . . . Freedom and imprisonment were mixed together in an imprecise reality', *MI*, p. 184). This fear of semantic flux contrasts with the desire expressed in *Juan sin tierra* to shock the Spanish language out of its stagnation, an idea conveyed by the image of the resolutely constipated Alvarito (*JT*, p. 210; *JL*, p. 186). In this novel, the narrator openly seeks to set the language in motion, to jolt it out of the torpidity of orderly definitions, strict usage, grammatical structure: 'liberar las palabras de su obediencia a un orden pragmático . . .: conmutando la anomalía semántica en núcleo generador de poesía . . .: manipulación improductiva (onanista) de la palabra escrita, ejercicio autosuficiente (poético) del goce ilegal' (*JT*, pp. 296–7; 'delivering words from their subservience to a pragmatic order . . .: transmuting semantic anomaly into the generative nucleus of poetry . . .: unproductive (onanistic) manipulation of the written word, self-sufficient (poetic) enjoyment of illicit pleasure', *JL*, pp. 261–2). Unlike Antonio, who is perhaps somewhat immature in his attitude, or if not immature, more conditioned by *esquizofrenia colectiva* than he realizes – he can function only if he can perceive a clear boundary setting him unequivocally apart from established values – the narrator of *Juan sin tierra* finds that to create a literary and linguistic reality in a constant state of flux, to blur as many semantic boundaries as possible, is itself an extremely effective form of rebellion and subversion.

So it is that the fundamental difference between *Señas de identidad* and the subsequent novels emerges, in this theme of metamorphic fluidity. Antonio and Alvaro in this first novel of the trilogy cannot cope with the creative and subversive potential of a thorough-going rejection of order. They can already perceive the psycho-social damage done by the order they know, but wish for a different one, rather than perceiving the possibilities for liberty and fertility of an order-free society. Whilst Alvaro deplores the 'orden brutal' of Spain under Franco (*SI*, p. 420; 'brutal order', *MI*, p. 350), and the industrial order of north-western Europe, he expresses his love for Dolores in terms of a divinely ordered plan: 'vuestra unión reposaba sobre una armonía preestablecida (*SI*, p. 327; 'your union was built on a pre-established harmony', *MI*, p. 271). And when the love affair finally collapses, as he realizes that she is flirting with Antonio, it is in utter despair that he contemplates the metamorphosis of his world of perfect order to complete chaos:

Bruscamente tuviste la impresión de estar de más.
El paisaje se transformó .... la nada se abrió a tus pies. Tran-
seúntes y automóviles circulaban caóticos, privados de finalidad y
de sustancia .... Irremediablemente solo.

(SI, pp. 356–7)

(You had the sudden feeling that you were intruding.
The countryside changed .... Nothingness opened up at your
feet. Pedestrians and cars were circulating chaotically, deprived of
finality and substance .... Irremediably alone.)

(MI, pp. 296–7)

This shift in attitude towards order and chaos may be seen as an explanation for the dramatic stylistic move from *Señas* to its successors. It could be asserted that once chaos is found to be the principle of ideal liberty and creativity, the style of the novels changes, for as we have seen, the order–chaos question has an important semantic dimension too. In *Señas*, where Alvaro is searching for some clarity in his past and that of his family and country, struggling to create some order out of jumbled memories, papers, and photographs, the reader, like him, is permitted gradually to piece snatches of anecdotes together, along with their accompanying emotional import. After *Señas* though, the narrator abandons his search for a better order than the one he was brought up to revere, discovering the delights of a society based on a chaotic lack of differentiation: that of the Maghreb. On the linguistic level, this revelation metamorphoses the style of the post-*Señas* fiction too, for now the narrator is deliberately seeking to destroy rigid boundaries of definition and usage, restrictive laws of grammatical structure, and also, on the literary level, stultifying conventions of genre and style. It is this attempt at what might be termed lawless literature that makes *Don Julián* and *Juan sin tierra* difficult for the reader. We can take nothing for granted: not the meanings of words and set expressions, not even conventions of punctuation and lay-out. So the thematic shift post-*Señas* away from a yearning for clarity and order, reflected both in the content and the style of the trilogy, can be attributed to the overall *raison d'être* of the trilogy: namely, the protagonist's struggle to cut loose from his

Spanish origins. At the beginning of this struggle, Alvaro's upbringing still has enough of a hold over his mentality for him to accept unquestioningly the equations of order equals good and chaos equals evil. One should not misinterpret his exhortation to himself at the end of *Señas*:

cuanto te separa de ellos cultívalo
lo que les molesta en ti glorifícalo
negación estricta absoluta de su orden esto eres tú

(*SI*, p. 419)

(cultivate everything that separates you from them
glorify whatever in you bothers them
the strict and absolute negation of their order that is what you are)

(*MI*, p. 349)

It is still only the rejection of '*su* orden' ('*their* order') that he can see as desirable; he has not yet realized that the key to their order is the veneration of order itself.

By the end of the trilogy, Alvaro will have thrown off his background sufficiently to perceive that his psychological metamorphosis must not transform his mind into just a differently ordered one, but rather, into an infinitely fluid condition. Only by rejecting the concept of order itself, will he find true freedom. This revelation is most clearly expressed after the trilogy, in *Makbara*; perhaps it is only having created a character – Mendiola – who made the journey, that Goytisolo can invent a new narrator to explain the destination. It is in the context of literary objectives that the ideal of infinite flux, not merely an exchange of one order for another, is posited:

vivir literalmente del cuento : de un cuento que es, ni más ni menos, el de nunca acabar : ingrávido edificio sonoro en de(con)-strucción perpetua : lienzo de Penélope tejido, destejido día y noche : castillo de arena mecánicamente barrido por el mar . . .
lectura en palimpsesto : . . . infinitas posibilidades de juego a partir del espacio vacío

(*Ma*, pp. 219–20 and 222)

(to live, literally by storytelling: a story that, quite simply, is never-ending: a weightless edifice of sound in perpetual de-

(con)struction: a length of fabric woven by Penelope and unwoven night and day: a sand castle mechanically swept away by the sea . . .

a palimpsestic reading: . . . infinite possibilities of play opening up in the space that is now vacant)

(Mb, pp. 265 and 270)

# 2
## *Esquizofrenia colectiva:*
## The Attack on Duality

Dualism governs perhaps the most immediately striking network of symbolism in Goytisolo's later novels. Even on first reading, the innumerable allusions to good and evil, white and black, cold and heat, virtue and vice (amongst other opposing pairs), are bound to strike the reader. The prominence of these symbols in the texts makes them a readily accessible starting-point for an analysis of Goytisolo's underlying ideology, beneath the surface plots and themes, which have been thoroughly examined by many critics already (see Introduction).

The appearance of the term *equizofrenia colectiva* towards the end of *Juan sin tierra* does not make it any less apt a heading under which to subsume Goytisolo's varying depictions of dualism and his attitude towards it, either earlier in *Juan sin tierra* or in *Don Julián* and *Señas*. Chapter 1 has considered the embryonic presence of *esquizofrenia colectiva* in the first novel of the trilogy; in this chapter, the development of the concept post-*Señas* will be studied. Once again, the reader is reminded that the texts are treated outside their chronological order in the belief that parallels and divergences emerge more powerfully by this method.

It would seem most logical to begin by considering dualism in its religious manifestation, for this predominates in *Juan sin tierra*; essentially, *esquizofrenia colectiva* may be defined in this context as the dichotomy between sin and purity. Although these are opposite concepts in traditional works of Catholic moral theology, Goytisolo succeeds in bringing them so close together in *Juan sin tierra* as to render them almost indistinguishable. He achieves this principally by means of two devices. One is to level the same razor-sharp criticism and sarcasm at both, and the other is the use of the historical perspective. This last is exploited in order to shed doubt on modern standards that confidently declare some actions, words, and thoughts sinful, and others, pure, by giving the conventional Christian argument used to justify acts of barbarism in the past. For example, the defense of the *auto-da-fé* is a faithful representation of traditional Church teaching. Having compared the short-lived pain of being burnt at the stake with the eternal tortures of hell, the apologist asks: 'quiénes serán entonces los bárbaros?: nosotros o ellos [los espíritus hipócritamente humanitarios]?' (*JT*, p. 186; 'so who are the real barbarians then?: we or they [the hypocritically humanitarian]?', *JL*, p. 167). Etienne Gilson summarizes Saint Bernard's ascetic message in one of the latter's sermons in just the same terms: 'Who spares his flesh the better, – the Cistercian who mortifies to save it, or the man we call carnal who condemns his own to eternal punishment?'[1] In this way, Goytisolo draws attention to the monstrous carnage of the Inquisition, not in the framework of a lamentable fact of less enlightened times, but rather, as a true application of Christian teaching.[2] This focus on the Church as the cause of such barbarism makes the reader contemplate whether the fundamental tenets of Christianity – which, after all, are the same today as they were then – may not remain a threat to civilized, humane society. Goytisolo is unequivocal in his affirmation of this possibility throughout *Juan sin tierra*, showing that the division of society and of the individual into two separate parts, one good and the other evil, threatens the mental health of the whole of Christendom. The same point is forcefully made in the non-fictional context of an essay in Goytisolo's 1978 collection *Libertad, libertad, libertad*, which presents in straightforward terms what is perhaps more obscure in the fiction:

Por espacio de décadas, desde las altas esferas del poder, nuestros programadores culturales y morales se esforzaron en inculcar en nuestro pueblo, con el deliberado propósito de transformar a la masa de los españoles en un rebaño de seres mutilados, culpables y enfermos, encerrados en la problemática sin salida de una lucha permanente y estéril contra su propio cuerpo.

(For decades, from the upper echelons of power, our moral and cultural programmers exerted themselves to inculcate our people, with the deliberate purpose of transforming the Spanish masses into a herd of mutilated beings, guilty and sick, locked into the dead-end problematics of a sterile and permanent struggle against their own bodies.)[3]

The imagery that is used throughout *Juan sin tierra* is as traditional as the apologetics. Saint Bernard – to whose writings the narrator repeatedly refers – draws the same parallel between purifying gold and purifying the soul as may be found in the novel when the apologist for the *auto-da-fé* preaches: 'conocéis la existencia de piritas auríferas que es preciso extraer, lavar y batir para que cedan al fin su noble sustancia amarilla?: pues así se acrisola y mejora el alma' (*JT*, p. 180; 'you know, do you not, of the existence of goldbearing ore that it is necessary to extract, wash, and beat in order that it may at last yield up its noble yellow substance?: in like manner the soul ... is purified and refined', *JL*, p. 162). Pure gold as an image for the pure soul is not, however, the one most commonly used in the novel. Goytisolo prefers another equally traditional network of metaphor and simile: that of whiteness for purity, blackness for evil, and stains or blemishes for individual sins.[4] In this regard, Spires draws attention to the symbolic unity of *Juan sin tierra* with his perceptive observation about the ending of the novel: 'With the end of the linguistic process, exterior reality imposes itself, and the text and the text speaker are returned to static black markers on a white page. Thus the novel ends where it began, with a black-white binary opposition'.[5]

This imagery is not exclusive to *Juan sin tierra*, but is to be found throughout the trilogy and in *Makbara*, as we shall see. In *Don Julián*, the Baby Jesus in a church is described as 'un muñeco de pelo rubio natural peinado a lo Shirley Temple' (*DJ*, p. 108; 'a doll with natural blond hair combed in Shirley Temple corkscrew curls', *CJ*, p. 89, adapted). This combines the traditional religious significance of blondness with its modern, secular manifestation, Shirley Temple, the Hollywood film industry's personification of the charms of childhood innocence and purity, and as much an object of adult veneration and love as the child saint in medieval times. At the same time, the use of the term *muñeco* ('doll'), implies an ideal devoid of any real humanity, and because fabricated by human beings to appeal to public taste, equally devoid of divinity. The *muñeco* is merely a mercenary creation dependent for its saleability on human fantasies and yearnings after purity and conventional prettiness. Furthermore, the choice of a little girl as parallel to Baby Jesus stresses the asexuality of both. This draws attention to the component of the veneration of child saints that accords them a special purity because they are supposed to be as yet untainted by sexuality. The concept of a lack of sexuality in children is dismantled at the end of *Don Julián*, when the protagonist's child self is drawn – 'irresistiblemente atraído' (*DJ*, p. 218; 'irresistibly attracted', *CJ*, p. 184) – to the sexual fulfilment offered by the adult self.

The same pattern is to be found in the case of the *carpetovetónico*'s daughter, who is first described as 'muy blanca y rubia' and as 'casta, continente' (*DJ*, pp. 162–3; 'very fair-skinned and blond' and 'chaste and continent', *CJ*, p. 137), linking pale colour to moral purity once again. Here, though, the destruction of the image follows straight on, when she is revealed as having as much of a sexual identity as the narrator's child self will do later in the text. Significantly, when this becomes apparent, she is no longer described in terms of whiteness, but attention is drawn to her 'pijama de seda negra' (*DJ*, p. 163; 'black silk pajamas', *CJ*, p. 138) and far from having a fair skin, her stomach is called 'bruñido' (*DJ*, p. 164; 'tan', *CJ*, p. 138). Thus, Goytisolo exploits traditional colour imagery by showing that the whitest-seeming person may be black underneath. This links up with the broader dualistic theme, which I term the *cáscara/pulpa* ('shell/pulp') phenomenon, the imagery of shells, masks, and disguises, which conceal the fleshly interior more or less adequately. The significance of this *topos* will be studied in the next chapter, dealing with the pariah figure. In brief, however, it is worth stressing the importance and endurance of the symbol, for although it perhaps reaches its climax at the end of *Don Julián*, with the tortured child self 'interiormente dividido en dos: por un lado la cáscara y por otro la pulpa . . .: ángel mentido: y real demonio: y el mundo, igualmente partido en dos: a un lado, casa y aula, piedad y holgura, Sagrada Mesa y mesa bien surtida: al otro, cabaña y fango, vergajo y lecho' (*DJ*, pp. 224–5; 'secretly divided in two: an outer shell and an inner pulp . . . : a spurious angel and a genuine demon: and the world likewise divided in two: home and school, piety and material comforts, the Lord's Table and groaning family board on one hand: on the other hand, a shack and mud, the whip and the cot', *CJ*, p. 190), it may be traced back to *Señas* and the 'rígido corsé' (*SI*, p. 18; 'rigid corset', *MI*, p. 13) discussed in chapter 1. Moving forward from *Don Julián*, the theme emerges once more in *Juan sin tierra*, when the black slaves on the sugar-plantation cast a spell on their owner's family, whereby the parents will start to sweat profusely and uncontrollably, and the little girls will begin menstruating. All are dressed in white and fair-skinned. With the spell's realization, the depiction of bodily fluids staining white skin and garments stresses the horror of those concerned: 'un klínex, quién tiene un klínex?, exclamarán a coro las niñas' (*JT*, p. 45; 'a Kleenex, who's got a Kleenex?, the girls will exclaim in chorus', *JL*, p. 34). This serves to underscore the artificial superimposition of whiteness or purity and the inevitability of 'body' or *pulpa* seeping through (see *JT*, pp. 44–5, *JL*, pp. 33–4, for the passage in full) and implies a reversal of the Platonic and Christian concept of the body imprisoning the soul, for here Goytisolo depicts the ideal of ethereal purity imprisoning and attempting to conceal the flesh.[6]

As these bloodstains demonstrate, white does not only appear in juxtaposition with black. It may be opposed to red, as a specific colour of carnality, rather than the more general black of evil. In *Don Julián*, yet another contrast is posited. In the Moorish re-invasion of Spain, part of the metamorphosis of the peninsula consists of colour transformation: 'el pardo será verde : el blanco será verde : el amarillo y gris serán verdes' (*DJ*, p. 147; 'the dun will turn to green: the white will turn to green: the sere yellows and the somber grays will turn to bright greens', *CJ*, p. 123, adapted). Pale colours are here to be turned to green, suggesting a number of symbolic overtones. In its association with fertility, the lush vegetation sought by the metamorphosis indicates, by extension, the aridity of the veneration of paleness and hence, purity. Next, in its colloquial value of 'licentious' (analogous to 'blue' in English), *verde* stands as an alternative to black in its association with the pleasures of the flesh. Green is also the colour emblematic of the Islamic Revolution, which fits in with the preference in the text for Islam over Christianity. Lastly, green is the colour of putrefaction and, in this meaning, reminds the reader of the narrator's love for the 'olores densos, emanaciones agrias' of Tangier in *Don Julián*, leading him to declare exultantly, 'todo lo que sea secreción, podredumbre, carroña será familiar para ti' (*DJ*, p. 44; 'everything that is secretion, rottenness, carrion will be your chosen realm', *CJ*, p. 32).

In the examples discussed hitherto, Goytisolo finds value in retaining conventional colour symbolism: white remains the colour of purity and spirituality, whilst black retains its equivalence to evil and carnality, with red and green as traditional alternatives. All that he changes is the supposition that purity is good and impurity bad. However, this is not his only method, for in *Don Julián*, the fleshly Arabs are also associated with whiteness, making unexpected bedfellows with Baby Jesus, Shirley Temple, and the *carpetovetónico*'s daughter in her chaste manifestation. The Arabs wear 'blancos turbantes' (*DJ*, p. 144; 'white turbans', *CJ*, p. 120) and Julián in particular has a 'níveo turbante' as well as the 'afilada blancura de unos dientes habituados al mordisco, al beso varón' (*DJ*, p. 185; a 'snow-white turban' and 'sharp white teeth made for love bites, for passionate, virile kisses', *CJ*, p. 157). The favourable tone of this description contrasts sharply with the derision heaped on the *Parejita Reproductora* (the 'Reproductive Couple') of *Juan sin tierra*, who appear in toothpaste advertisements, presumably because they like white teeth as much as Julián does: 'la acendrada blancura y perfumado aliento de la pasta dentífrica subrayan su natural armonía' (*JT*, p. 68; 'the perfumed, snow-white purity of toothpaste emphasizes their natural harmony', *JL*, p. 54).

The apparent inconsistency of this colour symbolism may be explained by giving some consideration to the shifting meanings of purity exploited by Goytisolo. There are those characters who are white and pure in the way the narrator loathes: that is to say, in the conventional, religious sense of virtue or in the post-religious sense of hygiene. The *Parejita Reproductora* of *Juan sin tierra* belong in this group, as do the narrator's child self and the *carpetovetónico*'s daughter in *Don Julián*, before their purity is destroyed. Conversely, there are those who are good in the narrator's view, which is to say, untainted by either the Church or Western consumer society. In this group may be placed the white-clad Moors and of course Julián himself. As Arabs, they are clearly free of the influence of Christian doctrine and as inhabitants of Tangier, they are removed from post-Christian Western society: 'los beneficios de la ínclita sociedad de consumo no se manifiestan aún en estas tierras' (*DJ*, p. 21; the marvelous benefits of the consumer society have not yet reached these parts', *CJ*, p. 12). As long as the reader is aware of the distinction between those who are 'white' by conventional standards, on the one hand, and by the narrator's, on the other, the colour symbolism can be appreciated.

In *Makbara*, the same dual significance for colour symbolism is also to be found: indeed, the split values of pale and dark colours are carried to the ultimate in this text, for the very same white dress that represents the loathsome variety of purity at the 'Salon du Mariage' becomes an emblem of the narrator's own idea of good when it is worn by the angel. The *Pronuptia* stand at the Salon is described as coldly white – 'níveo' (*Ma*, p. 80; 'snow-white', *Mb*, p. 84) – and, ironically, as 'sicodélico' (*Ma*, p. 80; 'psychedelic', *Mb*, p. 84), for the only colours are pastels. Artificiality is also emphasized, with the description of 'docenas de maniquís inmovilizados en posturas esbeltas y gráciles' (*Ma*, p. 80; 'dozens of mannequins frozen in lithe, graceful postures', *Mb*, p. 84), echoing the *muñeco* ('doll') image of Baby Jesus (*DJ*, p. 108; *CJ*, p. 89), who, incidentally, is in the arms of a Madonna described as 'un maniquí de madera articulado' (*DJ*, p. 108; 'a wooden mannequin with moving joints', *CJ*, p. 89). Later in *Makbara*, the imagery of the *Pronuptia* wedding dress takes on converse symbolic value, when it forms part of a depiction of uninhibited sexual pleasure: 'tu jarabe es espléndido, bendigo al médico que lo recetó, lo apuro, rebaño la cuchara, . . . para ti me voy a quitar la ropa, el modelo Etincelle de Pronuptia, la falda con cola de volantes, el décolleté anticonvencional . . . deseo utilizarlo de asiento, trabajar con codos y rodillas, no hay niña más flexible y elástica que yo' (*Ma*, p. 158; 'your syrup is splendid, I bless the doctor who prescribed it, I down every last drop of it and lick the spoon, . . . I'm going to take off my clothes . . . for you, the Etincelle model from Pronuptia, the skirt with the ruffled train, the unconventional low-cut neckline . . . I want to ride it like a saddle, pump with my knees and elbows, there's no young chick more lithe and supple than I am', *Mb*, p. 186).

At the beginning of *Juan sin tierra* especially, with reference to the sugar plantation community, but to a lesser extent throughout the later novels, colour imagery serves an additional aspect of duality, namely, racial prejudice. In one of the preacher's harangues to the slaves, he says, for example: 'qué bello habría sido el espectáculo de unas almas inocentes y blancas bajo el modesto disfraz de una piel morena e indigna!' (*JT*, p. 26; 'how beautiful a spectacle it would have been to see innocent lily-white souls beneath the modest disguise of a dark and unworthy skin!', *JL*, p. 15), and later in the same sermon, he refers to 'diablos tiznados' (*JT*, p. 27; 'sooty devils', *JL*, p. 17). It is of incidental interest to note that, according to my interview with Goytisolo (Paris, August 1985, unpublished), the contents of the sermons on the sugar plantantion were taken from a certain Canon Estrada's 'catecismo para negros bozales' (catechism for newly imported black slaves), and were not a fabrication or even an exaggeration by Goytisolo. Indeed, Estrada is mentioned in *Juan sin tierra* (p. 34). Mary is repeatedly called, not Blessed or any of the other well-used epithets, but *La Virgen Blanca* ('The White Virgin'), emphasizing the association between whiteness and purity. Furthermore, the depiction of the Virgin as white stands as a symbol of

virtue in juxtaposition with the blackness of the slaves, symboli-
zing vice or evil in generalized form, and the alternative epithet for
her, *inmaculada* ( *JT*, p. 53; 'immaculate', *JL*, p. 41), is counterposed–
more powerfully in Spanish than in English–to the *máculas* ('stains')
of individual sins, a term used by the preacher when he tells the
slaves that if they are virtuous, 'ingresaréis en el Cielo con una
blancura exquisita y sin mácula' ( *JT*, p. 36; 'you will enter the
Kingdom of Heaven with an exquisite, immaculate [stainless] whiteness', *JL*, p. 25). Synonyms expressing the same idea that sins are
stains or blemishes on the soul are common in *Juan sin tierra*: 'taras'
( *JT*, p. 35; 'defects', *JL*, p. 25), 'escoria', 'inmundicia', 'suciedades'
(all *JT*, p. 37; 'dross', 'impurities', 'dirty marks', *JL*, p. 26, adapted),
for example.

This dual counterpoint–purity/goodness to impurity/evil on the
one hand, and purity/stainlessness to impurity/sins on the other–
follows Christian doctrine: the twin concepts of redemption and
original sin corresponding to the first, and that of absolution and
individual sins committed for the second. The Church teaches that
original sin, in spite of Christ's redemption of mankind as a whole,
still leaves concupiscence–the tendency to lust–which means that to
be virtuous entails a constant struggle against what seem to be
natural inclinations, but which are really the distortion of man's
essentially–that is, pre-lapsarian–good nature. The translation of
this precept into the division of body from soul, with everything
associated with the body seen as detrimental to the soul and vice
versa, may be attributed to the influence of Plato on Paul. In *Phaedo*,
the former puts these pithy comments into Socrates's mouth:

> The philosopher's soul utterly despises his body and flees from
> it . . . . So long as we have the body accompanying our reason in
> its enquiries, so long as our souls are befouled by this evil
> admixture, we shall assuredly never fully possess that which we
> desire, to wit truth . . . . When soul and body are conjoined,
> Nature prescribes that the latter should be slave and subject, the
> former master and ruler . . . . The lover of knowledge recognizes
> that . . . his soul is a veritable prisoner fast bound within his body
> and cemented thereto.[7]

A similar repugnance towards the body is expressed in Paul's Epistle
to the Romans:

For I delight in the law of God after the inward man:
But I see another law in my members, warring against the law of my mind, and bringing me into captivity to the law of sin which is in my members. O wretched man that I am! who shall deliver me from the body of this death?
... With the mind I myself serve the law of God; but with the flesh the law of sin.

(Romans 7.22–25)

As we have seen in chapter 1, the Manichæans opposed matter to God, defining matter as concupiscence and regarding the soul as its prisoner; this was also influential in the evolution of Christianity.[8] Whatever the sources for the Christian dichotomy between body and soul, however, there can be no doubt that it has long been of fundamental importance. Pascal puts the matter succinctly in his *Pensées*: 'Nous sommes composés de deux natures opposées et de divers genre, d'âme et de corps'.[9] This is of course what Goytisolo calls *esquizofrenia colectiva* in *Juan sin tierra*. The meaning that he attaches to the psychiatric term *esquizofrenia* ('schizophrenia'), would seem to be the etymological rather than the technical one, that is to say, *esquizo-* meaning 'split' and *-frenia* meaning 'soul'.

At this point he departs from the vocabulary and tone of treatises on moral theology, for instead of limiting discussion of bodily desires to sexuality, sleep, food and drink, with their sinful counterparts, lust, sloth, and gluttony, he adds another, namely, excretion. The theme is used in a multitude of ways; the image of sweat and blood seeping through white skin and garments in *Juan sin tierra* has been discussed above. In addition, he attacks the taboo nature of the subject of defecation, which, as he explains in an essay about Quevedo, he sees as a type of collective self-deception in the interests of 'los grandiosos edificios "racionales" erigidos por credos, religiones, ideologías' ('the grandiose "rational" edifices erected by credos, religions, ideologies').[10]

The theme of defecation is employed principally with relation to concupiscence. Its link with the taboos of sodomy and homosexuality bestow upon it an emblematic significance representing forbidden sexual practices. At the same time, as a completely natural and inescapable human function, Goytisolo's persistent references to it tacitly undermine the Christian concept that it is possible and indeed essential to control the sexual urge, for the implication is that sexual activity is as irrepressible as the need to defecate and any attempt to

abstain from the former is as pointless and even ludicrous as to
forswear the latter. He pours scorn on the idea of sexual repression
by means of this parallel with defecation in the section of *Juan sin
tierra* where the 'bienaventurado niño Alvarito' (*JT*, p. 203; 'the
blessed child Alvarito', *JL*, p. 180) overcomes the carnal desire to
defecate (*JT*, pp. 203–8; *JL*, pp. 180–4).[11] Whilst the reader is aware
throughout this episode that defecation is specifically associated with
sodomy and homosexuality, he is also bound to notice the wider
value of the symbol: its representation of the whole concept of the
flesh, as carnal activity *par excellence*, utterly devoid of any spiritual
component. Thus, Goytisolo's narrator is specifically drawing attention to the absurdity, as he sees it, of limiting sexual activity to 'la
cópula normal, el acto creador que excusan los cánones' (*JT*, p. 29;
'normal copulation, the act of generation pardoned by canon law',
*JL*, p. 19), but he is simultaneously pointing to the entire mental
apparatus that seeks to repress everything connected with the body,
showing it to be an enterprise as unhealthy as it is futile.

In this wider application of the episode, Alvarito's desire to
become a saint echoes his earlier, doomed attempt in *Señas de
identidad* (*SI*, pp. 22–31; *MI*, pp. 16–24). In both cases, it is the
child's dissatisfaction with his body that leads him to yearn for
martyrdom and in symbolic terms the dissatisfaction is identical: in
*Señas* he is unhappy about his dark colouring and robust constitu-
tion: 'preguntándote con angustia si los niños morenos y saludables
como tú podían aspirar no obstante al favor y protección de las
potencias celestes' (*SI*, p. 23; 'wondering with anguish whether dark
and healthy children like you could still aspire to the favor and
protection of the heavenly powers', *MI*, p. 17). In *Juan sin tierra*, it is
his bodily functions: 'su aguda conciencia de la naturaleza corrupta
del cuerpo humano, con su fuerte inclinación al desahogo animal y
sus secreciones impuras' (*JT*, p. 203; 'his acute awareness of the
corrupt nature of the human body, with its strong inclination toward
animal-like alleviation and its impure secretions', *JL*, p. 180). As we
have seen, dark colours and defecation both serve as symbols for
carnality. In other words, the child seeks to annihilate the fleshly part
of himself, which his Christian upbringing has taught him to depre-
cate in both novels; the difference lies only in the realistic style
of portrayal adopted in the first novel of the trilogy, compared with
the fantastic tone of the third. Thus, in the former, Goytisolo depicts the inevitable disillusionment caused by such aspirations,
whereas in the latter, the discourse remains within the child's world
of fantasized identification with hagiographical fable. The fantasy

element is reflected in the style chosen to describe Alvarito, as well as in the successful outcome of his battle against the flesh. The reader is told, for example, that 'en vez de entregarse a los juegos . . . prefería refugiarse en el oratorio . . . absorto en meditaciones graves y abstrusas' (*JT*, p. 203; 'instead of giving himself over to . . . games . . . , he preferred to retreat to the . . . chapel, . . . absorbed in grave and recondite meditations', *JL*, p. 180). This is typical of the tone of traditional accounts of saints' childhoods, such as those quoted in *Señas* and without exaggeration, it must be said. Let us recall part of one description: 'Frecuentemente desaparecía de su casa para postrarse ante el Sagrario. Hallábanla allí sonriente y como en éxtasis, respetuosamente inmóvil y transportada de amor. A pesar de su niñez, comprendía ya' (*SI*, pp. 23–4; 'She would often disappear from home to prostrate herself before the Sanctuary. They would find her there, smiling and as if in ecstasy, respectfully motionless and carried away by love. In spite of her early years, she already understood', *MI*, p. 17).

In *Don Julián*, the *carpetovetónico* is the mouthpiece for this Christian idea of making the flesh suffer in the interests of the soul: 'hay que desterrar las actitudes cómodas e intranscendentes : someter la realidad a los imperativos absolutos del espíritu : a un orden jerárquico, vertical' (*DJ*, p. 81; 'we must do away with complacent, pedestrian attitudes: force reality to obey the categorical imperatives of the spirit: to submit to a hierarchical, vertical order!', *CJ*, p. 66); 'el carpeto concibe la historia como un lento proceso de auto-depuración, como un continuo ejercicio ascético de perfeccionamiento : en el fondo del alma ibera hay un residuo indestructible de estoicismo que, hermanado íntimamente con el cristianismo, ha enseñado a los hombres de la Meseta a sufrir y aguantar' (*DJ*, p. 111; 'the Hispano conceives of history as a slow process of self-perfection: in the depths of the Iberian soul there is an indestructible residuum of stoicism which, acting in intimate conjunction and perfect harmony with Christianity, has taught the men of the Meseta to suffer and endure', *CJ*, p. 92). These sentiments are taken almost verbatim from the extreme right-winger, Manuel García Morente, who of course was in earnest.[12] It is important to be aware that they are no exaggeration of García Morente's ideas; the potency of Goytisolo's parody lies in the fidelity of his reproduction of ideals held genuinely by a respected writer as recently as 1938. Born in 1931, Goytisolo's childhood must have been affected by the climate of opinion that García Morente's writings reflect.

Furthermore, when Goytisolo writes that 'el pequeño Séneca

siente insaciables afanes de inmortalidad y quiere abolir toda distancia entre el ser temporal y el ser eterno' (*DJ*, p. 114; 'little Seneca feels an insatiable thirst for immortality and is eager to bridge forever the gap between temporal being and eternal being', *CJ*, p. 95), this again is just how García Morente describes the attitude of the *caballero cristiano* (the 'Christian gentleman').[13] Goytisolo's use of Seneca to stand for the ideal Spaniard, in place of García Morente's Christian gentleman, adds a layer of sarcasm to the attack, for the Spanish establishment's admiration for the Roman Stoic, and their claim to his Spanish identity at a time before Spain existed as a national entity, ridicules the angle taken by conventional Spanish historians, stressing the Latin and Germanic but ignoring the positive contribution of the Semitic component.[14] García Morente is quoted yet again when the adult Séneca — now called Figurón (the Figurehead) — declares that 'la materia, el cuerpo, los cuerpos están o deben estar a las órdenes del espíritu: si se niegan a obedecer a éste es preciso obligarles por la violencia, la penitencia o el castigo sobre sí mismo y sobre los demás' (*DJ*, p. 118; 'matter, the corporeal, physical bodies in general, obey, or ought to obey, the dictates of the spirit: should they refuse to obey, it is then necessary to force them to do so, through violence, penitence, or the punishment of oneself and others', *CJ*, p. 99).[15] In these sentiments, García Morente is not revealing himself as a fanatical freak, but is following in the revered footsteps of Saint Thomas Aquinas, who states in the *Summa Theologiae*:

> Now for the young apt for deeds of virtue by good natural disposition or by custom or, better still, by divine gift, all that is required is the fatherly discipline of admonition. Not all the young, however, are like that; some are bumptious, headlong in vice, not amenable to advice, and these have to be held back from evil by fear and force.[16]

The purpose of the mortification of the flesh in Catholic doctrine is clearly conveyed by the commentator on the penitential procession depicted in *Don Julián*: the penitents 'ponen a dura prueba sus febles sentidos para hacerse dignos de entrar un día, purificados y limpios en la Morada Celestial' (*DJ*, p. 183; 'they mortify their senses in order to make themselves worthy of one day entering the Kingdom of Heaven with souls purified of all sin', *CJ*, p. 155). Goytisolo's protagonist attacks this monopoly of respect accorded to ethereal considerations when he proclaims, 'dioses y reyes a la basura' (*DJ*, p. 157; 'gods and kings, into the garbage can', *CJ*, p. 132).

The fact that patriotism is condemned as vehemently as religion – kings as well as gods are to be discarded – refines the attack in *Don Julián* to one against García Morente and writers of his ilk, who class *hispanidad* ('Spanishness') with Christianity as equally lofty ideals:

> La hispanidad es consustancial con la religión cristiana. Los que por especial favor de la Providencia hemos nacido en esta vieja y amada piel de toro ... o en las fabulosas tierras de allende los mares, que la savia hispana ha vivificado hasta los tuétanos, gozamos de un privilegio único en el orbe: el de que nuestra naturaleza nacional se identifique con nuestra espiritualidad religiosa. Español y católico son sinónimos.

> (Spanishness is consubstantial with the Christian religion. Those of us upon whom Providence has bestowed the especial favour of being born and living on this old, beloved bull's skin [an affectionate term for Spain arising from the shape of the country] ... or in the fabulous lands over the seas which Hispanic sap has vitalized to the very marrow, enjoy a privilege unique on earth: the fact that our national nature is identified with our religious spirituality. Spaniard [or Spanish] and Catholic are synonyms.)[17]

Thus, the shock-value of Goytisolo's onslaught on the Church and on Spain is reduced to some degree, if the reader is acquainted with García Morente's writings, for it then becomes apparent that the principal butt of the attack is this writer's narrow-minded dogmatism, rather than the entire ethos of Roman Catholicism, plus the whole of Spain and everything it represents. Furthermore, García Morente was widely read in the 1930s, especially in Spanish schools, so it is not unreasonable for Goytisolo to expect readers to be acquainted with his writings and therefore recognize the quotations, realizing that he is the specific target.[18] Whether the individualized nature of Goytisolo's attack should be regarded as a weakness or as a strength of *Don Julián* is bound to depend on each reader's standpoint. A patriotic Spanish Catholic would no doubt be relieved to discover that the author is condemning one approach to patriotism and the Church – albeit one which was very popular in the post-Civil War years – whereas an unpatriotic atheist could feel disappointed at this. However, it remains implicit in the attack that it is the Church and Spain that are responsible for producing and nurturing opinions and ideals such as those espoused by García Morente, so that the condemnation is tacitly aimed at a broader target.

The same holds true for the references to the blood-letting of the Spanish nation, an image taken from Angel Ganivet's *Idearium español*. In *Don Julián*, Figurón 'somete el país a una prudente terapéutica de sangrías y purgas que restablece lentamente ... su comprometida salud' (*DJ*, p. 118; 'he subjects his country to a carefully administered series of therapeutic blood-lettings and purges which ... restores its once dangerously threatened health', *CJ*, p. 98). Compare this with Ganivet's proud declaration:

> España sola sobrepuja a las demás naciones juntas, por el número y excelencia de sus sangradores .... El supremo doctor español es el doctor Sagredo .... Y jamás en la historia de la humanidad se dio un ejemplo tan hermoso de estoicismo perseverante como aquél que nos ofrece la interminable falange de sangradores impertérritos, que durante siglos y siglos se han encargado de aligerar el aparato circulatorio de los españoles.

> (On her own Spain surpasses all other nations put together, for the number and excellence of her blood-letters .... The supreme Spanish doctor is Dr Sagredo .... And never in the history of humanity has there been such a fine example of stoical perseverance as that which we are offered by the interminable phalanx of imperturbable blood-letters, who for centuries on end have taken it upon themselves to lighten the circulatory apparatus of the Spanish.)[19]

Whilst explicitly attacking Ganivet, the narrator implicitly condemns the society that created and held him in high esteem.

The concept of blood-letting is put to a different purpose elsewhere in the text. Rather than the sanguinary Dr Sagredo of Lesage's *Gil Blas*,[20] Goytisolo creates a linguistic purist who echoes Sancho Panza's fanatical doctor in *Don Quixote*, an eccentric dietician who prevents Sancho from eating anything on the Insula Baratoria for the sake, so he claims, of Sancho's own health: 'Lo principal que hago es asistir a sus comidas y cenas, y a dejarle comer de lo que me parece que le conviene, y a quitarle lo que imagino que le ha de hacer daño y ser nocivo al estómago' ('My prinicipal duty is to be present at his dinners and suppers, to let him eat what seems to me fitting, and to take away from him what I presume may do him harm and be injurious to his stomach'). The linguistic purist of *Don Julián* says: 'lo principal que hago es asistir a sus comidas y cenas, y dejarle comer de lo que me parece castizo y quitarle cuanto etimológicamente es extraño' (*DJ*, p. 197; 'my principal concern is watching over his meals and repasts, allowing him to partake of only those dishes that seem to me to be of native origin and forbidding him everything that is etymologically foreign to him', *CJ*, p. 166).[21] Just as Sancho would starve if he had to follow the doctor's directives on pure food, Goytisolo implies that the Spanish language would soon be bled dry if ideals of linguistic purity were to be realized: 'hay que rescatar vuestro léxico: desguarnecer el viejo alcázar lingüístico: adueñarse de aquello que en puridad os pertenece: paralizar la circulación del lenguaje: chupar su savia: retirar las palabras una a una hasta que el exangüe y crepuscular edificio se derrumbe como un castillo de naipes' (*DJ*, p. 196; 'your lexicon must be rescued: the age-old linguistic fortress must be dismantled: the circulation of language must be paralysed: its sap must be sucked dry: words must be removed one by one until the crepuscular edifice, bled dry, collapses like a house of cards', *CJ*, pp. 165–6). This rejection of Arabic-derived words gives an ingeniously ironic twist to the 'destrucción de la España sagrada' (*DJ*, p. 52; 'the destruction of Sacred Spain', *CJ*, p. 39), for writers like García Morente and Ganivet are hoist with their own petard of anti-Arabism, as it were. It is with their hatred of the Moors that Goytisolo's narrator forges the weapon of their destruction, by showing how the Arabic component of their beloved language is vital to its survival. To remove it for the sake of purity would be as misguided as the belief in blood-letting.

García Morente states: 'el moro es siempre el otro ... en los dos sentidos inseparables de la *otra* religión y de la *otra* nacionalidad'; ('The Moor is always the other, in the two inseparable senses of the *other* religion and the *other* nationality').[22] Goytisolo recognizes this vision of the Arab as the quintessential Other: 'El Islam ha representado de cara al mundo cristiano occidental un papel autoconcienciador en términos de oposición y contraste: el de la alteridad, el del Otro'; ('To the Western Christian world, Islam has played a role of fostering self-awareness, in terms of opposition and contrast: the role of differentness, the role of the Other').[23] But García Morente adds: 'España, que es cristiana y española en contraposición del moro, tiene que conquistar su propio cuerpo y su propia alma ... a la punta de la espada cristiana .... España está hecha de fe cristiana y de sangre ibérica'; ('Spain, which is Christian and Spanish as opposed to the Moor, has to conquer her own body and her own soul ... at the

point of the Christian sword . . . . Spain is made of Christian faith
and Iberian blood').[24] Through the blood–letting image combined
with the re–working of the Cervantine dietician, Goytisolo shows
that this call to arms is literally suicidal to the concept of *hispanidad*,
which is inextricably and essentially bound up with Arabism. The
same point is made in more straightforward style in the non–fictional
framework of an article by Goytisolo published in the Spanish
newspaper *El país*:

> La vieja y tenaz propensión nuestra a interrogarse sobre lo que es
> España, a permanecer absortos en el examen arrobado y doloroso
> de la supuesta 'españolidad' produjo, como sabemos, una implac-
> able sucesión de podas, supresiones y descartes de cuanto no era
> genuinamente hispano–lo musulmán, judío, luterano, afrance-
> sado y un largo etcétera–que desarbolaron la rica y compleja
> cultura medieval y renacentista, arramblaron con los elementos
> supuestamente foráneos y nos transformaron en los felices prop-
> ietarios de vasto y castizo erial.

> (That old, tenacious propensity of ours to question ourselves over
> what Spain is, to sit absorbed in the painful and ecstatic examina-
> tion of supposed 'Spanishness' produced, as we know, an implac-
> able succession of pruning, suppressing, and casting aside what-
> ever was not genuinely Hispanic–whatever was Muslim, Jewish,
> Lutheran, Frenchified, and a long et cetera–which dismantled the
> rich and complex medieval and renaissance culture, did away with
> the supposedly foreign elements and turned us into the happy
> owners of a vast, pure wasteland.)[25]

Although it is clear from such a statement as this, as well as the
etymological purgation episode in *Don Julián*, that Goytisolo recognizes the dependence of *hispanidad* on its important Moorish component, within the texts of the later novels he exploits the idea of the
Moor as Other to the full. The knife-sharpener described in *Don
Julián* exemplifies this approach:

> la boca emboscada en una barba de varios días, el pantalón
> remendado, los faldones de la camisa por fuera : . . . rezagado
> morisco . . . : antes de llevar otra vez la flauta a los labios y ejercitar
> especialmente para ti, se diría, la melodiosa, perspicaz tentación :
> augurio de una vida mejor y más libre, lejos de la funesta Península
> y de su aletargada fauna

(DJ, p. 17)

(his mouth hidden from view in a thick growth of beard many days old, his shirttails hanging out over a much mended pair of pants:... a Hispano-Moorish vagabond ...: before raising the flute to his lips again and once more casting his melodious subtle spell, apparently meant especially for your your ears: the portent of a better, freer life, far from the dreary Peninsula and its lethargic fauna)

(*CJ*, p. 8)

The beard suggests the Arab's uncomplexed attitude towards his carnal, animal component; his occupation of knife-sharpener, violence, and the phallic flute that he seductively puts to his lips, all evoke the eroticism associated with Arab otherness. As a whole, the depiction presents a symbolic picture of fleshliness *par excellence*. The narrator ends the piece by clearly stating a preference for the Other, attributing to this shadow-ego of the Spaniard a better, freer life. Thus, this little vignette expresses in microcosm the author's attitude to *esquizofrenia colectiva* as applied to the question of Arabism. Within the mentality that classes the Moor as opposite of the Spaniard – an illusory classification, as the linguistic purge of *Don Julián* demonstrates – the Arab is preferable, in just the same way as black is depicted as preferable to white, flesh to spirit, and underworld to heaven.

Claudia Schaefer-Rodríguez criticizes Goytisolo's depiction of the Arab world:

Los árabes nunca tienen realidad social para él [Alvaro]; sólo son el epítome del 'enemigo' .... El árabe es la imagen del 'otro' .... Mendiola prefiere y necesita que se mantenga [la división Oriente/ Occidente (cristianos/musulmanes)] ... para que él pueda brincar al 'otro lado' así formado (con los parias, los marginados, el 'tercer mundo') cuando le convenga .... En fin, no fomenta una comprensión del hombre moderno, ni árabe ni español.

(The Arabs never have social reality for him [Alvaro]; they are just the epitome of the 'enemy' .... The Arab is the image of the 'other' .... Mendiola prefers and needs [the Orient/Occident (Christians/Muslims) division] to be maintained so that he can hop over to the 'other side' which is so created (with pariahs, the marginalized, the 'third world') whenever it suits him .... Finally, he does not foster an understanding of modern man, either Arab or Spanish.)[26]

This seems a little unfair, as Goytisolo never purports to depict Arabs as they really are, but rather to breathe life into the traditional image of the Arab, a process that emerges most clearly in the character of the North African of *Makbara*: oversexed, deaf (to reason), incomprehensible. Goytisolo comments:

> El mundo musulmán y más concretamente el marroquí se integran [en *Don Julián*, *Juan sin tierra*, y *Makbara*] . . . en una escenografía mental en la que la realidad empírica y las observaciones directas inciden casi siempre de modo secundario . . . . Los actores y comparsas que cruzan los espacios imaginarios de Tánger, Fez o Marraquech no son, o no son sólo marroquís 'de carne y hueso' sino sombras o máscaras creadas por una tradición occidental embebida de represiones, temores, deseos, animosidad, prejuicios.

> (The Muslim, and more particularly, the Moroccan worlds are integrated [into *Don Julián*, *Juan sin tierra*, and *Makbara*] . . . in a mental scenario into which empirical reality and direct observations almost always enter in a secondary position . . . . The actors and extras who cross the imaginary spaces of Tangier, Fez, or Marrakesh are not, or are not only 'flesh-and-blood' Moroccans, but shadows or masks created by a Western tradition steeped in repressions, dreads, desires, animosity, prejudices.)[27]

It may at first seem contradictory that Arabism is shown to be both an inherent part of *hispanidad* and its opposite. However, this may be resolved by distinguishing between what Goytisolo thinks himself and expresses through his protagonists and in articles such as the one from *El país* quoted above, and on the other hand, what he parodies through the various Spanish stereotypes, namely, the belief in a pure *hispanidad*, divorced from Moorish influences. Furthermore, a psychological approach to the apparent contradiction offers another solution. The Moor may be apprehended both as inherent to the Spanish self and in opposition to it, in the same sense that the shadow is part of the whole person and yet in opposition to the conscious portion of the psyche. Indeed, Goytisolo recognizes this in an essay, saying, 'El Otro soy yo . . . . El rodillo compresor del progreso, al dislocar cortezas y superficies, rescata los elementos subyacentes con los que podemos recomponer . . . la identidad integral perdida'; ('The Other is me. The bulldozer of progress, by dislocating crusts and surfaces, rescues the underlying elements with which we can put our lost integral identity back together again').[28] Or, as Jung puts it, if man 'turns his gaze inward upon the recesses of his own mind, he will discover a chaos and a darkness there that he would gladly ignore'; 'I must have a dark side also if I am to be whole'; 'every civilized man . . . is still an archaic man at the deeper levels of his psyche'.[29] This psychological angle would seem to offer both an explanation of, and a justification for, the apparent double focus of Goytisolo's depiction of impurity. On the one hand, it is what the Spaniards consciously consider to be alien to themselves and, in this aspect, the Arab world represents vice, carnality. On the other hand, it lies within the very people who shun it consciously and, in this *cáscara/pulpa* aspect, impurity is seen as escaping, now through the child self's irresistible attraction to Julián at the end of the second novel of the trilogy, or through Séneca's need to defecate in the same work (*DJ*, pp. 153–4; *CJ*, p. 129), now through the oozing sweat and blood in *Juan sin tierra* (*JT*, pp. 44–5; *JL*, pp. 33–4).

Whilst Goytisolo's attack on the spirit/flesh duality concentrates on the Church's role in its propagation, he also points to the survival of *esquizofrenia colectiva* in secular society, where the spiritual ideal of purity or saintliness becomes hygiene, and its opposite, impurity or sinfulness, becomes dirt. Thus, in *Juan sin tierra*, he derides modern consumer society in these terms:

> la orquestada promoción de detersivos, blanqueadores, desodorantes destinados a eliminar toda culpable huella de su más neta y substancial función: autonegación despiadada, implacable, cuya impronta morbosa revela el temple agresivo, compensatorio de las modernas sociedades omnívoras y su aparato de represión eficaz: coacciones, propulsas, censuras que atrofian el organismo humano y brutalmente lo escinden en dos: arriba: lo visible, racional, tolerado: abajo: lo infando, indecible, oculto
>
> (*JT*, p. 226)

> (the well-orchestrated promotion of detergents, bleaches, deodorants destined to efface every guilty trace of its most obvious and most basic function: implacable, merciless self-denial, whose morbid imprint reveals the aggressive, compensatory nature of omnivorous modern societies and their efficient repressive apparatus: compulsions, contractions, censorships that cause the human organism to atrophy and brutally divide it in two: above: what is

visible, rational, tolerated: below: what is abominable, unspeakable, hidden)

(*JL*, p. 200)

Indeed, the extreme proximity between Christian concepts of desirability and post-Christian society's consumerist ideals is humorously indicated in *Don Julián*, with the description of a picture of the Annunciation:

> el rubio, rollizo y salutífero enviado del Señor transmitiendo a la ruborizada Virgen la improbable unidad comunicativa y, por tanto sustanciosísima información, acerca de los inesperados beneficios de la visita de una paloma que, por lo gorda, blanca, lustrosa, entretiene en el piadoso contemplador del mural una excusable confusión de ideas entre el Holy Ghost invocada por la opulenta Mahalia Jackson y el anuncio en colores de Avecrem

(*DJ*, p. 205)

> (the blond, plump, auspicious messenger of the Lord transmitting to the blushing virgin the improbable, and therefore very substantially informative, unit of communication having to do with the unexpected benefits of the visit of a dove which, because of its plumpness, whiteness, and brightness, gives rise to an excusable confusion in the mind of the pious contemplator of the mural, who is uncertain as to whether it is the Holy Ghost as invoked by the buxom Mahalia Jackson or an advertisement for Maggi chicken bouillon)

( *CJ*, p. 173)

In addition to the post-Christian dualism of hygiene versus dirt, Goytisolo also brings to light a different modern manifestation of *esquizofrenia colectiva*, namely, the concept of being in or out of fashion: 'la muy urbana, anónima, mass-media multitud: vestida de paño catalán, encuadernada en ante mallorquín, con elegantes mocasines de trovadoresca línea italiana: flamante, impecable, endomingada, agrupada bajo el común denominador de una radical y estrepitosa novedad ...: sociedad de consumo! ...: resueltamente IN: Carnaby Street, corbatas Pierre Cardin, gorros y sombreros Bonnie and Clyde' (*DJ*, p. 187; 'the very urbane, anonymous, mass-media-conditioned multitude: dressed in Catalan wool, bound in Mallorcan suede, shod in elegant Italian-troubadour style moccasins: resplendent in their brand-new, impeccably tailored Sunday best, all of them capable of being summed up under the common denominator of the radically and startlingly new: . . . a consumer society!: . . . determined . . . to be IN: Carnaby Street, Pierre Cardin ties, Bonnie and Clyde berets and fedoras', *CJ*, p. 158). This element of fashion is picked up and expanded considerably after the trilogy, in *Makbara*, with whole passages written in advertising jargon and, perhaps most effectively of all, in the Salon du Mariage section. However, the seeds of this later development of the theme are decisively sown in *Don Julián*, with the newspaper advertisements for Rolex watches and holiday homes in the Guadarrama, first transcribed when the narrator tries to bury his head in a newspaper to avoid speaking to the *carpetovetónico*, and later repeated in the 'Little Red Riding Hood' parody, where the repetition provides a structural link with earlier sections of the text (*DJ*, pp. 56–7 and 208–9; *CJ*, pp. 44–5 and 175–6). In *Juan sin tierra*, the odious Parejita Reproductora combine their spiritual purity, conveyed through their resolve to 'perpetuarse conforme a los cánones del rito sacramental' (*JT*, p. 69; 'perpetuate themselves in accordance with the canons of the sacramental ritual', *JL*, p. 55, adapted), with their fashion-conscious modern dualism, for the doomed consummation of their marriage is destined to take place on an 'extra-firm lace-tied mattress that assures proper support and lasting comfort . . . : this week only at savings that are terrific' (*JT*, p. 69; *JL*, p. 56). The American English in which the sales patter is couched underlines the powerful American influence and origin of the post-Christian *esquizofrenia*, in contrast to the use of Latin when dealing with the religious variety.

With the 'Little Red Riding Hood' version of *Don Julián*, which is interspersed with secular advertisements, the child's piety is stressed, albeit mockingly. On his way through the wood, 'realiza diversas acciones y obras pías . . . : fustiga suave pero firmemente la escandalosa impudicia de dos moscas vinculadas ex commodo en fulmínea y sonora copulación : . . . y rezando también' (*DJ*, p. 207; 'he does a number of good deeds, performs several charitable acts . . . : he gently but firmly fustigates two scandalously immodest flies locked together *ex commodo* in fulminous, sonorous copulation: . . . and he prays as well', *CJ*, pp. 174–5). As with the Parejita Reproductora of *Juan sin tierra*, Goytisolo mingles the two modes – pious and consumerist – in order to stress their underlying similarity. The Church and the mass media seek to instil a sense of right and wrong – be it on ethical or fashionable grounds – in society. Both seek to perpetuate their power and authority through their imposition of a dualistic thought-system. Individuality and independence are bound to be discouraged, for they weaken the hold of each on the community.

It is in the light of rebellion against authority, and a defiant statement of the potential for pleasure rooted in the self, that Goytisolo's use of the theme of masturbation may be considered. Whilst the Moor appears as the most central symbol of carnality in *Don Julián*, this fades somewhat in *Juan sin tierra*, to be replaced by a conglomeration of interlinked sexual and anal figures. Some of the implications of the defecation motif have been discussed above. As well as these and in its association with sodomy, the concept links up theologically with masturbation, for the Roman Catholic Church classifies both as the worst type of vice. They are graver sins than fornication, adultery, or incest, for example, because sperm is spilt without any possibility of procreation.

There is another connection between the images of defecation and masturbation though, which bypasses the sin of sodomy. Unlike the latter, but in common with defecation, masturbation can stand as a symbol of individualistic self-gratification. Indeed, Goytisolo explicitly brings the two together in his utilization of them both as images for literary creativity. Masturbation is likened to the writer's art: 'el inveterado, improductivo acto de empuñar la pluma y escurrir su filiforme secreción genitiva según las pulsiones de tu voluntad' (*JT*, p. 209; 'the inveterate, unproductive act of clutching the pen and letting its filiform generative secretion flow in accordance with the impulses of your will', *JL*, p. 185). In a logical extension of this metaphor, the Church's censure of masturbation is paralleled with Church-dominated state censorship. At this point, masturbation and defecation fuse to form a single symbol, for the effect of such censorship is described as a kind of national constipation. Just as Alvarito suppresses his bodily needs for the sake of his illusory aspirations to sainthood, his compatriots crush their equally natural creativity for similarly misguided ideas of literary and/or ideological purity: 'la imagen del blondo, angelical infante majestuosamente posado en su dompedro te orienta quizá por la buena vía y te inspira de paso la solución: la de un país (el suyo) secularmente estreñido' (*JT*, p. 210; 'the image of the blond, angelic heir apparent majestically sitting on his chamber pot has perhaps set you on the right path and given you a hint of the correct answer: that of a country (his) that has been constipated for centuries', *JL*, pp. 185–6). Constipation as an image for the effect of censorship suits Goytisolo's purpose particularly well, as it conveys both the exterior social cause–

corresponding to the 'error de diagnóstico y falta de tratamiento adecuado' (*JT*, p. 211; the 'faulty diagnosis and . . . lack of proper treatment', *JL*, p. 187) – and an internal 'pertinaz anomalía digestiva' (*JT*, p. 211; 'persistent digestive anomaly', *JL*, p. 187), which, remembering Alvarito's behaviour in the previous section of the text, expresses the efforts of individuals indoctrinated with guilt, to overcome their desire to succumb to the free creative impulse.

On this literary and linguistic level of creativity versus censorship, Goytisolo highlights an additional layer of repression in *Juan sin tierra*: not only does he attack the repression of the body itself, but also the censorship of description of carnal activities, and here too the same interplay between external and internal forces is at work. In the language of the chaplain on the sugar-plantation, played by the Protean representative of the establishment, Vosk, the external pressure to censor on the one hand, and his own squeamishness towards using the vocabulary of fleshly gratification on the other, emerge clearly. From without, comes the Virgen Blanca's plea: 'en latín, en latín, suplicará' (*JT*, p. 45; 'in Latin, in Latin, the White Virgin will beg', *JL*, p. 34), interrupting his description of the slaves' sinful habits. Besides this, though, he cannot bear to enunciate their sins in the vernacular because of his own internal scruples: 'el capellán parece a punto de asfixiarse: . . . la descripción de los vicios nefandos del almacén trae a sus labios una florida fraseología latina destinada a paliar con un velo de tenue pudor, tal vez con un precario barniz de cultura, la cruda y espantosa realidad de los actos' (*JT*, pp. 29–30; 'the chaplain appears to be on the point of suffocating: . . . the description of the abominable vices of the warehouse brings to his lips a florid Latin phraseology destined to cast a thin veil of modesty, or perhaps a tenuous veneer of culture, over the crude and frightful reality of the acts committed', *JL*, p. 19).

Another of Goytisolo's figures further ridicules the whole dualistic thought-system that divides everything into pure and impure, good and bad, and by implication reinforces his attack on censorship. This – like *esquizofrenia colectiva* in general – is, after all, based on a belief that human beings can know what is sinful in God's eyes, and are therefore in a position to pass judgement on other people and their actions. The device that is used to explode this presupposition is the computation of statistics providing exact numbers of those in heaven, hell, purgatory, and limbo: 'únicamente un veinte por cien de nuestros compatriotas fueron sentenciados el pasado año a las penas sin fin del infierno' says the voice of the Establishment in *Juan sin tierra* (*JT*, p. 183; 'only some twenty per cent of our citizens were condemned this past year to the eternal sufferings of hell', *JL*, p. 164). Similarly, in *Don Julián*, Caperucito's prayers on his way through the wood are 'jaculatorias en latín y oraciones ricas en indulgencias cuyo cómputo aproximado, frais deduits, se eleva a la astronómica cifra de 31273 años: ... resultado: quince almas del purgatorio redimidas o aliviadas de sus penas de daño y de sentido según la fidelísima y dulce contabilidad IBM: y hasta el posible rescate del limbo de algún niño mongólico o subnormal' (*DJ*, pp. 207–8; 'brief ejaculations in Latin and prayers rich in indulgences, the approximate total of which, with expenses deducted, adds up to the astronomical figure of 31,273 years: ... as a consequence: fifteen souls in purgatory are relieved of their spiritual and corporeal punishments or have them reduced according to the most faithful and most obedient calculations of the I.B.M. machine: and there is even the possibility that a mentally retarded or Mongol child may be rescued from limbo', *CJ*, p. 175, adapted). The technique used here, as elsewhere, is to render a Christian principle absurd by simplistically taking it literally and then carrying it to a logical but ludicrous extreme. Indeed, Goytisolo confirmed his predilection for the device in my interview with him: 'Me gusta mucho', he said, 'mostrar el absurdo de las cosas, llevándolas siempre al extremo' ('I like very much to show up absurdities by carrying things to an extreme'). In this instance, the target of the attack is the thinking behind confession and absolution, which presupposes that certain human beings – the clergy – can have access to divine standards of judgement and are able to exercise them on God's behalf.

It is in this framework of belief in the accuracy of the Church's understanding and interpretation of divine standards that the complacent, self-assured attitude of Vosk towards succumbing to sin is portrayed in *Juan sin tierra*. Like the protagonist, he recognizes the inevitability of the flesh's victory over the spirit, time and time again, the 'flaqueza de nuestra frágil voluntad humana que nos somete a su tiranía fatídica [del diablo]' (*JT*, p. 201; the 'frailty of our human will which subjects us to his fateful tyranny [the devil's]', *JL*, p. 178); but the radical difference in their approaches is that Vosk sees this as an unfortunate fact of life for which one can and should atone and of which one can and should be absolved time and time again. His recommendation is the standard Christian one: 'surge rursum, plange, suspira, humiliate' (*JT*, p. 201; *JL*, p. 178). The protagonist, on the other hand, sees the whole process of sin-remorse-confession-absolution as not only pointless but also psychologically harmful, for the constant pulling in opposite directions of fleshly needs and spiritual aspirations diametrically at odds with them is at the root of the *esquizofrenia* that ravages Christendom. He offers another course of action altogether with his 'habitúese a la propia materia' (*JT*, p. 225; 'accept your own material condition', *JL*, p. 199); as we saw above, Goytisolo himself criticizes the attitude typified by Vosk in 'Remedios de la concupiscencia según Fray Tierno'.

The solution proposed by the protagonist of *Juan sin tierra*, to accept the carnal aspect of man, is the basis of the utopian vision posited in the text: 'paraíso, el tuyo, con culo y con falo' (*JT*, p. 218; 'a paradise, yours, with an ass and a phallus', *JL*, p. 192).[30] Even though Goytisolo admits elsewhere that 'devolver la voz al cuerpo nos parece todavía una empresa quijotesca' (to give the body its voice back still strikes us as a quixotic enterprise'),[31] it would seem that this is precisely what he is trying to do in the novel, with his deliberate use of plain language and his untiring treatment of 'lo infando, indecible, oculto' (*JT*, p. 226; 'what is abominable, unspeakable, hidden', *JL*, p. 200); surely this is an attempt to dismantle the *esquizofrenia colectiva*, by rendering the unmentionable mentionable and stripping away the white coverings to reveal the throbbing *pulpa* underneath.[32]

Together with the twin themes of defecation and masturbation, which have been shown to encompass in symbolic terms sexual sin as well as carnality in general, not to mention the state of Spanish society and literature, there is another *topos* that is linked doctrinally with these two as it also entails the spilling of sperm without any chance of procreation and therefore falls into the gravest category of sexual vice. This is bestiality. For Goytisolo, this theme has the advantage of retaining its ability to inspire revulsion even in a modern reader who may well regard masturbation and sodomy with tolerance. In an essay, the author recognizes that 'la represión actúa todavía con mayor fuerza sobre el excremento que sobre lo pro-piamente sexual' ('repression acts with greater force on excrement than on what is strictly sexual')[33] and in this opinion may lie the key to his choice of defection as an emblem of sodomy, rather than a straightforward treatment of the sin itself. But, be that as it may, in bestiality he has found one powerful source of revulsion at actual sexual practice and one that he re-uses to equal effect in *Paisajes después de la batalla* with the 'Llamamiento a la opinión' section (*PB*, pp. 37–9; 'Appeal to Public Opinion', *LB*, pp. 24–7), an indignant letter to the editor claiming an individual's right in a free and supposedly tolerant society to be sexually attracted by dogs.

Returning to *Juan sin tierra*, though, the figure of King Kong lends itself readily to a symbolic value of frightening, monstrous aspects of sex. It supports the defecation motif in the repugnance that it inspires and its unmentionable status, but it also brings some additional associations into the symbolic fabric of the text. Unquestionably a twentieth-century character, King Kong's appearance in the novel reminds the reader that *esquizofrenia colectiva* is as much a feature of modern, Americanized Western society in its hygiene/dirt and fashionable/unfashionable manifestations as in a Church-based environment, such as Spain under Franco, in the spirit/flesh, virtue/vice dualism. It is also worth recalling that in the film a certain sympathy for Kong is built up, so that when he must be exterminated at the end because he is causing havoc in New York, it is with some regret tinged with rational resignation to his fate that the audience watches the closing scenes. Goytisolo thus draws the reader's attention to an undeniable fascination with – and even perhaps attraction towards – monstrosity, which is nevertheless stifled by expediency: King Kong will destroy New York – which is to say, civilization – unless he is destroyed himself. In an interview given to José A. Hernández, Goytisolo discusses King Kong and asserts that the plot of the film has nothing to do with his use of the image of the giant ape, but rather that Kong stands autonomously for 'el sexo con mayúsculas. Lo descomunal, aberrante, enorme, imposible' ('sex in capital letters. The out-of-the-ordinary, aberrant, enormous, impossible').[34] However, I would argue that the creature cannot be totally divorced from the narrative setting, so that even if he has a powerful independent value, his appearance in *Juan sin tierra* is bound to evoke memories of the film in the reader's mind.

Now, in addition to the literal implications of King Kong (his monstrosity and the plot of the film), there is a level of psychological symbolism that is not confined to the specific vice of bestiality, but in which the gigantic ape stands for carnality in general, as opposed to spirituality. The resemblance to humankind, coupled with powerful animality, make the ape a particularly apt image for fleshly man, the body without the spirit. In his *Diccionario de símbolos tradicionales*, Juan-Eduardo Cirlot claims that 'los simios tienen un sentido general de fuerza inferior, sombra, actividad inconsciente' ('apes have a general sense of inferior force, shadow, unconscious activity') and that 'se identifica monstruo con libido' ('monster is identified with libido').[35] The ape that is also a monster, therefore, may be seen as the symbol of the shadow with its uncontrolled sexual appetite, and in this sense King Kong takes on the role played by the Moor in *Don Julián*: the *otro* that is nevertheless part of the self.

As a creature of African climes, King Kong also may be linked with wider concepts of heat as opposed to cold, and he is therefore a more apposite choice of image for *Juan sin tierra* than, say, a pig or a wolf, both of which are also traditional symbols for the animal side of man. The use of the wolf in the parody of 'Little Red Riding Hood' in *Don Julián* is, however, harmonious with that novel, where heat is associated with the arid Spanish climate and so does not carry the positive value of the fertile jungle developed in *Juan sin tierra*, or the liberating desert sands of *Makbara*. Indeed, heat and cold are not depicted as symbolic opposites in *Don Julián*, one being endowed with positive and the other with negative value, since both are features of the enemy Castilian weather: 'esa Castilla árida y seca, requemada por el sol en verano, azotada en invierno por las ventiscas' (*DJ*, p. 140; 'barren, arid Castile, seared by the summer sun, lashed by winter's bitter-cold blasts', *CJ*, p. 117). It is only as of *Juan sin tierra*, when Castile moves out of the spotlight as principal object of attack, that this manifestation of duality may be exploited.

Thus, in the third novel of the trilogy, the fertility associated with the heat of the jungle is contrasted sharply with the coldness of white purity. Moreover, the symbolic link between temperature and the spirit/flesh, virtue/vice dualism is fused with the black/white colour imagery in the first section of the text, when the white owners of the sugar plantation are depicted in front of the purified, snow-white sugar, and this in turn leads to the narrator's vision of them in a snowscape:

> el bisabuelo-nicolás y la zarina posan inmóviles, felices de abarcar con la mirada el símbolo inmaculado de su poder, la mentida, pero deslumbrante cosecha de azúcar : . . . todo límpido y albo, irreprochable, puro : sin ninguno de los vicios y achaques que el clima de los trópicos acarrea en los cuerpos aun más delicados y ebúrneos : manchas, transpiración, calor
>
> (*JT*, p. 39)

> (great-grandfather Nicolas and the tsarina stand there motionless before the camera, pleased to be gazing upon the immaculate symbol of their power, the illusory but dazzling sugar

harvest: ... everything is clean and white, irreproachable, pure:
with none of the vices and indispositions visited by a tropical
climate upon bodies that are even more delicate and ivory-like:
stains, perspiration, heat)

(JL, p. 28)

By contrast, the black slaves on the plantation are not associated with
the whiteness of the purified sugar and its implications of coldness,
but with the heat and dust of the Cuban setting: 'el sol del trópico cae
a plomo sobre sus cabezas ... : reunidas aparte, las hembras se
abanican con femíneos gestos, coquetas siempre a pesar del polvo, la
suciedad' (*JT*, p. 15; 'the tropical sun beats down on their heads ... :
standing in a group apart, the females fan themselves with feminine
gestures, eternal coquettes despite the dust, the filth', *JL*, p. 6).

The concept of the fertility of the jungle is not absent from *Don
Julián*; although there is no reference to temperature, for, as we have
seen, this is not a symbolic figure of the text, the wild – and hence
natural – quality of the jungle is stressed: 'dulces acogedores montes
donde quisieras descansar para siempre! : como Mowglie, sí: lejos
de la afeitada civilización hispana : en la vellosa, intrincada jungla
poblada de fieras' (*DJ*, p. 152; 'soft, sheltering mountains where you
would like to stay forever! : yes, like Mowgli: far from the meticulously barbered civilization of the Hispano: in the hairy, impenetrable jungle, inhabited by fierce wild beasts', *CJ*, p. 128). The choice
of the adjective *afeitado* ('barbered' in the translation), to contrast
civilization with the *velloso* ('hairy') of the jungle, is significantly
ambiguous. In its modern meaning of 'shaven', it suggests the efforts
made by members of civilized society to remove all traces of their
kinship with the animal world. In this meaning, it links up with the
bearded Tangerine knife-sharpener discussed above and the mous-
tached Tariq of *Don Julián*. At the same time, though, the reader
should be aware of the older meaning of *afeite*, namely, 'sustancia
con que se embellecen la cara las mujeres' ('substance with which
women beautify their faces'). This raises the question of *cáscara/pulpa*
once again, for in the sense of wearing make-up, the implication is
that in civilized society human beings conceal their animal nature
beneath a mask of cosmetics.

Moving from tropical to Mediterranean climes, the theme of the
animal as image for the carnal aspect of the flesh/spirit dichotomy
may be pursued, with Goytisolo's use of the Minotaur in *Don Julián*.
This creature's human body joined to an animal's head serves the

same imagistic purpose as the ape's overall resemblance to human-kind combined with its unmistakable animality. According to Cirlot's *Diccionario de símbolos tradicionales*, 'la inversión que da a la cabeza la forma de animal y al cuerpo la de persona lleva a las últimas consecuencias ese predominio de lo inferior' ('the inversion which gives the head the animal form and the body the form of a person carries that predominance of the inferior to its ultimate conse-quence').[36] Moreover, the Minotaur's status as a freak of nature may be linked with King Kong's equally freakish magnitude. Thus the Minotaur of *Don Julián* may be regarded as a symbolic prefigura-tion of the King Kong image of *Juan sin tierra*. Now, in the classical myth of course, the Minotaur is slain by the heroic Theseus, repre-senting spiritual man, but Goytisolo inverts this, for the protagon-ist's child self, representing the purity of childhood innocence – and therefore as devoid of carnality as the classical hero – is:

> ofrendado inerme
> en holocausto
> al monstruo encerrado por el rey de Minos
>
> (*DJ*, p. 210)

> (sacrificed
> helpless and defenceless
> to the monster shut up . . . by King Minos)
>
> (*CJ*, p. 177)

And in case the reader might have construed the Minotaur as some external evil force, it is planted much earlier in the text 'que el laberinto está en ti: que tú eres el laberinto: minotauro voraz, mártir comestible: juntamente verdugo y víctima' (*DJ*, p. 52; 'knowing that the labyrinth lies within: that you are the labyrinth: the famished minotaur, the edible martyr: at once the executioner and the victim', *CJ*, p. 40). Thus, the figure unequivocally dramatizes the engulfing of the individual's spirit by the flesh, the victory of *pulpa* over *cáscara*.

Annie Perrin and Françoise Zmantar make some illuminating observations about this motif of the labyrinth and the Minotaur, which are worth quoting at some length:

> Tradicionalmente, el laberinto consiste en circunscribir en el espa-cio más reducido, la amalgama más compleja de senderos para retardar la llegada del viajero a su centro. Mientras que el hilo de Ariadna conduce al hallazgo del camino, el laberinto permite

acceso a un lugar, al mismo tiempo que obstaculiza la llegada. El diseño del laberinto une el motivo cerrado del trazo generador de angustia y el trazo abierto dinámico del espiral, en la que el ritmo vertiginoso conduce a un centro. En el centro del laberinto el Minotauro devora a los jóvenes, pero, a su vez, es abatido por Teseo, con lo que se convierte así en víctima y verdugo al mismo tiempo. Ir al encuentro del Minotauro es recorrer como Teseo el camino que conduce al interior de sí mismo; asesinar al Minotauro en un abrazo normal, sacrificar una parte de sí para que renazca la otra, reencontrar aún [sic] la perdida unidad del ser.

(Traditionally, the labyrinth consists of circumscribing the most complex amalgamation of paths in the smallest space in order to delay the traveller's reaching the centre. Whilst Ariadne's thread leads to finding the path, the labyrinth allows access to a place at the same time as impeding arrival there. The design of the labyrinth unites the closed motif of the anxiety-generating line and the dynamic open line of the spiral, in which the spinning rhythm leads to a centre. In the centre of the labyrinth the Minotaur devours youths, but in his turn, he is slain by Theseus, with which he becomes victim and executioner at the same time. To go to meet the Minotaur is, as Theseus did, to tread the path which leads to the inside of oneself; to murder the Minotaur in a normal embrace, to sacrifice a part of oneself so the other may be reborn, to find once more yet the lost unity of being.)[37]

While I am broadly in agreement with this, it could be argued that the Minotaur is not *verdugo* and *víctima* (executioner and victim) simultaneously, but first *verdugo* and then *víctima*, an order that is reversed by Goytisolo, for Alvaro first feels victimized by his *pecado de origen* (sin of origin) in *Señas* and then becomes the merciless, vengeful *verdugo* of his enemies—*hispanidad*, the Church, the bourgeoisie—in *Don Julián* and *Juan sin tierra*. Hence, we have an instance here of the battle between beast and slayer, but with its outcome reversed.

Indeed, the subversion of the traditional battle between the schizophrenic adversaries recurs throughout the trilogy. Already in *Señas*, the process is underway with the treatment of the bullfight at Yeste. The scene depicted is one of sordid aggression, far from lofty symbolism or even vivid local colour; this crushed people 'es un público elemental y hosco sin turistas lectores de Hemingway' (*SI*,

p. 145; 'It is an elemental and rough audience, without tourists who read Hemingway', *MI*, p. 121). If there is any symbolic representation of animality in the tableau, it belongs with the human beings, not the bull. Moreover, the bullfighters are anything but symbols of ethereal heroism and spirituality, 'con ojos insomnes, atontados todavía por el calor y la fatiga. La mayoría de ellos viaja a pie, duerme al raso, sigue como puede el duro trote de los encierros', 'con sus improvisadas muletas, sus capotes sucios y ajironados' (*SI*, pp. 134 and 141; 'with sleepless eyes, still stupefied by heat and fatigue. Most of them travel on foot, sleep in the open, follow as best they can the difficult rounds of the runnings', 'with their improvised *muletas*, their dirty and tattered capes', *MI*, pp. 112 and 117). Later in *Señas*, the animal imagery for the Spanish people, rather than for the brute in the ring, is picked up, reaffirmed, and expanded. The people under Franco are seen as 'toros . . . y ni siquiera eso, mansos felices . . . , triste rebaño de bueyes . . . , pueblo heroico en su día . . . , reducido al cabo de veinticinco años . . . a una vana sombra del pasado, a un retintín muerto' (*SI*, pp. 231–2; 'bulls . . . and not even that, happy tame bulls . . . , sad herd of oxen . . . , a heroic people in their day . . . , reduced after twenty-five years . . . to a vain shadow of the past, to a dead jingle', *MI*, pp. 192–3). Deprived even of the bull's qualities of ferocity and sexuality, all heroism lost too, they are nothing but a 'retintín muerto'.

In *Don Julián*, the undermining of this quintessentially Spanish manifestation of the spirit's victory over animality gathers momentum, when the narrator draws attention to the Moorish origin of the exclamation ¡*Olé!* The Arabic-derived word magically wreaks havoc on the scene, making the bull the victor:

el olé, Julián, el olé!: el bello y antiquísimo wa-l-lah!: saca el adocenado orín que lo cubre, restitúyele el lustre original!: que las gargantas mesiánicas que los emiten se atrofien y enmudezcan de golpe: sin su místicovisceral acompañamiento la danza filosófica del torero perderá su magistral señorío, sus movimientos devendrán torpes, el pánico le dominará: . . . el traje de luces abatirá su brillo . . . : el Thur arábigo embestirá entonces con retenida furia y sus cuernos no apuntarán la sofística capa de brega'

(*DJ*, pp. 200–1)

(the *olé*, Julian, the *olé*!: the marvelous age-old wal-l-lah! remove the vulgar rust that has corroded its surface, restore its original

luster! may the messianic throats uttering it suddenly atrophy and
fall silent: without this mystico-visceral accompaniment the philosophical dance of the *torero* will lose its majestic dignity, his
movements will become awkward, he will be suddenly panic-
stricken: . . . his suit of lights will dim . . . : the Arab Thur will
then launch his attack, with all the force of his long-contained
fury, and his horns will not be aimed at the sophistic cape)

(*CJ*, p. 169)

Finally, the destruction of the traditionally positive response to the
beast's defeat at the hands of man's superior nature reaches its
apotheosis in *Juan sin tierra*, when the brutish nature of a people who
can practise bullfighting is ironically conveyed through the apologetics for the *auto-da-fé*:

ceremonia fúnebre y sin embargo alegre, incomparable ritual de
vida y de muerte que arrebata los ánimos más serenos y justifica el
clima litúrgico, de atención religiosa de los incontables familiares,
consultores y aficionados . . .: pues para comprender exactamente
el auto de fe resulta indispensable abarcarlo en su trágica y reden-
tora totalidad: ciertamente, el espectáculo de un hombre achichar-
rado en la estaca parece a primera vista insoportable y atroz: . . .
las convulsiones, los gritos, el olor de la carne quemada son meros
ingredientes accesorios de la tragedia y sólo el verdadero aficionado a los autos puede calibrarlos en su justo valor

(*JT*, pp. 173 and 176)

(a gloomy ceremony and yet at the same time a joyous, incomparable ritual of life and death that sends the most serene souls into
raptures and justifies the liturgical atmosphere, the religious atten-
tiveness of the countless familiars, advisers, and aficionados . . .: in
point of fact, in order to properly appreciate the auto-da-fé it is
indispensable to embrace it in its tragic and redeeming totality:
admittedly, at first glance the spectacle of a man roasting on a stake
seems unbearable and horrifying: . . . the writhing, the screams,
the odor of burning flesh are mere accessory details of the staging
of the tragedy and only the true aficionado can judge them at their
proper worth)

(*JL*, pp. 156 and 159)

That the *auto-da-fé* stands for the bullfight as well as the public
burning of heretics is confirmed by the reference (just after the

quoted passage) to Hemingway as 'el egregio autor de "Muerte en la tarde"' (*JT*, pp. 176–7; 'the celebrated author of *Death in the Afternoon*', *JL*, p. 159).[38]

As well as exploiting the traditional correspondence between the beast and man's animal side, Goytisolo also attacks *esquizofrenia colectiva* in *Juan sin tierra* by tampering with a member of the animal kingdom that is identified with untainted spirituality, namely the dove that represents the Holy Ghost. Goytisolo transforms the Virginal Conception into a boldly sacrilegious portrayal of bestiality. Mary's 'arrobos y éxtasis' (*JT*, p. 57; 'expressions of rapture and ecstasy', *JL*, p. 45) are not those of mystical union with God, but of physical pleasure arising from sexual intercourse with the dove. Mingled with the bestial aspect is incest too, another type of sexual activity that still remains taboo today. The would-be redeemer yet to be born is miraculously present at the conception, during which he kills the dove and takes its place, thereby committing incest with his future mother. In this way, Mary's pure relationship with the Holy Trinity is parodied acerbically, the suggestion being that her status as both bearer of God's Son and His mother makes her guilty of incest. Genaro Pérez judges *Don Julián* to be the cruellest novel of the trilogy in its treatment of the Church;[39] yet this scene can surely compete with any from the second novel of the trilogy. Indeed, a passage more offensive to a Christian would be hard to imagine and even a non-Christian reader is likely to be shocked. But this reaction forces him to ask himself why he is horrified and that in turn leads him to recognize the presence of religion-based sexual taboos and aversions within himself. This serves as a preparation early in the novel for an attack on his own mentality, on his own contribution to *esquizofrenia colectiva*, jolting him out of any expectations of some sort of cosy complicity with the narrator, in which relationship they will scoff together at the folly of the masses.

In conclusion, the Christian notions of sin and purity, whether seen in their primary religious context or in the form of their secular descendants, which exalt hygiene and fashion, dreading dirt and tastelessness, amount to a dualism that may be traced back to the doctrine of original sin with its legacy of concupiscence. This creates a lifelong tension between the pull in one direction of the tainted body and in the other of the potentially pure soul, yearning for salvation. As long as a constant war is waged against the flesh, the Church teaches that God will forgive any number of individual defeats. Once the doctrine of original sin is rejected, however, the justification for this endless fight is seriously undermined if not negated altogether. Once it is no longer accepted that mankind is in a fallen state and therefore tends to evil, then natural inclinations need no longer be suppressed or guilt-ridden. Furthermore, if the doctrine of judgement after death is also discarded, then the effects of the constant battle against carnality may be measured in wordly rather than eschatological terms. Goytisolo does so and finds society gravely sick, racked with hidden complexes, yet constipated with its self-assured complacency that never questions the violence done to its members through external controls nor the psychological torture inflicted through its imposition of the duty to exercise self-repression both physical and ideological.

The concept of damaging dualism denominated *esquizofrenia colectiva* in this chapter is not by any means a purely abstract feature of the symbolic fabric of Goytisolo's later novels. Specific characters are depicted as its victims and its victors, so providing a concrete context for the imagery discussed above. Because these personages rebel against or are alienated by the 'schizophrenic' Establishment, they may be regarded as pariahs or outsiders. It is to this motif of the pariah that I now shall turn.

# 3
# The Pariah:
# Outsider or Uplifter?

The term *pariah* derives from the name of one of the untouchable Hindu castes. Whilst Hinduism is not a dominant theme in Goytiso-lo's novels, references are occasionally to be found in *Juan sin tierra*, besides the recurrent use of the word *paria* ('pariah') itself in all the texts. Particularly striking, because they are the opening words of the third novel of the trilogy, is this observation: 'según los gurús indostánicos, en la fase superior de la meditación, el cuerpo humano, purgado de apetitos y anhelos, se abandona con deleite a una existencia etérea, horra de pasiones y achaques' (*JT*, p. 11; 'according to Hindustani gurus, in the superior phase of meditation the human body, purged of its appetites and desires, abandons itself with delight to an ethereal existence, freed from passions and vices', *JL*, p. 2). Later, in the sacrilegious parody of the Virginal Conception, the narrator alludes to the Kama Sutra: 'la vedada posesión materna se llevará a cabo en la más peregrina de las posturas: las láminas de una edición ilustrada del Kama-Sutra te inspiran' (*JT*, p. 56; 'the forbidden maternal possession will take place in the strangest possible position: the plates of an illustrated edition of the Kamasutra inspire you', *JL*, p. 44). More importantly, however, the concept of untouchability does play an important role, since it is one aspect of the broader theme of *esquizofrenia colectiva*, the dualistic phenomenon comprising a horror of the flesh, on the one hand, and a yearning for pure spirituality, on the other. Now, in addition to the two-way opposition represented by the twin concepts of touchability and untouchability, the Hindu caste-system is a complex and rigidly hierarchical structure; Goytisolo's recurrent use of the term *paria* therefore serves – albeit in a capacity secondary to the *esquizofrenia* theme – as one of the many weapons that he employs in his war on order seen as a desirable psycho-social objective. Thus, the pariah motif may be regarded as the link that joins the concept of *esquizofre-nia colectiva* to that of order and chaos, in the thematic chain that I am arguing may be traced through the later novels. Before turning to a discussion of the treatment of order and chaos, therefore, it would seem opportune to consider the pariah motif and its contingent implications.

Untouchability is inextricably bound up with the concept of pollution; untouchables in India are avoided because contact with them pollutes. But a fear of pollution with the corollary of untouch-ability is immensely widespread in societies ranging from the most primitive to the most sophisticated. Sir James George Frazer's *The Golden Bough* enumerates countless examples of such taboos in primitive communities; Mary Douglas in *Purity and Danger* makes some striking observations about modern manifestations of pollu-tion fears:

> When we honestly reflect on our busy scrubbings ... we know that we are not mainly trying to avoid disease .... If we ... send the men to the downstairs lavatory and the women upstairs, we are essentially doing the same thing as the Bushman wife [who sticks a rod in the ground to divide the home into male and female quarters] .... Both we and the Bushmen justify our pollution avoidances by fear of danger. They fear that if a man sits on the female side his male virility will be weakened. We fear pathogenic-ity transmitted through micro-organisms. Often our justification of our own avoidances through hygiene is sheer fantasy.[1]

At first sight, Christian doctrine might appear to be free of pollution fears; papal decrees of 1734 and 1744 denounced untouch-ability as alien to Christianity, and Jesuit missionaries in India were criticized for their policy of accommodation towards it.[2] However, whilst ritual impurity may have been rejected by the Church, psychological contamination by heretics and unbelievers has always been and still is recognized and feared. As recently as 1979, a Christian may be found who takes the extreme view that 'you can become less chaste by reading that column in your Sunday paper', for example.[3] As this warning demonstrates, Christianity has, in a sense, fuelled the fear of pollution, by refining and extending it beyond the concrete – eating, marrying, touching whatever or whomever is forbidden – to the merest impure thought. One of the points that Jesus makes in the Sermon on the Mount is: 'Ye have heard that it was said by them of old time, Thou shalt not commit adultery:/But I say unto you, That whosoever looketh on a woman to lust after her hath committed adultery with her already in his heart' (Matthew 5.27–28). This is of course part of Jesus's general policy towards the legal intricacies of Judaism. He felt – as numerous Jewish teachers both before and after Him have done – that precise observation of the law is futile unless the feelings and intentions of the faithful are godly and that practical obedience to the law should not create an attitude of complacent self-righteousness. However, the psychological effect of this abstraction is to introduce an element of unsettling uncontrollability; at any moment a wicked thought may appear uninvited in the mind and this can be seen as a real sin for a Christian, capable of altering his eternal destiny, not merely a reprehensible occurrence to be discouraged as, for example, in Judaism. So if the essentially uncontrollable psychic processes must nevertheless be restrained as much as possible, the sense in a Christian's advocating zealous avoidance of anything or anyone that might spark off an impure train of thought becomes apparent.

In *Señas de identidad*, Antonio sees himself as just such a person to be avoided. Like Mary Douglas, he is aware of the similarity between moral contamination fears and the modern dread of bacteria. He says: 'La cárcel es una enfermedad peligrosa . . . . Cuando uno pasa por ella todo el mundo teme el contagio' (*SI*, p. 197; 'Jail is a dangerous disease . . . . When somebody catches it, everybody is afraid of contagion', *MI*, p. 164). This, it should be borne in mind, is the opinion of a pariah in his own words; however accurate or otherwise his appraisal of the public's attitudes to him might be, it stands as an important guide to his own psychology; this is how he has interpreted the behaviour of those around him and these are the words and imagery that he has chosen to describe it. Furthermore, it is as well to remember that this entire section of the narrative is based on Antonio's account of it, so that third-person description has also been filtered through his own self-image. This is explicitly stated by Alvaro at the beginning of the fourth chapter of *Señas* (the one in which Antonio's experiences are described), for this component of the chapter is said to be 'el relato de Antonio sobre su detención y confinamiento (rehecho luego por ti con ayuda de Dolores)' (*SI*, p. 160; 'Antonio's story of his arrest and imprisonment (all put together again later on by you with Dolores's help)', *MI*, p. 134). Alvaro also makes it clear that his re-working deals only with superficialities and does not interfere with the core of the account, which remains Antonio's: 'Sometida a los cánones imperiosos de lo real tu imaginación se resarcía componiendo con morosidad las situaciones, limando las aristas del diálogo, atando cabos y rellenando huecos' (*SI*, p. 160; 'Submitted to the demanding canons of reality, your imagination compensated for it by slowly putting situations together, polishing the edges of dialogues, tying up loose ends and filling holes', *MI*, p. 134). In the light of this indication that the narration of Antonio's vicissitudes is essentially based on his own version of events, the implications, for example, of the episode in which he deliberately alienates the establishment figures of the doctor and Don Gonzalo, appear more complex than on first reading. It is stated in the third person that Antonio 'de nuevo podía pasear por el pueblo como un proscrito, adivinando en la condena muda de los otros la señal indeleble que le marcaba' (*SI*, p. 231; 'once more he could walk through town like an outlaw, sensing in the mute condemnation of the others the indelible sign that marked him', *MI*, p. 192); but it is Antonio who has interpreted the villagers's silence as condemnation, rather than some other emotion such as fear, or perhaps even sneaking admiration and it is he who has seen himself as indelibly marked.

This depiction of the pariah places the emphasis on *esquizofrenia colectiva*; the position held by Antonio, as the lowest member of the village hierarchy, is never elaborated explicitly; instead, the description revolves around the character's bold re-affirmation of his own untouchability. It is his deliberate self-detachment from the society of touchables that dominates the episode, although the distasteful social hierarchy is suggested perhaps, by the depictions of Don Gonzalo's family, recognized collectively by the locals as the highest in the community, and of the prostitute at the opposite end of the scale (barring Antonio himself), with the doctor and the Civil Guard somewhere in between. The former presumably reflects public opinion when he reverently describes Don Gonzalo as 'el extraordinario hombre de negocios de hoy: él, y nadie más que él, ha sabido crear una industria en el pueblo, ha revalorizado la tierra, ha atraído el turismo. Si la gente vive mejor que antes se lo debe a don Gonzalo' (*SI*, p. 206; 'the extraordinary businessman we have today: he and nobody else was able to build up an industry in this town, make land more valuable, attract tourists. If people are better off, they owe it to Don Gonzalo' (*MI*, p. 172). As for the prostitute, it is worth noting that despite the traditionally low status of those in her profession, even she is embarrassed when Antonio confronts her: '"Cuando me hablaron de usté no imaginé que un día le vería por mi casa . . ." la muchacha sonreía azorada. "Uy, si me da apuro hasta mirarle"' (*SI*,

p. 208; '"When they told me about you I didn't imagine that one day I'd see you in my house . . . "the girl was smiling, disturbed. "Gosh, it's even hard for me to look at you"', *MI*, p. 174).

The protagonist of *Makbara* is a pariah of modern, secular society; hence, he meets with fears of pathogenicity rather than moral contagion: 'alejémonos de él, no nos roce su aliento, cubramos prudentemente narices y bocas con suaves pañuelos esterilizados' (*Ma*, p. 17; 'let us move away from him so his breath doesn't touch us, let us prudently cover our mouths and our noses with soft sterilized handkerchiefs', *Mb*, p. 8). Since the style of this text is not so straightforward as that of *Señas*, the reader never knows either who is speaking or whether indeed anyone is speaking at all, rather than just thinking. Comments such as those quoted above could be the thoughts of the Parisians, reported by an omniscient narrator; or the thoughts of the pariah imagining what people are thinking, also reported by an omniscient narrator; or else, they could be comments spoken aloud by passers-by, either heard by the protagonist and reported by him in a narrator role, or lastly, and bearing in mind that he has no ears, they could be comments spoken aloud by passers-by, but not heard by him and reported instead by a separate (and not necessarily omniscient) authorial voice. Presumably, Goytisolo wishes to keep all these possibilities open simultaneously, in order to comment on diverse issues economically. If the passage is taken as a faithful representation of the behaviour and reactions of bourgeois society, and by the same token, if it is assumed that Antonio's interpretation of the villagers' attitude as condemnatory in *Señas* is accurate too, it could be said that Goytisolo's pariahs have much in common with their namesake caste in India, inasmuch as they have to cope with inspiring repugnance and being avoided by those around them.

However, if we shift the focus from the rest of society's behaviour towards the pariah, to the pariah himself, treating the *Makbara* discourse and Antonio's opinions as symptomatic of their own mentality and not necessarily as accurate interpretations of others' reactions towards them, the same pieces of text fall kaleidoscopically into a different pattern altogether. Now the crucial difference between Goytisolo's untouchables and their Indian counterparts becomes apparent, for whilst the essence of the caste-system rests rigidly on heredity, Goytisolo's pariahs have deliberately assumed their outcast status. They make themselves unacceptable to bourgeois society by their behaviour in the full knowledge that this will be its effect. Even though the vocabulary commonly used –

*outcast*, *rejected*, and *stigmatized*, for instance – suggests that it is
society that takes the active part, by throwing out or branding a
person, in the case of these pariahs, they have pulled themselves out,
or more precisely, they have deliberately pushed society into pushing
them out. It is therefore hard to see how Schaefer-Rodríguez comes
to her opinion that in *Señas* Alvaro rejects 'con venganza una
sociedad que él percibe que le ha rechazado' ('vengefully a society
which he perceives as having rejected him'), when he has taken the
active role by leaving the country.[4]

The phenomenon of a character who makes himself unacceptable
to others is not, of course, an innovation on Goytisolo's part.
Joaquín Monegro in Unamuno's *Abel Sánchez* admits that since
childhood, 'era él [Abel] simpático, no sabía por qué, y antipático yo'
('he [Abel] was the nice one, I did not know why, and I the
unpleasant one'). He tries not to face this fact, preferring to cast the
blame on those around him – 'todos, todos me amargaron la vida'
('everyone, everyone embittered my life') – yet Unamuno depicts
him throughout the novel as creating his own misery, making
himself unpleasant.[5] Herman Hesse's Steppenwolf does likewise in
the novel of that title, although unlike Joaquín, he recognizes that he
is the only person responsible for his outcast status: 'Let no one think
that I blame other men . . . or that I accuse them of the responsibility
of my personal misery'.[6] As these quotations make clear, both
Joaquín and the Steppenwolf, though somehow impelled to make
themselves unacceptable to others, are unhappy because of this and
would rather fit into society unproblematically. This is where Goytisolo's pariahs differ significantly from such literary antecedents as
these, for they are content to be outcasts: Antonio of *Señas* has his
first good night's sleep in the village where he is exiled, only after he
has destroyed the locals' goodwill towards him, thus re-affirming his
untouchability:

> El médico le dio la espalda y Antonio se sintió inmensamente
> feliz . . . .
> Estaba transportado por un arrobo indecible . . . . Al recogerse,
> por primera vez en muchos meses, durmió a sueño suelto, sin
> necesidad de recurrir a los somníferos.
> (SI, pp. 224–5)

The doctor turned his back and Antonio felt immensely
happy . . . .

[He was] carried away by a rapture that could not be described . . . . When he went to bed, for the first time in many months he fell fast asleep without the need of sleeping pills.

(*MI*, p. 187)

One cannot help but be struck by the depth of feeling conveyed here through the choice of *feliz*, a far stronger word for 'happy' than *alegre* or *contento*, not to mention the ecstatic 'arrobo indecible' ('rapture that could not be described').

Why, the reader inevitably wonders, do Goytisolo's pariahs want wholeheartedly to be rejected by society? Some critics have addressed themselves to this question, but their suggestions are often too superficial to be really helpful. José Miguel Oviedo, for example, describes Goytisolo as 'un maldito que maldice a los suyos – porque son como él' ('a cursed man who curses his own – because they are like him').[7] Apart from the confusion of the author with his character, this statement, though striking, is of little use: in what sense are they like him and why should he curse them because they resemble him? Surely it is more usual to like people similar to oneself. Besides, even accepting Oviedo's identification of the writer with his creature in this respect, Goytisolo's personal testimony contradicts the critic's assertion; in the 'Presentación crítica' of Goytisolo's translation of José María Blanco White, he claims to feel akin not to his own class but to social outcasts: 'Si algún impulso de solidaridad siento, no es jamás con la imagen del país que emerge a partir del reinado de los Reyes Católicos, sino con sus víctimas: judíos, musulmanes, cristianos nuevos, luteranos, enciclopedistas, liberales, anarquistas, marxistas' ('If I feel any impulse of solidarity, never is it with the image of the country which emerges as of the reign of the Catholic Monarchs, but with their victims: Jews, Muslims, New Christians [those newly converted to Christianity and for that reason victims of discrimination], Lutherans, Encyclopedists, liberals, anarchists, Marxists').[8]

In search of more satisfactory suggestions as to the motivation that drives Goytisolo's voluntary pariahs, works on the social psychology of conformity and deviance propose some useful theories. Baron and Byrne claim that 'other people like you better when you conform to their beliefs and judgements' while Sykes and Matza state that one way for a deviant to cope with rejection 'would appear to involve a condemnation of the condemners . . . . His condemners, he may claim, are hypocrites, deviants in disguise, or impelled by

personal spite'.[9] If the thrust of these two assertions is reversed, one
might say that Goytisolo's pariahs voluntarily assume their status as
such because they do not wish to be liked by a society they deplore,
regarding its members as hypocrites, deviants in disguise, and impelled by spite, amongst other criticisms. The concept of establishment figures being deviants in disguise is especially stressed in *Don
Julián* and *Juan sin tierra*, with, for example, the *carpetovetónico*'s pious
daughter in the former, revealed to be an erotic go-go dancer in
secret, and the depiction of Saint Simeon Stylite in the latter as being
covertly in a state of permanent sexual ecstasy on the phallic symbol
of his column (*DJ*, pp. 162–6; *CJ*, pp. 137–40; *JT*, p. 118; *JL*,
p. 105). The protagonist of *Paisajes después de la batalla* too, is 'de
puertas afuera, un caballero muy bien educado' (*PB*, p. 23; 'on the
outside, . . . a perfect gentleman', *LB*, p. 13), whatever his revolutionary and erotic fantasies within his flat. Moreover, it is in a spirit
of condemning the condemners that Alvaro declares at the end of
*Señas*:

> aléjate de tu grey tu desvío te honra
> cuanto te separa de ellos cultívalo
> lo que les molesta en ti glorifícalo

(SI, p. 419)

> (get away from your flock your detour honors you
> cultivate everything that separates you from them
> glorify whatever in you bothers them)

(MI, p. 349)

Presumably, for Goytisolo's pariahs to allow themselves to be liked
and accepted would be tantamount, in their view, to wanting to be
liked and accepted.

Proof of despising society's opinions, then, provides one motive
for deliberate assumption of outcast status. Indeed, this is Linda
Gould Levine's interpretation: 'En la obra posterior de Goytisolo, . . . el autor comprende que los valores falsos de la sociedad
tienen que ser rechazados y aniquilados, que la única liberación
posible consiste en asumir dentro de uno mismo la identidad del
desposeído' ('In Goytisolo's later work, . . . the author understands
that society's false values must be rejected and wiped out, that the
only possible liberation consists of assuming within oneself the
identity of the dispossessed').[10] However, another reason may be
found in the conflict within the pariah himself. Kiesler and Kiesler

distinguish between two types of conformity that they term 'compliance' and 'private acceptance'.[11] The doctor and the civil guard in the village of Antonio's exile in *Señas*, preach the benefits of compliance without private acceptance. In the civil guard's words, 'Una cosa es el uniforme que uno viste y otra muy distinta las convicciones personales' (*SI*, p. 202; 'The uniform you wear is one thing, but your personal ideas are something else again', *MI*, p. 169); or, in the doctor's slightly more sophisticated mode of expression, 'Uno puede someterse en apariencia como yo, y, por dentro, ser libre' (*SI*, p. 206; 'A person can appear to submit like me, but inside he can be free', *MI*, p. 171, adapted). For these two personages, this is a satisfactory *modus vivendi*. However, Antonio and subsequent pariahs in *Don Julián*, *Juan sin tierra*, and *Makbara*, not only condemn such a dichotomy between outward behaviour and inner opinions as contemptible hypocrisy, but also find that it creates unbearable ambiguity and conflict. Such disharmony between outer and inner selves is shown to be linked with *esquizofrenia colectiva* and, in the closing scenes of *Don Julián* especially, the psychological torment of feeling obliged to present an image of virtue, whilst having a completely opposite fleshly identity underneath, is dramatized to harrowing effect. Alvarito is tortured by his divided self until he is driven to killing the compliant exterior, seen as deceitful: 'sólo el rostro infantil y sin bozo se mantiene *engañosamente* intacto' (*DJ*, p. 226, my italics; 'only the childish face without the slightest trace of a beard remains *deceptively* unchanged now', *CJ*, p. 191). Worth noting too, perhaps, is the mention here and recurrently of the still beardless nature of the youth. This picks up the concept of facial hair being associated with carnality, as with the 'afeitada civilización hispana' (*DJ*, p. 152; 'the meticulously barbered civilization of the Hispano', *CJ*, p. 128) and the unshaven Tangerine knife-sharpener (*DJ*, p. 17; *CJ*, p. 8), discussed in chapter 2. However, nightmare-like, the beautiful child is at the same time an insect with a hard exoskeleton: 'Por un lado la cáscara y por otro la pulpa' (*DJ*, p. 224; 'an outer shell and an inner pulp', *CJ*, p. 190). This image hauntingly reinforces the earlier vision of Alvarito, depicted as the prey of a carnivorous plant (*DJ*, pp. 211–12; *CJ*, pp. 178–9). Finally, the torment ends when exterior is aligned with interior at the end of the episode: 'apuras la brevedad del milagro: abrazándote a él: ... en simbiosis fulmínea: impugnando la muerte que os cierne: ... tú mismo al fin, único' (*DJ*, p. 230; 'you will hasten the miracle: pressing him to your bosom: ... in a fulgurating symbiosis: impugning death threateningly hovering over-

head: . . . you yourself at last, become one and indivisible', *CJ*,
p. 195).

The necessity to clothe the vicious flesh in spiritual robes of purity,
respectively denominated *pulpa* and *cáscara* in this episode of *Don
Julián*, has a parallel in *Juan sin tierra*, when bodily fluids seep
uncontrollably through the pure white skin and garments of the
virtuous: 'el suave mador del escote de la zarina impregnará poco
a poco el blanco satén de sus pechos: imposible contener la
sudación!: . . . tres máculas bermejas, simultáneas ultrajarán el acendrado blancor de sus faldas [de las niñas]' (*JT*, pp. 44–5; 'the slight
moisture trickling down the neckline of the tsarina's dress will little
by little impregnate the white satin of her breasts: impossible to
contain the perspiration!: . . . three bright-red spots will stain the
immaculate whiteness of their skirts [the girls']', *JL*, pp. 33–4,
adapted). In both of these depictions, the link between the pariah
notion and *esquizofrenia colectiva* is extended to the metaphysical: the
child self of *Don Julián* and the mother and daughters of *Juan sin tierra*
suggest that within each socially acceptable individual, there lurks an
imprisoned pariah, held in check by a *cáscara*. This raises a new set of
questions in the reader's mind, for the concept of the fleshly *pulpa*
concealed within the apparently virtuous person, taken together with
the depiction of the pariah as predominantly a corporeal creature,
combine to imply that the overt pariah differs from the socially
respected only in his refusal to participate in the *esquizofrenia colectiva*.
Suddenly, the social outcast appears in a new light: he becomes the
frank expression of what other people are trying to conceal within
themselves. He thus ceases to rank as an essentially different type of
being; he is a daunting figure not for his strangeness, but on the
contrary, for his disturbing familiarity, as is suggested by the pariah
of *Makbara*, when he is called the 'monstruo del más acá venido' (*Ma*,
p. 13; 'monster from inner space', *Mb*, p. 1, adapted). One is reminded of Goytisolo's 'Vicisitudes del mudejarismo' once again: 'El
Otro soy yo; es decir, bajo la escritura borrada, el palimpsesto nos
muestra una imagen impensable: la propia' ('The Other is me; that is
to say, beneath the erased writing, the palimpsest shows us an
unthinkable image: our own').[12]

After *Señas*, there is a shift in emphasis that highlights another
aspect of the pariah condition: not only are Goytisolo's outcasts
intent on being rejected by the bourgeois society that they detest, but
they also want to be accepted by a society of natural pariahs (as
opposed to other voluntary ones like themselves). According to

Baron and Byrne, quoted above, acceptance comes with conformity, but there are certain insurmountable barriers here for Goytisolo's prospective untouchables. Until *Makbara*, they lack the qualifying physical attributes, because they are not black or of Semitic complexion, nor are they sufficiently crippled or otherwise mutilated to compensate for their bourgeois socio-racial identity. In an ingenious switch of conventional ideals of physical appearance, these protagonists feel stigmatized by their European, healthy appearance, because this causes them to be excluded from the group of their choice, that of natural pariahs: 'blanco de mierda: abucheado al unísono por la indignada dotación: cortado para siempre de los parias y los metecos' (*JT*, p. 59; 'a motherfucking white: jeered at in chorus by all the indignant assembled blacks: cut off forever from the pariahs and the halfbreeds', *JL*, p. 47). It might be added, incidentally, that this is a reality faced by the author as well as by his characters. In an interview given to José Miguel Ullán in 1981, he says: 'Por mucha simpatía que sienta por el mundo musulmánico, por grande que pueda ser el conocimiento que de él tenga, sería absurdo pretender que podría integrarme en él totalmente' ('However fond of the Muslim world I feel, however great my knowledge of it may be, it would be absurd to claim that I could be totally integrated in it').[13]

The desire to be accepted by natural pariahs is motivated in part by the same feelings as those discussed above, which make Goytisolo's characters want bourgeois society to reject them. However, there is another important factor, which should not be overlooked. The protagonist of *Juan sin tierra* does not only want to be a pariah in order to be as non-bourgeois and as repugnant to bourgeois society as possible, he also sees his role as redeemer of pariahs: 'así también al bajar Alvarito a este mundo para redimir del pecado a todos los parias de la tierra ...' (*JT*, p. 53; 'in like fashion Alvarito, on descending to this earth to redeem all the world's pariahs from sin ...', *JL*, p. 41).

The redeemer concept throws a whole new aspect of the outsider motif into relief. The inferior pariah and the superior redeemer are often indistinguishable in the eyes of the society of their own time. In his study of deviance, Wilkins states:

All societies tend to reject deviants. Both saints and criminals have been excluded from the cultures into which they were born, and the majority of saints have suffered exactly similar fates to the deviant sinners. Many saints were, in fact, *defined* specifically by their current society as criminals. Their society recognized deviance, but not the direction of the deviance.[14]

In the New Testament, Jesus provides the definitive example of not being afraid to stand alone for what is believed to be truth, against a society felt to be misguided. Furthermore, Jesus also actively associated with the social pariahs of the times: prostitutes, lepers, beggars. The figure of the outcast who is proud to stand alone because he is convinced that he has found some truth of which the rest of society is ignorant links up with the attitude of Goytisolo's pariahs. As the protagonist-pariah of *Makbara* turns his back on the shocked bystanders of the 'Salon du Mariage', he thinks: 'abandonarlos al disfrute tardío de la reprobación y la burla, caminar orgullosamente ceñida en desdén como a más alta dignidad promovida' (*Ma*, p. 83; 'leaving them the pleasure of exchanging reproving and mocking remarks about you once you have gone, proudly walking away, girded in lofty disdain as though promoted to a more exalted rank', *Mb*, p. 89). The same sentiment dominates the section appropriately if sacrilegiously entitled 'Sic transit gloria mundi', in which the grotesque lover is ridiculed as she fantasizes about her past. She reacts 'con el empaque y circunspección de una dama, serena y consciente de lo efímero de las glorias, epopeyas mundanas' (*Ma*, p. 58; 'with the dignified and decorous air of a lady to the manner born, serene and intimately aware of the ephemeral nature of all wordly glories and epic endeavors', *Mb*, p. 57).

The model of self-sacrifice provided by the Redeemer, and the Christian doctrine of His redemption of mankind by His assumption of original sin upon Himself, stands in a more complex relation to Goytisolo pariahs. The term *pecado original* or *pecado de origen* ('original sin' or 'sin of origin') is habitually used to refer to the protagonist's bourgeois Spanish roots, from which one might assume that it is other middle-class Spaniards who are similarly burdened and therefore need to be redeemed, not Moroccan tannery-workers and their like. Why then does the protagonist of *Juan sin tierra* explicitly state that his vocation is to redeem pariahs and not the bourgeoisie? A possible solution to the paradox would appear to lie in the ambiguity that surrounds the relationship between protagonist and author in all the later novels, between the actions of the protagonist within the text and the action of the author in writing it. If a certain fluidity between protagonist and author is accepted, if the two are permitted to fuse and split as convenient, the redeemer figure may be seen in double focus. Within the texts, the protagonist does indeed take up the pariahs' cause, pointing out the injustice of their wretchedness: 'huérfano, sucio, andrajoso ... : envuelto en el desdén y reprobación de los selectos, contaminando sin querer su aire' (*Ma*, p. 68; 'an orphan ... , filthy, in tatters ... : enveloped in the scorn and reproof of the elect, unwittingly contaminating their air', *Mb*, p. 71). Yet, at the same time, the texts themselves are not likely to be read by Moroccan cripples and the author is undoubtedly aware of this fact, as the dedication of *Makbara* to 'quienes la inspiraron y no la leerán' ('those who inspired it and will never read it') shows. It is surely the intellectual bourgeoisie that will constitute his readership. By highlighting the hypocrisies, prejudices, and other failings of the very group to which his readers are almost bound to belong, is he not opening their eyes, attempting to save them from their wicked ways? And in the process, is he not crucifying himself in literary terms, by making enemies of the very people upon whom his success as a writer depends?

Indeed, he has made enemies of many of his compatriots, who have accused him of being what amounts to a traitor to his country and, tacitly though equally significantly, to his class.[15] It is hardly surprising, therefore, that the figure of the traitor looms large in the novels, as the title of *Reivindicación del conde don Julián* underscores. The opening passage of *Señas* also plays its part in this context, scornfully parodying the type of criticism directed at Goytisolo in the early 1960s:

> anunciado fuera de nuestras fronteras a bombo y platillo con el internacional y resobado repertorio de alharacas y garambainas con que se saluda siempre en algunos círculos a lo que de lejos o de cerca huela a anti-español ... revela tal catadura moral que mejor es no mencionarlo aunque nos bastaran dos sustantivos y una preposición ... visión fugaz y trashumante más propia de un Mérimée de pacotilla que de un vástago de familia acomodada y respetable ... educada en veterana institución religiosa
>
> (*SI*, pp. 9–11)

(announced beyond our borders with the bass drum and cymbals of that international and well-worn repertory of noise and show with which anything from far or near that smells anti-Spanish is always greeted in certain circles ... [he] reveals such moral taste that it is best not to mention him even though all we need is a preposition, two nouns, and the indefinite article . . . a fleeting and hazy vision more worthy of a second-rate Mérimée than that of the heir of a wealthy and respectable family . . . with a Christian education in a long-established religious institution)

(*MI*, pp. 5–7, adapted)

Moreover, Genaro Pérez rightly points out that in *Señas*, 'the betrayal motif is encountered throughout', not just in these opening passages.[16]

The traitor stands in sharp contrast to the redeemer figure, as far as the motivation of each is concerned – the latter an essentially good character, often unrecognized as such; the former, essentially bad, but undiscovered until after the damage has been done – yet they can both be subsumed under the concept of pariah. One might say that it is the time factor which distinguishes the two, for the redeemer is pariah first, until his heroism comes to be recognized, whereas the traitor only assumes pariah status last, after his true villainous nature has been perceived. In short, the redeemer starts as a pariah whilst the traitor ends as one.

Despite this temporal contrast between the redeemer-pariah and the traitor-pariah, their shared status as social outcasts remains a factor that invests them with a certain degree of unity. Hyam Maccoby, in *The Sacred Executioner*, analyses another significant point of contact between the two figures in his discussion of Jesus and Judas: 'The commensality of Judas with Jesus makes him one of Jesus's spiritual family . . . . Viewed merely as a story of betrayal, this . . . is an instance of the "wicked brother" motif so common in folk stories. But from the standpoint of myth, the close family relationship between the sacrificial victim and his betrayer . . . is of thematic importance'.[17] To this specific observation one could add that the traitor is bound by his nature to be closely related – whether physically or spiritually – to the victim of betrayal, for two inescapable reasons. Firstly, a wholly detached figure will not have access to the information with which to betray the victim; and second, even if he does somehow bring about his ruin or death, this cannot be classified as betrayal, since he owes the victim no loyalty and has therefore in no way abused a position of trust.

In the light of these introductory observations concerning the traitor in general, let us now consider Goytisolo's treatment of the figure, bearing in mind that it stands in the novels as one manifestation of the broader motif of the pariah.

As chapter 1 showed, the traitor was already an important figure in the earlier fiction; However, Don Julián is surely the first traitor that springs to mind on contemplation of the later novels. With reference to the necessarily close ties between betrayer and betrayed, it is worth noting that the legendary Count Julián was supposed to be a Christian, for he was a Visigoth. Had he been a Muslim, the story of how he permitted the Moorish invasion of Spain to take place in revenge for the King of Spain's deflowering of his daughter (by letting Tariq's hordes cross his territory on the North African coast and thus cross the Straits of Gibraltar) could never have been considered an act of treachery, but only a straight-forward invasion and occupation by a foreign army. It is because he was turning against his spiritual mother – the Church – that he became the wicked traitor *par excellence* of Spanish legend and folklore. It is interesting to notice that the account of Spain's betrayal told in the relevant *romances* does not place the blame solely on Don Julián, but also, ambivalently, on the King, Don Rodrigo and La Cava, Julián's daughter. Responsibility is imputed to Julián in the title of the fourth *romance*, 'La traición del conde don Julián' ('The Treachery of Count Don Julian'), but in the second, which recounts the illicit love of Rodrigo and La Cava, the closing lines clearly – if wryly – point to these two as blameworthy too:

De la pérdida de España
fue aquí funesto principio
una mujer sin ventura
y un hombre de amor rendido.
    Florinda [La Cava] perdió su flor,
el rey padeció el castigo;
ella dice que hubo fuerza,
él que gusto consentido.
    Si dicen quién de los dos
la mayor culpa ha tenido,
digan los hombres: la Cava
y las mujeres: Rodrigo.

('A luckless woman and a lovesick man were the ill-starred beginning of the loss of Spain. Florinda [la Cava] lost her flower, the king suffered punishment; she says she was forced, he that it was pleasure with consent. If they say which of the two was more to blame, let the men say: la Cava, and the women: Rodrigo.')[18]

However, Rodrigo is exonerated in the popular imagination, presumably because of his famous penance with the snake; indeed, the seventh *romance* ends on an optimistic note as far as the ex-king's eternal destiny is concerned:

Las campanas del cielo
sones hacen de alegría;
las campanas de la tierra
ellas solas se tañían;
el alma del penitente
para los cielos subía.

('The bells of heaven are joyfully pealing; the bells on earth were ringing on their own; the soul of the penitent was rising up to the heavens.')[19]

Julián, therefore, stands as the symbol of impenitent treachery and also of course as vengeful destroyer of Christian Spain, and it would seem to be these additional associations that attract Goytisolo to resurrect him in the second novel of the trilogy. Betrayer of his Christian heritage, ally of the Moors, traitor to his fellow Visigoths and their land; these are the specific characteristics of Julián that surely lead the author to wish to vindicate him, not just plain treachery.

Despite these overtones, Julián remains a relatively simple symbol of the traitor, compared with the more complex patterns that emerge on analysis of the protagonist of the trilogy. Alvaro is a double traitor: not only does he betray his country and his class, he also betrays his fellow traitors – people like Antonio of *Señas* – because he leaves Spain instead of staying to fight the regime with them. It is as if Julián had let the Moors into Spain and then turned on them too. Alvaro refuses to identify with other voluntary pariahs like himself, be they his rebel friends still in Spain or his fellow exiles in Paris:

Tu aventura propia y la de tu patria habían tomado rumbos divergentes: por un lado ibas tú, rotos los vínculos que te ligaran antaño a la tribu, borracho y atónito de tu nueva e increíble libertad; por otro aquélla, con el grupo de tus amigos que persistían en el noble empeño de transformarla pagando con su cuerpo el precio que por indiferencia o cobardía habías rehusado pagar tú.

(*SI*, p. 159)

Poco a poco Alvaro había espaciado los encuentros [con emigrados en París] simulando imprescindibles obligaciones .... Fingía absorberse en ocupaciones urgentes si le llamaban por teléfono, no respondía al sonido del timbre que anunciaban sus pisadas inconfundibles, se eclipsaba en cuanto los veía merodear por los alrededores de su casa .... Alvaro había huido de su contacto o de su simple proximidad física, deseoso de olvidarse para siempre de su existencia.

(*SI*, p. 242)

(Your own adventures and those of your country had taken divergent directions: you went one way, the bonds that had once linked you to your tribe having been broken, drunk and astonished at that new and incredible freedom of yours; along the other way, your country and that group of friends who were persevering in their noble efforts to change it, paying with their persons the cost that from indifference or cowardice you had refused to pay.)

(*MI*, p. 133)

(Little by little, Alvaro had spaced out the meetings [with Spanish emigrés in Paris], pretending pressing obligations .... He pretended to be involved in urgent business if they called him on the telephone; he would not answer the bell that their unmistakable footsteps foretold; he would duck out of sight whenever he saw them prowling around his house .... Alvaro had fled from contact with them or their simple physical proximity, wishing to forget about their existence forever.)

(*MI*, p. 200)

The rejection of a protagonist's fellow bourgeois-born rebels resurges powerfully in *Paisajes después de la batalla*, with the guilt that such acquaintances heap on him and the depiction of his own feelings towards them: '¿Qué diablos haces a solas, jubilado del mundo, encerrado en tu celda como un anacoreta? ... ¿Te desentiendes de nuestros anhelos y luchas?' (*PB*, p. 79; 'What the devil are you up to, keeping to yourself, withdrawn from the world, shut up in your cell like a hermit? ... Is it your wish to dissociate yourself from our aspirations and struggles?', *LB*, p. 61). For the protagonist, they are grotesquely childish; indeed, he finds their 'desviación infantil izquierdista' ('infantile leftist deviation') a depressing spectacle (*PB*, p. 81; *LB*, p. 62).

Rather than remaining loyal to the group of bourgeois rebels, 'muchachos de excelente familia . . . educados todos cristianamente en colegios de pago' (*SI*, p. 283; 'boys from good families . . . all having had a Christian education in private schools', *MI*, p. 234), Goytisolo's protagonists are traitors to them, as well as to the background they all have in common. Instead, they turn to natural pariahs: blacks, Arabs, cripples, beggars. Alvaro is a traitor to his country and his class in the eyes of the Establishment and betrays his fellow traitors too in his own and their eyes, yet he seeks to become the redeemer of his chosen group, 'redimir del pecado a todos los parias de la tierra' (*JT*, p. 53; 'to redeem all the world's pariahs from sin', *JL*, p. 41). However, he is rejected by them, 'abucheado al unísono' ('jeered at in chorus') because of his white skin, 'cortado para siempre' (*JT*, p. 59; 'cut off forever', *JL*, p. 47), barred from anchoring his floating loyalties to them. That leaves him in a state of total isolation, having turned his back on his heritage and those who have done likewise, in the hope of joining a new group, but thwarted in this objective. What is left to him can only be to attach his loyalty paradoxically to the concept of treachery itself: 'abandonarse al excitante juego de las combinaciones y extraer de cada operación un beneficio cualquiera: económico, físico o espiritual: o, en último término, por pura gratuidad, por la fulgurante satisfacción del acto en sí: traición grave, traición alegre: traición meditada, traición súbita: traición oculta, traición abierta: traición macha, traición marica: hacer almoneda de todo' (*DJ*, p. 135; 'becoming totally absorbed in this exciting game in which all sorts of winning combinations may turn up, and reaping some measure of profit from every operation: economic, physical, spiritual: or, in the end, for the sheer, gratuitous pleasure, the heady satisfaction inherent in the act in and of itself: solemn treason, joyous treason: premeditated treason, spontaneous treason: overt treason, covert treason: he-man treason, pansy treason: liquidating everything, putting everything under the auctioneer's hammer', *CJ*, p. 112). His isolation takes on an aspect of defiant bravery: 'sólo tú, Bond, caminando impertérrito' (*DJ*, p. 186; 'you alone, James Bond, nonchalantly striding across the room', *CJ*, p. 157, adapted).

James Bond is an interesting symbol of bravery and heroism to have chosen here, in the context of a discussion of redeemers and traitors. Although depicted as a hero, it is worth noting that he is far from the straightforward type of, say, a war film, but in a profession – espionage – the very essence of which is duplicity. In a sense, Bond is the traitor-redeemer motif personified, for he combines the treachery of his methods with the redemption of innumerable hapless victims, tricking his enemies into defeat by means of outlandish gadgetry and quick wits.

Thus, it may be asserted that in some ways, the redeemer and the traitor are not only closely related, but may be seen as two aspects of the same *topos*. Indeed, this is Maccoby's proposition in *The Sacred Executioner*, as he concludes his discussion of the Jesus-Judas relationship: 'the sacred executioner is simply another aspect of the sacrificed victim. After taking upon himself all the community's sins, he assumes in addition the sin of performing the sacrifice . . . . The brotherhood or twinship of the sacrificer and victim may thus express not merely the kinship of the community with the victim, but the identity of victim and sacrificer'.[20]

This would seem to be the concept suggested by the *verdugo-víctima* (executioner-victim) motif, which runs right through the trilogy. In *Señas*, Alvaro laments pointless bloodshed in these terms: 'evocados unos y olvidados otros, fusilados del verano del 36 y de la primavera del 39 eran todos, juntamente verdugos y víctimas, eslabones de la cadena represiva' (*SI*, p. 110; 'some were remembered, and others were forgotten, shot during the summer of 1936 and the spring of 1939, all of them, executioners and victims, were links in the repressive chain', *MI*, pp. 90–1, adapted). The theme is powerfully dramatized in *Don Julián*, when, in the final section of the text, the adult self acts as the executioner of his own child self, but this is foreshadowed earlier with these words: 'y desdoblándote al fin por seguirte mejor, como si fueras otro: ángel de la guardia, amante celoso, detective particular: consciente de que el laberinto está en ti: que tú eres el laberinto: minotauro voraz, mártir comestible: juntamente verdugo y víctima' (*DJ*, p. 52; 'finally splitting in two to tail yourself better, as though you were another person: a guardian angel, a jealous lover, a private eye: knowing that the labyrinth lies within: that you are the labyrinth: the famished minotaur, the edible martyr: at once the executioner and the victim', *CJ*, p. 40). Then, in *Juan sin tierra*, 'tras las huellas del Père de Foucauld' ('in the footsteps of Father Foucauld'), the narrator declames: 'la perfección del amor es la perfección de la obediencia!: entregado al fin, sin inhibiciones, al crudo y amoroso deliquio: a los arrebatos y éxtasis inefables que unen en arpegio común verdugos y víctimas, comisarios y oposicionistas, herejes e inquisidores' (*JT*, p. 151; 'the perfection of love is the perfection of obedience!: finally surrendering, without inhibitions, to the exquisite, amorous swoon: to the ineffable ecstasies and raptures that unite in a single soaring arpeggio executioners and victims, yogis and commissars, heretics and inquisitors', *JL*, p. 138).[21]

There are two characters who differ significantly from the rest of Goytisolo's *verdugo-víctima* outsiders and consequently merit separate consideration. They are Jerónimo of *Señas* and the protagonist of *Paisajes*.[22] They are both solitary men, and in this sense could be said to resemble the other pariahs, but the difference lies in the fact that they both make a point of not being provocative towards other people. In Jerónimo's case, notwithstanding his detachment from the other farm-hands, 'la seriedad y el escrúpulo inhabituales que ponía en la tarea le habían granjeado en seguida todas las simpatías' (*SI*, p. 42; 'the unaccustomed seriousness and scruple that he put into his work had immediately brought him everybody's liking', *MI*, p. 33). In *Paisajes*, the reader is told that the protagonist is 'de puertas afuera, un caballero muy bien educado' (*PB*, p. 23; 'on the outside, . . . a perfect gentleman', *LB*, p. 13). In spite of their innocuous appearance, however, both are active in their respective subversive activities: Jerónimo is involved in a resistance movement against the regime in Spain and the hero of *Paisajes* is running some sort of obscure freedom-fighting campaign in Paris.

Jerónimo says little and there is no omniscient narrator to reveal his thoughts, but there is some insight into the mentality of the protagonist of *Paisajes*, which it might not be too presumptious to imagine would be similar to Jerónimo's. As we have seen, the former regards the vociferously anti-establishment behaviour of his old friends as 'desviación infantil' (*PB*, p. 81; 'infantile . . . deviation', *LB*, p. 62). This suggests that a need to be seen to stand apart from establishment values may be indicative of immaturity rather than heroism, if such overt self-stigmatization in itself serves no practical purpose save self-satisfaction. The clique of Parisian intellectuals whom Alvaro meets in *Señas* is typical of this self-righteous nonconformism that accomplishes naught; after all the discussion of Spain's problems, these people do nothing, turning instead to new – and, no doubt, equally unrealized – plans to save other oppressed groups: 'tu país había desertado definitivamente de la esfera de sus preocupaciones . . . . Gérard Bondy . . . había ido a pasar varios meses a Málaga sin organizar por ello, como pretendiera entonces, la insurrección armada . . . . Se limitó a escribir una novela comercial con pretensiones metafísicas' (*SI*, p. 219; 'your country's problems had abandoned the sphere of his preoccupations for good.... Gérard Bondy... had gone to spend several months in Málaga without having organized, as he had planned, his armed insurrection.... He limited himself to writing a commercial novel with metaphysical pretensions', *MI*, p. 182).

Unlike these earnest and loquacious non-achievers, both Jerónimo of *Señas* and the protagonist of *Paisajes* produce effective results before society catches up with them. Jerónimo disappears mysteriously, killed, Alvaro imagines, but having fought physically for his beliefs; the protagonist of *Paisajes* has helped to sow unrest in Le Sentier before he is caught at the end of the book. Neither of them feels a need to display his disapproval of the Establishment, but carries out his plan of destruction under cover. Returning to the vocabulary of Kiesler and Kiesler, both find positive value in maintaining outward compliance together with private non-acceptance. Are these two, then, like the hypocritical doctor and civil guard in Antonio's village? It would seem not; they differ fundamentally because they are *acting* behind a front of compliance rather than just retaining anti-establishment views in secret, with no intention of ever doing anything about them.

In these two characters, Goytisolo would seem to be expressing his recognition of the value of outward compliance without private acceptance, providing as it does the freedom to realize effective subversion undisturbed. In *Makbara*, there is the idea that the obvious pariah is free because society avoids him and he is therefore left to himself: 'el paria, el apestado, el negro se mueve libremente' (*Ma*, p. 16; 'the pariah, the plague carrier, the black moves about freely', *Mb*, p. 6, adapted). However, this apparent liberty is shown subsequently to be illusory, for the PB Radio broadcasters dog the *trogloditas* for their sensational news value, and the American intellectuals who capture the North African deprive him of his freedom, callously treating him not as a human being but a mere anthropological specimen (*Ma*, pp. 141–60 and 161–75; *Mb*, pp. 162–89 and 190–209, respectively).

The overt pariah's pitched battle against society would seem to be a futile one. And yet Goytisolo's opinion, as expressed in his essay, 'Marginalidad y disidencia: la nueva información revolucionaria', does not accord with this reading of the later novels:

Como premisa indispensable, el marginal deberá *descalificarse moralmente* mediante la asunción voluntaria de todas las transgresiones y rupturas que lo convertirán a ojos del intelectual humanista en un paria o un apestado, y elaborar, a partir de dicha asunción, un lenguaje distinto, *deliberadamente provocador*. Sólo desnudándose podrá desnudar a los demás y apuntar a la insuficiencia y precariedad de un orden social y moral que elimina o pone entre paréntesis lo ajeno, inasimilable, excluido.

(As an indispensable premise, the marginalized person will have to *disqualify himself morally* by voluntarily assuming all the transgressions and ruptures which, in the eyes of the humanist intellectual, will turn him into a pariah, a plague-carrier, and to elaborate with that assumption as the starting-point, a different, *deliberately provocative* language. Only by baring himself, will he be able to lay the others bare and to indicate the insufficiency and precariousness of a social and moral order which eliminates or brackets off what is alien, incapable of assimilation, excluded.)[23]

However, it is worth noting that this essay was published in 1978, which is to say, between *Juan sin tierra* and *Makbara*, well before *Paisajes*, where the concept of private non-acceptance coupled with outward compliance is developed. Be that as it may, it seems clear on the evidence of the texts themselves that the pariah's attempts to shock society's respectable members into awareness fail; indeed, his determination to slough his outer *cáscara* of appearance and behaviour in order to reveal his *pulpa* of inner beliefs might be seen as a form of immature self-indulgence, not to say evidence of a deep insecurity: he can believe that he stands apart only when he sees this reflected in others' reactions to him. The covert pariah, on the other hand, needs no such reassurance because he can see the tangible results of his clandestine activities. However, is it valid to call anyone a covert pariah? Surely this is a contradiction in terms. If Jerónimo is liked by his workmates and if the protagonist of *Paisajes* appears to be a perfectly respectable member of Parisian society, to what extent is it justifiable to call either of them a pariah or social outcast? As with the redeemer-traitor motif, it is the time factor that qualifies them for inclusion in a chapter concerning pariahs. Both are retrospective pariahs, as it were, for whether they be seen as redeemers or traitors, this status is unrecognized until after they have acted. It is only with the benefit of hindsight in Jerónimo's case, and insight in that of the protagonist of *Paisajes*, that their true nature can be revealed.

Untouchability, in the final analysis, is unproductive, because while people will not touch someone, he cannot come close enough to touch – to have a real effect on – them. The effective pariah – be he traitor, redeemer, or both simultaneously – needs to balance precariously on the knife-edge of outer compliance in order to gain access to the masses, and inner but active subversion, in order to change them; he must be willing to remain unrecognized until after his task is completed. Returning to the double focus of Goytisolo's later novels, arising from the blurring of the boundaries between author and protagonist, between action within the text and the act of writing it, an analogy suggests itself: where the protagonists are overt pariahs from the outset – that is to say, in *Don Julián, Juan sin tierra*, and *Makbara* – the style of writing is as deliberately off-putting, as uncompromising towards the reader as the protagonists are towards society. *Paisajes*, on the other hand, is much more compliant on the surface, with its normal punctuation and light-hearted, almost jocular tone. Yet, perhaps together with *Señas*, it achieves more as far as subversion is concerned, for the reader is drawn into a complicitous relationship with the text, rather than driven, as it were, into the enemy camp, and he is therefore more receptive to the condemnation of society. Once the open pariah, Goytisolo seems to have donned the cloak of compliance with *Paisajes*, but owing to his overtly non-conformist stance in the trilogy and *Makbara*, there will be no surprise revelation of a traitor-redeemer after the event. On the contrary, the reader who knows his previous novels approaches the amenability of *Paisajes* with suspicion, so that when, towards the end, it transpires that the apparently conventional narrator is none other than the subversive protagonist himself (*PB*, p. 119; *LB*, p. 94), it is with a nod of recognition rather than a sense of having been tricked that the discovery is met. As an autonomous text, therefore, *Paisajes* might be successfully deceptive, but as a link in the author's chain of production, the reader will not be taken in.

In sum, it could be asserted that the pariah motif in the later novels bestrides the concepts of *esquizofrenia colectiva* on the one hand, and condemnation of ordered hierarchies on the other. Admittedly, the most immediately striking feature is Goytisolo's depiction of the dualistic mentality of Western civilization, which categorizes certain people as untouchable, in contrast to socially accepted individuals who mask their fleshly *pulpa* in one kind of *cáscara* or another. In contrast to this dualism, Arab society is described as lacking in such compartmentalization: 'colectividad fraterna que ignora el asilo, el

ghetto, la marginación : orates, monstruos, extraños campan a sus
anchas' (*Ma*, p. 204; 'a fraternal community with no notion of
asylums, ghettos, outcasts: lunatics, freaks, monsters set up camp
wherever they choose', *Mb*, p. 243). However, at the same time as
condemning the untouchable/touchable dualism, attention is also
implicitly drawn to the pariah as standing on the bottom rung of the
hierarchical ladder of Western society.[24] On this more complex level
of interpretation of the *topos*, the characters who wish to assume
pariah status are rejecting the concept of a society structured according to spiritual worth. Their wish to join the ranks of natural pariahs
fits in with the broader theme of deliberate descent in the ordered
hierarchy of Western convention, based on a refusal to accept the
basic tenet that spirit is superior to flesh. Like the desire to reinstate
bodily functions – 'habitúese a su propia materia' ( *JT*, p. 225; 'accept
your own material condition', *JL*, p. 199) – like the desire to create a
'paraíso, el tuyo, con culo y con falo' ( *JT*, p. 218; 'a paradise, yours,
with an ass and a phallus', *JL*, p. 192), like the love of the underworld, the favourable treatment of pariahs contributes to the thrust
of all the later novels: to blur the notion of metaphysical ascent and
descent to the point of meaninglessness, thus destroying order itself
and replacing it with a complete lack of evaluative differentiation.
This attack on structured hierarchies needs to be examined next,
therefore.

# 4
## *Reivindicación del caos:** Depictions of the Good Place

Common usage has distorted the term *utopia*. Coined by Thomas More in 1516 with the publication of his work of that name, it is a pun on the Greek prefixes *ou-* and *eu-*, meaning respectively 'not' and 'good', with the rest of the word meaning 'place'. If More's country was therefore a good place that was nowhere, it was not depicted as a perfect place. The inhabitants were not Christians, a fact which, given that the author died for his faith, necessarily precluded perfection. The existence of slavery and warfare in Utopia further distanced it from a vision of the ideal. Needless to say, this is not a criticism of the work, since Utopia is nowhere declared perfect by the author. Be that as it may, though, *Chambers Twentieth Century Dictionary* gives as a definition of *utopia*, 'any imaginary state of ideal perfection', which, whether derived from a misunderstanding of More's book or not, is what the word has come to mean nowadays. Northrop Frye puts it thus: 'The popular view of the utopia, and the one which in practice is accepted by many if not most utopia–writers, is that a utopia is an ideal or flawless state, not only logically consistent in its structure, but permitting as much freedom and happiness for its inhabitants as is possible to human life'.[1]

In response to utopian literature, the genre known as dystopianism has developed, made famous by such works as Aldous Huxley's *Brave New World* (1932) and George Orwell's *Nineteen Eighty-Four* (1949). The technique of such writers as these involves a distortion of the utopian perspective, so that they depict a society organized according to typical utopian values, but by shifting the focus, the

*'Vindication of chaos'

dystopian author reveals it to be more like a ghastly nightmare than a beautiful dream.

The dystopians play the utopians at their own game, as it were, countering the latter's rational, dispassionate, and above all feasible vision of a perfect society, with an equally feasible one of a nightmare. Goytisolo boldly departs from this response to the utopian genre. If dystopians such as Huxley and Orwell hold up a grotesquely distorted mirror to utopians like More and H. G. Wells, Goytisolo does not even accord utopian constructs a serious, anguished reflection. In *Juan sin tierra*, his one foray into a utopian-style fiction (*JT*, pp. 215–34; *JL*, pp. 190–206), is openly humorous and clearly not to be taken seriously for a moment, for it does not attempt to create a plausible society. Whilst the dystopians construct a credible vision, making the reader think with a shudder that this dreadful society could just as easily be the outcome of human attempts to attain perfection as a blissful one, Goytisolo's attack on the utopian genre aims at the concept of plausibility itself. In the mocking utopian section of *Juan sin tierra*, he questions the set of conventions pertaining to plausibility for utopians and dystopians alike, suggesting that it is quite arbitrary and therefore ludicrous. The question tacitly posed is: why should it be considered plausible that people could be honest, not greedy, faithful to their spouses, happy with their lot, and yet laughable that they should wear clothes with a square cut out to expose their bottoms? If we are inclined to laugh at the latter, he suggests, then we should laugh at the former too.

In addition to this, Goytisolo utilizes his parody of the utopian genre in *Juan sin tierra* to make some further suggestions; whilst playfully mocking the genre itself, he nevertheless raises some serious questions. At the same time, for example, as laughing at the idea of portraits of famous people's bottoms adorning government office walls (*JT*, p. 223; *JL*, p. 197), the reader is reminded of the equally laughable pretence in Western society, which demands that respectable people behave as though they did not perform bodily functions nor possess the organs with which to do so. The literary device that brings this to light has been called the *contre-pied*.[2] This operates by making the reader aware that he has grown to accept purely arbitrary conventions as morally right and that had he been brought up differently, the exact opposite might seem proper. Samuel Butler uses this device in *Erewhon*, when he simply swaps disease and law-breaking, so that the former becomes a punishable offence

and the latter a misfortune attracting sympathy and professional help.[3]
Goytisolo, like Butler, 'ne fait que souligner le relativisme choquant
de nos raisonnements' (is only underlining the shocking relativism of
our reasonings), as Cioranescu observes about *Erewhon*.[4] In Butler's
case, he is not saying that the Erewhonians are right to punish diseased people, but that there is perhaps something to be said for
showing compassion and seeking cures for those who break the law,
rather than simply imprisoning or fining them. And, beyond the
particular example given by Butler, there is surely a general warning to beware of confusing convention with reason or with right.
The reader is told that the judge who sentenced a man suffering from
pulmonary consumption was 'a kind and thoughtful person . . . . Yet
for all this, . . . he could not emancipate himself from . . . the bond-
age of the ideas in which he had been born and bred'.[5] The same
message would seem to be conveyed by Goytisolo's reversal of *cara*
and *culo* ('face' and 'arse'). For him too, it is not the dark side of the
comparison that is advocated. Faces are not to be concealed or unmentionable in his utopia, but must relinquish their monopoly of
acceptability. Rather than outlawing what is deemed respectable in
present society, the emphasis is on redeeming the condemned: the
criminal will be cured and loved in Butler's work and the zealously
concealed bottom will be emancipated in *Juan sin tierra*. This point
is worth stressing, since a critic like Claudia Schaefer-Rodríguez
misjudges Goytisolo in this respect: 'El lector se da cuenta de que lo
que propone Alvaro es la "esclavitud" a las funciones corporales; el
orden dictatorial de obedecer, sin plan ni fin social, a los impulsos
"inferiores" corresponde al acto de aquéllos del mundo objetivo de
rendir homenaje a un caudillo' ('The reader realizes that what Alvaro
is proposing is "slavery" to bodily functions; the dictatorial order to
obey "inferior" impulses, quite without social objective or plan, is
on a par with the actions of those in the objective world who pay
homage to a caudillo').[6]
    The silliness of bottoms taking the place of faces serves another
purpose too, namely, to indicate the silliness of absolute equality as a
social objective. The bottom is seen as the 'mínimo común múltiplo
que anula la superior diferencia de rasgos' (*JT*, p. 223; 'the minimum
common multiple that cancels out the superior difference in
features', *JL*, p. 197). This concept is reinforced by the equally
impracticable idea of creating equality between all life, animal and
vegetable: 'no mantenemos ningún criterio elitista con respecto a la
flora y la fauna : auspiciamos por igual todas las especies vegetales y

animales . . . : no nos tomamos como antes solíamos, por reyes y señores de nadie' ( *JT*, p. 234; 'we apply no elitist criterion to the various flora and fauna; we give equal opportunities to all vegetable and animal species . . . : we . . . no longer take ourselves to be, as we once did, the lords and masters of anyone', *JL*, p. 206). The concept of man as ruler of Creation originates in the Old Testament, of course:

> And God said, Let us make man in our image, after our likeness: and let them have dominion over the fish of the sea, and over the fowl of the air, and over the cattle, and over all the earth, and over every creeping thing that creepeth upon the earth . . . .
> And God blessed them and God said unto them, Be fruitful and multiply, and replenish the earth and subdue it: and have dominion over the fish of the sea, and over the fowl of the air, and over every living thing that moveth upon the earth.
>
> (Genesis 1.26 and 28)

The *cara-culo contre-pied*, then, embraces several comments on utopian literature. First, and perhaps most obviously, *culo* ('arse') symbolizes corporality; its reinstatement condemns repression of the body: 'cara y culo parejos, libres y descubiertos, utopía de un mundo complejo, sin asepsia ni ocultación: . . . paraíso, el tuyo, con culo y con falo' ( *JT*, p. 218; 'the face and the ass equals, free and bare, the utopia of a complex world, without asepsis and concealment: . . . paradise, yours, with an ass and a phallus', *JL*, p. 192). In this respect, one might discern a shade of utopianism in Goytisolo's writing, albeit of an unconventional sort, for he is advocating an improvement in an imaginary society and at the same time pinpointing what he sees as a defect in his own; or, as Frye puts it: 'The utopia proper, is essentially the writer's own society with its unconscious ritual habits transposed into their conscious [rationally explicable] equivalents. The contrast in value between the two societies implies a satire on the writer's own society, and the basis for the satire is the unconsciousness or inconsistency in the social behaviour he observes around him'.[7]

Second, the patent silliness of the idea as a proposed reform demonstrates the silliness of attempting to create a perfect society: 'ensueños idílicos, ilusiones bucólicas que . . . permitían fantasear exquisitos planes de educación y vida común conforme a modelos de la antigüedad grecorromana, ajenos del todo a la masa ingente y hostil' ( *JT*, p. 215; 'idyllic dreams, bucolic illusions which . . . gave rise to fantasized plans for education and communal life, modeled on Greco-Roman antiquity and completely alien to the hostile, teeming masses', *JL*, p. 190, adapted). Here, Goytisolo follows the tradition of Jonathan Swift in *Gulliver's Travels*, who makes the same point by discovering an ideal society amongst horses, in the land of the Houyhnhnms, where the same environment has created a breed of human beings – the Yahoos – which is degenerate and vicious.[8] Both are saying, it would seem, that human nature is not compatible with the kind of perfect society dreamt up by utopians.

Third, and linked with this, Goytisolo pours scorn on the idea of equality, one specific detail of the sort of perfection with which human nature as he sees it is incompatible. Besides, even if it could be attained, equality is depicted as bringing with it the tedious uniformity typically dreaded by dystopian writers. With tongue-in-cheek, Goytisolo's narrator declares: 'la felicidad! : cuando sociedad e individuo dejan de ser términos antagónicos y el dañino individualismo se funde en un arpegio social unánime' (*JT*, p. 216; 'felicity! : as society and the individual cease to be antagonistic terms and pernicious individualism resolves into one unanimous, majestic social arpeggio', *JL*, p. 191).

Fourth, the *cara-culo contre-pied* highlights the arbitrary nature of social conventions; just as logical a case can be made for *culo* to stand as a dignified symbol of humankind as for *cara* to do so. This undermines the status of logic or reason as an unquestionably trustworthy criterion and in this function joins with all the jesuitical argumentation throughout *Juan sin tierra* in demonstrating how unreliable logic may be.[9]

Another striking feature of this utopian vision in the third novel of the trilogy is worthy of note. Goytisolo departs from conventional utopians and dystopians alike in his attitude to work. While the utopians either make it minimal or pleasurable and the typical dystopians make it tedious and inescapable, Goytisolo simply rejects it altogether: 'planes de trabajo?: ninguno' (*JT*, p. 230; 'work plans?: none:', *JL*, p. 202).[10] The concept of not needing to work at all harks back to the Garden of Eden before the Fall in the Judaeo-Christian tradition and the Greek Golden Age of classical mythology, as portrayed by Hesiod, for instance.[11] It is also a feature of the traditionalist Muslim vision of the afterlife in paradise.[12] However, in all three, as well as in the legendary Cockaigne – where the extreme example is found of meat presenting itself ready cooked – the world is a very different place, with correspondingly different

natural laws.[13] In his study of utopian literature, Cioranescu emphasizes the difference between the classical Golden Age and utopia; and
in this regard, Eden, the Muslim paradise, and Cockaigne could be
grouped with the Golden Age: 'Le mythe compte avec la collaboration totale et dévouée de la nature, entendue comme providence,
tandis que l'utopie ne compte qu'avec le travail des hommes' (the
myth can count on the total devoted collaboration of nature, understood as providence, whilst utopia can only count on men's
labour).[14] Goytisolo chooses to limit himself to the utopian scheme,
though he proposes a completely novel solution to the question of
work; he opts for 'saqueos, robo, pillaje de los pueblos laboriosos
vecinos' ( JT, p. 230; 'sacking, robbing, pillaging industrious
neighboring peoples', JL, p. 202). There is no point in complaining
of the non-feasibility of such a policy, objecting that there would be
retaliation and/or preventive measures taken by the neighbouring
communities; it must be remembered that Goytisolo has rejected the
twin principles of logic and plausibility in utopian constructs. It is no
use pleading immorality either, for throughout his fiction, the whole
notion of right and wrong is repeatedly attacked, shown to be
arbitrary, culture-bound, hypocritical, misguided, inhumane, and
psychologically damaging. Stealing food can hardly be more
blameworthy, it is tacitly suggested, than stealing freedom and
creativity from others.

Complementary to the utopian vision of *Juan sin tierra* is
Goytisolo's later invention, equally ironical and critical of this type
of fantasy world, which he calls *Disneylandia* in *Paisajes después de la
batalla* (*PB*, pp. 100–2; *LB*, pp. 79–80). It is described in terms
typical of the utopian fantasy, yet at the same time, there is a subtler
undercurrent that draws a parallel between this and heaven. It is 'un
mundo nuevo y armonioso, de una sociedad abierta al sueño y a la
esperanza, . . . un salto cualitativo al mañana . . . que sustituye la
realidad de un presente gris y zafio con un modelo ya existente en
otras latitudes, en tecnicolor fabuloso: Disneylandia' (*PB*, p. 101; 'a
new and peaceful world, of a society open to dreams and hopes, . . . a
qualitative leap into tomorrow, . . . replacing the reality of a gray and
vulgar present with an already existing model, in other latitudes,
projected in fabulous Technicolor: Disneyland', *LB*, p. 79). Indeed,
this extract encapsulates what heaven and utopia have in common:
perfection, future hope, a contrast with the wretchedness of the
present life, and a real, if distant, location.

It is interesting to note the traditional attitude adopted here by

Goytisolo towards space and time. He stays within the scheme used by Thomas More and his most faithful followers, by keeping the location of the utopia 'ya existente, en otras latitudes' ('already existing . . . in other latitudes'), rather than making the no-place into a no-time, that is to say, giving a futuristic vision of a genuine place, such as William Morris's London in *News from Nowhere* (1890), or Edward Bellamy's Boston in *Looking Backward* (1888). However, like More's creation, Goytisolo's Disneylandia is not devoid of a temporal dimension in the shape of hope for the future. As with *Utopia*, the fact that a more just society not only could but actually does exist can inspire the reader with the hope that his own society may become more like that one in time. The words with which More closes his book bring out this relationship between the currently existent good place located 'en otras latitudes' and hope for the author's own society in the future: 'There are many features of the Utopian Republic which I should like – though I hardly expect – to see adopted in Europe'.[15] The same element of temporality is suggested by the 'salto cualitativo al mañana' ('qualitative leap into tomorrow') of Disneylandia.

The heavenly undercurrent of Disneylandia is prefigured in *Makbara*, where there is a reference to the 'beatífico tecnicolor de Walt Disney' (*Ma*, p. 14; 'Walt Disney's beatific technicolor', *Mb*, p. 4). The English slogan of 'glorious Technicolor' also has heavenly associations, but these are less striking since the adjective *glorious* has slipped into common, secular usage. *Beatífico* revives the heavenly history of *glorious* and reminds the reader in so doing of the escapist, paradise-seeking implications of the Hollywood film industry, suggested by this choice of adjective. Although the slogan 'Glorious Technicolor' was not translated literally into Spanish, it may be familiar to Spanish film-goers who could have seen it written on the screen when dubbed American films were previewed. Indeed, for a Spaniard reading the English *glorious* and naturally associating it with the Spanish *gloria* (meaning 'heaven'), these implications would be far more powerful than for English-speaking audiences.

Both in *Makbara* and *Paisajes*, the cinema is seen as an escape from reality in which fantasies can be played out, whilst James Bond in *Don Julián* and King Kong in *Juan sin tierra* prefigure the motif. Even in *Señas*, Alvaro takes Dolores's nephew to see a Marx Brothers film while she is having her abortion (*SI*, pp. 352; *MI*, pp. 293–4), and as early as *Fiestas* (1957), there is a character, Pipo, who lives in a cinema-inspired fantasy world. Already here, the contrast between fun-filled, exciting Hollywood, and sordid, desolate reality is starkly delineated.

In *Don Julián*, repeated references are made to a poster advertising a James Bond film: 'la perfilada silueta de un hombre con un revólver tácito y elocuente: JAMES BOND, OPERACION TRUENO, última semana' (*DJ*, p. 28; 'the silhouette in profile of a man with a silent, eloquent revolver: JAMES BOND, THUNDERBALL, final week', *CJ*, p. 18). The escapist element is introduced in crescendo. First, there is the comment that follows straight on from the advertisement, principally referring to the narrator's walking away from the Spaniards at a nearby café, but necessarily associated with the Bond motif because of its position in the discourse: 'hasta perderse de vista y anular de golpe los remotos sueños incumplidos, las jamás satisfechas esperanzas de los broncos y bizarros carpetos' (*DJ*, p. 28; 'then at last disappearing from view, thereby suddenly destroying the vague dreams, bitterly disappointing yet again the hopes of those coarse Hispano males who like to think of themselves as irresistible Don Juans', *CJ*, p. 18, adapted). Then, there is the description of part of the film (*DJ*, pp. 75–9; *CJ*, pp. 61–4), when the narrator decides to go into the cinema, having just escaped 'una horda de mendigos que corren detrás de ti, te tiran de la manga, te rodean, amenazan, suplican, intentan cortarte el paso' (*DJ*, p. 74; 'a horde of beggars at your heels: surrounding you, tugging at your sleeve, threatening you, whining at you, attempting to block your path', *CJ*, p. 60). The contrast between this scene of squalor and the 'áureo esplendor de la noche antillana, dominio efímero de Su Majestad Carnaval y su séquito' (*DJ*, p. 75; 'the gilded splendor of nights in the Antilles, the ephemeral domain of His Majesty the King of the Carnival and his cortege', *CJ*, p. 61) is bound to strike the reader. finally, the escapism reaches a climax later in the text, when the narrator, departing momentarily from his Don Julián fantasy, actually sees himself as Bond: 'sólo tú, Bond, caminando impertérrito hacia la orquesta de calypsos, bajo la dorada luz de los focos' (*DJ*, p. 186; 'you alone, James Bond in the flesh, nonchalantly striding across the room toward the calypso orchestra, illuminated by gleaming spotlights', *CJ*, p. 157).

In *Juan sin tierra*, King Kong is removed from the cinema screen altogether, appearing only in the protagonist's fancy. The giant ape which, as the reader knows, originates in a film, is never seen there; it is as if this were a preliminary stage that might be eliminated. Instead, the discourse jumps straight into the full-blown reverie, the seeds of which must have been sown in the absent cinema: 'las raptadas doncellas tiemblan de inconfesable dicha sobre su vasta palma velluda y el antropomorfo las observará con arrobo' (*JT*, p. 75; 'the damsels he has carried off by force tremble with inexpressible happiness on his huge hairy palm, and the anthropomorph will contemplate them ecstatically', *JL*, p. 61). As with Bond in *Don Julián*, the cinema is seen to be fuel for fantasy, not an end in itself.

In *Makbara*, however, the focus shifts somewhat. Not only does the 'beatífico tecnicolor' kindle fantasy, but also the very experience of going into the cinema takes on its own significance. What Alvaro of *Señas* could not – or perhaps would not – appreciate, preoccupied as he was with Dolores's ordeal elsewhere, the narrator of *Makbara* drinks in with relish: 'la fetal, sedativa tiniebla' (*Ma*, p. 21; 'soothing, fetal shadow', *Mb*, p. 14). In *Don Julián* this aspect of the experience of going to the cinema was left undeveloped; the description of the auditorium was neutral – 'te acomodas como puedes en la butaca' (*DJ*, p. 75; '[you] plop down in [an empty seat]', *CJ*, p. 61) – whereas for the protagonist of *Makbara*, the experience is likened to a return to the womb, not only because it is warm and dark, but also – and perhaps most importantly – because it allows to be 'abolido el infierno, el mundo de ellos' (*Ma*, p. 22; (because) 'the inferno, their world, has disappeared', *Mb*, p. 15).[16] Here the emphasis is on the auditorium itself as the source of solace, but the action on the screen does not decrease in value for all that. On the contrary, it is because the members of the audience are absorbed by a horror film that the protagonist feels relaxed and comfortable. The spectacle of the film draws the public's attention away from him: 'cerrar los ojos, descansar, dormir, soy yo, no miran, me ampara el horror de la película' (*Ma*, p. 22; 'closing my eyes, resting, sleeping, being who I am, they're not looking, the horror of the film is protecting me', *Mb*, p. 15). The combination of darkness, warmth, protection from the masses, and fantasy, is a recurrent *topos* from *Juan sin tierra* onwards, for these are the attributes of the underworld good place, which I shall consider presently.

To return to the cinema, though, Disneylandia in *Paisajes* depicts the same sort of 'edén engañoso, embustero' (*JT*, p. 217; 'deceptive, fake eden', *JL*, p. 192) that Goytisolo attacks in the utopian parody of the third novel of the trilogy. Just as he takes exception there to the way in which utopian literature tends to portray a world 'sin culo: marea infinita de rostros que ríen, cantan, . . . pero no joden ni cagan, no empalman, no expelen: ciegos del ojo inferior' (*JT*, p. 217; a world 'without asses: a boundless sea of faces that laugh, sing, . . . but neither fuck nor shit, neither couple nor excrete: blind in their inferior . . . eye', *JL*, p. 192), Disneylandia is a place of 'esparcimientos honestos, expansiones sanas, leve y espontánea alegría' (*PB*, p. 119; 'healthy recreation, light-hearted, spontaneous effusion', *LB*, p. 95), but with the same criticism that it overlooks the true nature of humanity: 'Un solo detalle superfluo: tu puñetera picha' (*PB*, p. 119; 'Just one superfluous detail: your damned hard-on', *LB*, p. 95).[17] Furthermore, and as with his criticism of utopian literature, Goytisolo is not merely finding fault with the genre itself when he attacks Disney-type escapist cinema; more importantly, he deplores the mentality that creates the demand for it, the people who can wish for and find comfort in this type of ideal world. In none of the novels is the reader taken to a Hollywood film studio, in order that scorn may be heaped on the makers of this kind of film; but the queues outside the cinema in Paris are described: 'la interminable y hasta ahora paciente cola de espectadores, que aguarda con su prole el *anhelado* momento de entrar en el Rex' (*PB*, p. 100, my italics; 'the endless and heretofore patient line of moviegoers, awaiting with their offspring the *yearned-for* moment of entering the Rex', *LB*, p. 79, adapted).

In both the utopian parody of *Juan sin tierra* and the depiction of Disneylandia in *Paisajes*, there is a transformation of the ideal into the grotesque. From an albeit sarcastically treated description of the typical utopia 'sin culo', there is in both texts a shift to a grotesque negation of the vision. In *Juan sin tierra*, it is less disturbing, for the exposition of how the narrator's topsy-turvy utopian society would be is just as much a flight of fancy as the original conventional one; in addition, its sting is lessened by the bizarre humour of the piece. In *Paisajes*, however, the action moves down from the cinema screen and onto the streets; the rose-coloured fantasy becomes a bloody reality, as agitators disguised as Donald Duck, Pluto, and Mickey Mouse cause a riot. More alarming still, they are not just thugs who have used Disney disguises by chance; they are utopian activists, seeking to change the world into Disneylandia itself (*PB*, pp. 100–2; *LB*, pp. 79–80). In this way, Goytisolo draws attention to the violence perpetrated in the name of establishing a better or even perfect society, echoing his earlier attacks on the Spanish Inquisition, colonialism, and of course the Civil War, all justified as necessary in order to create a better society. In *Señas*, Alvaro meditates on the carnage of the Civil War and its equally bloody historical antecedents in these terms:

Por espacio de tres años un vendaval de locura había soplado sobre la piel del toro . . . completando la obra destructora emprendida siglo a siglo, con tesón y paciencia, por tus antepasados ilustres. Poseídos de oscuros e inconfesables instintos, íncubos y súcubos a la vez de sus aborrecidos apetitos y sueños, habían procedido con orden y minuciosidad a la poda cruel e inexorable de sí mismos, a la expulsión y exterminio de los demonios interiores, sin detenerse ante motivo o consideración de índole alguna, arruinando, por turno, *en aras del imposible exorcismo*, el comercio, la industria, la ciencia, las artes.

(SI, p. 154, my italics)

(For a period of three years a wind of madness had blown across the skin of the bull [Spain] . . . completing the destructive opus carried on with tenacity and patience down the centuries by your illustrious ancestors. Possessed by dark and inconfessable instincts, at once the incubus and succubus of their hated appetites and dreams, they had proceeded with order and thoroughness to a cruel and inexorable self-pruning, to the expulsion and extermination of their inner demons, stopping for no reason or consideration whatsoever, destroying in turn, *on the altars of an impossible exorcism*, commerce, industry, science, art.)

(MI, p. 128, adapted)

Similarly, the preacher in *Juan sin tierra* tells the slaves that 'la esclavitud es la gracia divina en virtud de la cual ingresaréis en el Cielo' (*JT*, p. 36; 'slavery is the divine grace by virtue of which you will enter the Kingdom of Heaven', *JL*, p. 25). This justification for suffering highlights a parallel between revolutionary propaganda on the one hand, which asserts that preliminary hardship and bloodshed are a necessary stage on the path to perfection, and on the other, the orthodox Christian mentality; both suffer from 'la vieja predisposición de la estirpe a suprimir la libertad viva de hoy en nombre la imaginaria libertad de mañana' (*JT*, p. 14; 'the age-old predisposition of the breed to suppress the living liberty of today in the name of the imaginary liberty of tomorrow', *JL*, p. 5).[18] Whether the imaginary liberty is a place in heaven after death, or a place in Disneylandia after the revolution, there is the same deplorable sacrifice (as the texts present it), of what happiness could be found in this albeit imperfect world, for the sake of an empty illusion.

That is not to say that illusions are portrayed as necessarily a bad thing. It seems to depend on how they affect the deluded person. If belief in an illusion makes life better in the here and now, then there is no condemnation. This is the case with the Muslim concept of the afterlife in paradise. For the tannery-worker in *Makbara*, for example, faith in a just reward after death is a 'compensación necesaria a la inhóspita, brutal realidad: . . . refugiarme en la certeza superior de la fe' (*Ma*, p. 68; 'necessary compensation in the face of a harsh, cruel reality: . . . taking refuge in the higher certainty of the faith', *Mb*, p. 70, adapted). The same positive attitude is to be found in the treatment of the Arab story-teller's world: 'reino ideal donde la astucia obtiene la recompensa y la fuerza bruta el castigo, utopía de un dios equitativo de designios profundos y honrados: antídoto necesario de la vida pobre y descalza, el hambre insatisfecha, la realidad inicua' (*Ma*, p. 220; 'an ideal realm in which cunning is rewarded and brute force is punished, the utopia of a just god whose designs are profound and honorable: the necessary antidote for a miserable, barefoot existence, empty bellies, a reality that is cruelly unjust', *Mb*, pp. 266–7). Christian faith does not, however, receive the same sympathetic treatment; Padre Vosk's consolatory sermon to the slaves in *Juan sin tierra* is presented in an inhumane, barbaric light and yet the essence of what he is preaching is very similar: 'defendiéndoos a vosotros contra vosotros mismos: a fin de que un día pudierais sentaros a la diestra del Padre . . . : allí concluirán de una vez vuestras tribulaciones y miserias' (*JT*, p. 35; 'protecting you against yourselves: so that one day you may sit at the right hand of God the Father . . . : up there your tribulations and miseries will come to an end once and for all', *JL*, pp. 24–5). In *Señas* too, there is a less aggressive but equally negative portrayal of Christian faith in the description of Alvaro's great-grandmother: 'resignada y muda, . . . desengañada e infeliz . . . sin más refugio que la práctica melancólica de una religión consoladora' (*SI*, p. 17; 'resigned and mute . . . disillusioned and unhappy . . . with no other refuge except the melancholy practice of a consoling religion' (*MI*, p. 12, adapted). Is this baseless prejudice against Christianity in favour of Islam, or is there some justification for the divergence in treatment within what is basically a feature common to both religions, namely, the belief in eternal reward and punishment after death?

Goytisolo goes some way towards explaining the difference in his attitude towards Christian and Muslim traditions concerning the afterlife in his essay 'Quevedo: la obsesión excremental' (Quevedo [great Spanish seventeenth-century poet, essayist, and picaresque novelist]: The Obsession with Excrement). It is worth quoting at some length:

Mientras la pintura del edén coránico cautiva la mente del musulmán con el colorido y sensualidad de su paleta, el cristianismo ha
fracasado de modo lamentable en su tentativa de representarnos el
cielo .... La abstracción y la insipidez de las descripciones del
fastidiosísimo reino de los bienaventurados establece una neta
separación entre la religión que rehusa el cuerpo y la felicidad de
los sentidos y otra que los prolonga y perpetúa en la vida
ultraterrenal. Religión y erotismo no son términos antagónicos
para el musulmán; su ley no le veda las satisfacciones del placer
físico y su paraíso es una condensación portentosa de todas las
fantasías y quimeras del hombre del desierto: jardines de volup-
tuosidad con frutas, palmeras, granadas; aguas que corren man-
samente; vino exquisito que no embriaga; lechos nupciales;
muchachas de ojos negros, grandes y cándidos, que ningún hombre habrá desflorado antes y que, aun después de ser poseídas,
seguirán siendo vírgenes; mancebos hermosísimos que seran siempre en la flor de la edad, etc.

(Whilst the picture of the Koranic Eden captivates the Muslim's
mind with the colours and sensuality of its palette, Christianity has
failed lamentably in its attempt to depict heaven for us .... The
abstraction and insipidness of the descriptions of the supremely
tedious abode of the blessed establishes a clear separation between
the one religion which rejects the body and the joys of the senses
and the other, which prolongs and perpetuates them in the afterlife. Religion and eroticism are not antonymous terms for the
Muslim; his law does not bar him from the satisfactions of physical
pleasure and his paradise is a portentous condensation of all the
fantasies and chimeras of the desert-dweller: gardens of volup-
tuousness with fruit, palm-trees, pomegranates; gently flowing
waters; exquisite wine which does not intoxicate; nuptial beds;
girls with big, black, innocent eyes, whom no man will have
deflowered before and who, even after being possessed, will
continue to be virgins; the most beautiful boys, who will always
be in the finest flower of youth, etc.)[19]

However, he does not ask why there should be this difference
between the unashamed sensuality of Islam and the guilt-ridden
attitude of the Christian world. This might be explained by one of
the greatest divergences between the two religions, namely, the
absence in Islam and the presence in Christianity of the doctrine of
original sin and the Fall. This is at the root of the Christian notion

that human souls have all been tainted and so, in order to be virtuous and thereby gain a place in heaven, life must be spent in a constant effort to overcome the tendency to lust, the temptation towards evil present in man because of his corrupted condition. Taken together with the influence on Paul of Hellenic concepts of the duality of flesh and spirit, and the baseness of the former compared with the latter, the virtue required of a Christian who wishes to go to heaven becomes a lifelong nightmare of repressing natural instincts (because human nature is supposed to be corrupt) and denying oneself pleasure (because the body is deemed base). For a Muslim, however, the hope of going to paradise does not entail suffering on earth. Admittedly, Muslim law lays down strict rules about fidelity in marriage, observance of holy days and many rituals, but throughout the Koran – which abounds in references to heaven and hell – the emphasis is on basic belief in the first place and personal integrity in the second. Believers will go to paradise and unbelievers to hell, where hypocrisy and dishonesty will also be punished. The following quotations from the Koran are but two examples taken from countless expressions of this type of sentiment:

And those that believe and do deeds of righteousness
them We shall admit to gardens underneath
which rivers flow, therein dwelling forever and ever.

(4.60)

As for the unbelievers who cry lies to Our signs,
those shall be the inhabitants of the Fire,
therein dwelling forever.

(2.36)[20]

In other words, the hope of bliss in the future is not condemned by Goytisolo unless it mars the present. If, on the contrary, it enhances life on earth, as in the case of the tannery-worker, so much the better. Only if belief in a glowing future brings about unwarranted suffering in the present, is it to be deplored. Nevertheless, such an interpretation of the author's stance regarding Islam and Christianity does not altogether eliminate the possibility of bias. The tannery-worker's belief in paradise is perhaps responsible, after all, for making him more unhappy in the present than he otherwise would be; maybe he would find some way of improving his lot on earth if he thought that was all there was to life. Conversely, perhaps Alvaro's great-grandmother is deeply and genuinely consoled by her

Christian faith. Is there in fact such a difference between the two? Both are unhappy; both find solace in their religion. Since the description of the great-grandmother comes from *Señas*, whereas the 'compensación necesaria' theory is in *Makbara*, published fourteen years later, perhaps Goytisolo changed his mind about religious faith and its potential for good in the intervening period.

Be that as it may, he does not tire of stressing the negative potential of the Christian conception of life after death. The emphasis is placed on the role of heaven, purgatory, and limbo during life on earth, more than on thoughts of going there oneself after death. Heaven has the inhibiting attribute of ever-watchful omniscience, 'ojos que todo lo ven' (*DJ*, p. 16; 'eyes that see everything', *CJ*, p. 7). This would seem to be a feature of doctrine commonly stressed in Spanish Catholic education. God as spying overseer is an image to be found in a poem included in a Spanish nursery-school anthology published as recently as 1962. Illustrated by a disturbing disembodied eye in the sky, the refrain is 'Buenos seamos: /¡que Dios nos ve!' ('Let us be good: /for God can see us!').[21] Purgatory and limbo provide the satisfying opportunity of rescuing souls by praying for them, as when Caperucito Rojo (Little Red Riding Hood) recites 'jaculatorias en Latín ricas en indulgencias . . . : quince almas del purgatorio redimidas . . . : hasta el posible rescate del limbo de algún niño mongólico o subnormal' (*DJ*, pp. 207–8; 'brief ejaculations in Latin and prayers rich in indulgences. . . : fifteen souls in purgatory are redeemed. . . : and there is even the possibility that a mentally retarded or Mongol child may be rescued from limbo', *CJ*, p. 175, adapted). Fear of hell does not seem to play a great part in the mentality of Goytisolo's characters; for the child self of the narrator of *Don Julián*, for instance, 'el eterno castigo le deja totalmente indiferente' (*DJ*, p. 230; 'eternal punishment leaves him totally indifferent', *CJ*, p. 195). More worrying are the earthly consequences of sin, such as the physical deformation described by an unnamed priest in *Don Julián*: 'el cuerpo del culpable se cubre de pústulas, una jaqueca tenaz no le concede un instante de reposo: poco a poco se manifiestan síntomas de contagio en la piel, en los párpados, en los intestinos' (*DJ*, p. 103; 'the body of the sinner becomes covered with pustules, he suffers constant wracking headaches which give him not a single moment's respite: little by little the telltale signs of his affliction manifest themselves, on his skin, on his eyelids, in his intestines', *CJ*, p. 85). Also, the fear of upsetting the Virgin Mary in heaven seems to be a deterrent to sin, as is found in the parodic vision of *Juan sin tierra*:

having persuaded Padre Vosk to tell her all the sins the slaves are committing, 'sacará un pomo de sales del corsé . . . para que no se desvanezca : los gemidos de la dotación son cada vez más roncos y, horrorizada, intentará cubrirse los oídos' ( *JT*, p. 32; '[she] will take a vial of smelling salts out of her corset . . . so that she doesn't faint: the moans from the plantation blacks are growing hoarser and hoarser, and filled with horror, she will try to cover her ears', *JL*, p. 22).

Thus, the Christian hell fails to terrify and heaven is portrayed as anything but an inspiring hope of future bliss; rather, it is the abode of a frightening, spying overseer, its pleasures being limited to the dubious joys of French Romantic poetry and eau-de-cologne. By contrast, the Muslim paradise embodies the hope of attainment of tangible pleasure: 'dulzura del reposo, fresco lugar para dormir en los calores del día, jardín sembrado de viñedos y árboles, glorietas umbrosas, sedas exquisitas, riachuelos de miel, frutos abundantes : . . . arroyos lentos, agua incorruptible, leche cuyo delicioso sabor no se altera nunca, doncellas en la flor de la edad, pabellones nupciales, vino que no embriaga' (*Ma*, p. 68; 'sweet repose, a cool place to sleep during the heat of the day, a garden full of trees and vines, shady bowers, exquisite silks, rivers of honey, abundant fruit: . . . gently flowing streams, incorruptible water, milk whose delicious taste never changes, maidens in the bloom of youth, nuptial pavilions, wine that does not intoxicate', *Mb*, p. 70).

The kind of self-delusion in which the tannery-worker indulges is depicted as harmless and beneficial, not only because it improves life in the present, but also, perhaps, because there is no danger of disillusionment. When an illuson concerns life on earth, damaging disillusionment can later occur, as with Alvarito's belief in the stories of child martyrs read to him in *Señas*. His disillusionment comes about when he attempts to realize this romantic ideal in the tough, down-to-earth setting of Barcelona during the Civil War: 'Sollozando, sin coronita ingrávida, tu traje blanco manchado, habías meditado con amargura sobre el irremediable fracaso' (*SI*, pp. 30–1; 'Sobbing, without a weightless coronet, your white outfit spoiled, you meditated bitterly about the hopeless failure', *MI*, p. 23, adapted). Similarly, Madame Heredia's belief in Frédéric as the embodiment of her ethereal, artistic ideal, also in *Señas*, leads to crushing disillusionment when he runs off with her son, plunging her cruelly back into 'la vejez ingrata y . . . la realidad arisca' (*SI*, p. 335; 'unpleasant old age and harsh reality', *MI*, p. 278). In sum, it would seem to be by virtue of the inevitability of disillusionment that Goytisolo attacks these fantasies, rather than because of their fanciful nature itself.

Associated with this question of illusion and disillusionment is childhood, an important element of the good place, whether this takes the form of Eden before the Fall, the afterlife in paradise, or utopia. In Kuhn's study of the child in literature, he notes that 'one popular conception of the child is that, as a personage living in the state of nature, he is basically good until the forces of civilization corrupt his naïve essence' and that 'the child as a prelapsarian Adam in his own garden of Eden is the tempting vision'.[22] He also acknowledges the special treatment accorded to children in Dante's *Paradiso*, which bears this out:

Fede ed innocenzia sono reperte
Solo nei pargoletti: poi ciascuna
Pria fugge, che le guancie sien coperte.

(Faith and innocence are found only in children: then
each takes flight, before the cheeks are covered.)[23]

Kuhn makes the point that this vision of the child represents the adult's nostalgia rather than the truth of childhood. This is powerfully illustrated in Goytisolo's fiction, which shows, moreover, the harmful effect on children of such adult fantasies.

Alvarito of *Señas* loves the stories of the child martyrs because of their bloodthirsty nature. He is delighted by the idea of becoming a martyr himself, seeing the prospect as the advent of 'el fabuloso mundo de las persecuciones y torturas' (*SI*, p. 26; 'the fabulous world of persecutions and tortures', *MI*, p. 19), not as an opportunity to bear witness to his pure and deep commitment to Christianity, as adults like Señorita Lourdes want to think. The supposedly innocent child is called 'pintoresco y falaz' (*SI*, p. 15; 'picturesque and deceitful', *MI*, p. 10, adapted) and when he is not aware that he is diverging from the adults' image of him, is seen to be down-to-earth and unromantic. Thus, when Señorita Lourdes attempts to create a Garden of Eden around her little prelapsarian Adam, the following exchange takes place. Having been taught by her that flowers are good, Alvarito asks: '"Y los pajaritos, ¿también son buenos?" "También, rey mío." "Entonces, ¿por qué pican las flores?"' (*SI*, p. 50; '"And the little birds, are they good too?" "Yes, my prince." "Then why do they peck the flowers?"', *MI*, p. 40). In keeping with the portrayal of childhood in *Señas* as far from the adult vision of innocence, the children observed by the protagonist at the beginning of *Don Julián* are playing cruel and complex games (*DJ*, pp. 17–18; *CJ*, pp. 8–9).

Often though, Goytisolo's depiction of childhood follows the traditional dystopian method: he turns the features that ought to be positive into sources of misery. Thus, comfort and stability are portrayed as boring, with the use of terms such as *vegetar* and *languidecer* ('to vegetate' and 'to languish'). The most enjoyable moments depicted are far removed from the adult's conception of infant purity: the endless war games and the 'concurso de tiro de pipí' ('peepee-shooting contest') in the South of France, for example (*SI*, pp. 156–7; *MI*, p. 131).

However, it is the effect on the child of adult illusions about him which are most sharply criticized, rather than the misapprehension itself. The agonized process of breaking out of this idealized image is portrayed in *Don Julián*, in terms of sado-masochistic homosexual activity and mental torture of the child by his adult self. The culmination of the sequence comes about when the adult demands that the child sell him his mother, having already blackmailed him into stealing from her. The episode suggests that the root of the agony lies in the necessity to strip the mother of her illusory picture of her son. The child is at pains to conceal his transformation from her; indeed, it is on threat of betrayal to her that the adult self finally induces the child to commit suicide: 'si no la traes, iré a verla yo y le contaré cuanto has hecho' (*DJ*, p. 229; 'if you don't bring her, I'll go see her myself and tell her all the things you've done', *CJ*, p. 194). To make matters worse, she has remained totally oblivious to the metamorphosis of her son: 'los agoreros estigmas ... visibles ya, palmarios : la madre, solamente, no los ve' (*DJ*, p. 224; 'the premonitory stigmata ... clearly visible already, strikingly evident: it is only his mother who does not see them', *CJ*, p. 190) and later, when 'las cicatrices se acumulan en la espalda y los regueros espesos de sangre negra : ... sus heridas supuran : ... la piadosa madre sigue sin darse cuenta' (DJ, p. 226; 'the whip marks on his back grow more numerous, and the thick trickles of black blood: ... his wounds ooze pus: ... the pious mother still suspects nothing' *CJ*, p. 191); ultimately, 'su rostro de sapo está cubierto de contusiones y hematomas que inspiran repulsión y piedad: pero la inocente madre sigue absorta en sus devociones' (*DJ*, p. 227; 'his toad's face is covered with bloody lumps that inspire pity and revulsion: but the child's innocent, unsuspecting mother, absorbed in her devotions as always', *CJ*, pp. 192–3). So when the revelation finally comes as it must, the reader can imagine that it will be rendered more painful for its unexpectedness.[24] Although the episode is played out as though the adult were the villain, the reader knows that he and the child are the same person – 'qué niño?: tú mismo un cuarto de siglo atrás' (*DJ*, p. 215; 'what youngster?: you yourself a quarter of a century ago' *CJ*, p. 182) – and is therefore aware of the inevitability of their relationship. When he asks himself why it is such a painful and anguished one, he is forced to recognize that it is due to the child's inner conflict between what he is supposed to be in his mother's eyes and what he feels he is becoming: 'por un lado la cáscara y por otro la pulpa' (*DJ*, p. 224; 'an outer shell and an inner pulp', *CJ*, p. 190). There would be no agony, no suffering, if he could slough the shell without fear of hurting his mother; indeed, the shell would never have formed in the first place.

For Goytisolo, then, the concept of childhood as a lost paradise is an adult illusion. In keeping with his attitude towards illusion in general, as I have interpreted it, his condemnation hinges not on its falsity but on the damage it causes, to the adult presumably, though this is not treated in any great depth in the later novels, and to the child, who is forced into a double life of concealed *pulpa*, the living matter, and superficial *cáscara*, lifeless and rigidly constraining.

My hypothesis that the author is not opposed to harmless illusions would seem to be borne out by his treatment of the Albania fanatics in *Paisajes*. For them, Albania is clearly the ideal place and in that sense a utopia. At first sight one might object that since it is a real country it cannot be a purist's utopia, as this should combine goodness of a place with non-existence. However, even if Albania appears on the map, it becomes increasingly clear, as one reads the eulogy to it, that it is no more than a name to which to attach a fantasy. The Albania utopians have closed their eyes to the aspects of the country that do not form part of their dream and embroidered whatever can be made to fit into it, so as to construct a living example of a utopia 'ya existente en otras latitudes' (*PB*, p. 101; 'already existing . . . in other latitudes', *LB*, p. 79). Once one comes to see them as neo-Hythlodays,[25] the location of the good place in Albania takes on the same value of literary premise as the details of Utopia's location being drowned by a well-timed cough, or the secrecy of *Erewhon*'s narrator regarding the whereabouts of that country because 'I prefer the risk of being doubted to that of being anticipated'.[26] Besides, the idealists of *Paisajes* use the most hackneyed utopian descriptions and imagery for so-called Albania, confirming that they are expounding on wishful thinking rather than any place in the real world. They claim, for example, that it is 'una sociedad definitivamente limpia de las taras, desviaciones, y prácticas revisionistas', that it is 'el mundo de mañana' and add that '¡la censura resulta allí innecesaria porque esta clase de libros . . . no interesa absolutamente a nadie!' (PB, pp. 43, 46, and 48; 'a society definitively free of the defects, deviations, and revisionist practices', 'the world of tomorrow', and 'censorship is unnecessary there because that sort of . . . book interests absolutely no one!', LB, pp. 30, 32 and 34). And yet, how does Goytisolo treat these self-deluding utopians? Does he reserve some terrible fate for them in the Otekan terrorist campaign? Does he launch one of his vitriolic diatribes on their dream? On the contrary, he accords them one of his least damning judgements, describing the look on the faces of the speakers and their audience as 'una beatitud o estado de gracia capaz de suavizar perfiles, . . . impregnar las fisionomías más cerriles e ingratas de un toque de alegría y fecunda receptividad' (PB, p. 46; 'a beatitude or state of grace capable of softening angles and profiles, . . . of infusing the most uncouth and unattractive physiognomies with a touch of joyous and fecund receptivity', LB, pp. 32–3). It is clear that, relatively speaking, he has no quarrel with these people, though the ironical use of religious terminology here suggests that he is amused by their ingenuousness. It seems, therefore, that this type of illusion is in the category of 'compensación necesaria', along with the tannery-worker's dreams of the afterlife and the story-teller's world of just reward and punishment in Makbara.

The people for whom Goytisolo has no time in Paisajes are not these harmless dreamers, but the celebrities who go to a charity gala in aid of the oppressed of Eastern Europe:

¡Los mineros encerrados en los pozos de Katowice se sentirían sin duda muy reconfortados si supieran que a mil kilómetros del lugar en donde siete de sus compañeros acaban de ser acribillados . . . , una brillante asamblea de vedettes y notables se emociona con su destino, vierte lágrimas por su suerte, solloza interiormente a la escucha de los compases del gran Frédéric [Chopin]!

(PB, p. 152)

(The miners deep in the shafts of Katowice would surely find it comforting to know that, a thousand miles from the spot where seven of their comrades have been felled by a hail of bullets . . . , a dazzling assembly of notables and celebrities is moved by their fate, shedding tears for their tragic lot, sobbing inwardly to the sound of the plangent measures of the great Frédéric [Chopin].)

(*LB*, p. 122)

These are the hypocrites who delude themselves that their own Western society is free of oppression. They are what Karl Mannheim calls *conservative utopians* in *Ideology and Utopia*. He says that for this group, 'the utopia . . . is, from the very beginning, embedded in existing reality . . . . Reality, the "here and now", is no longer experienced as an "evil" reality but as the embodiment of the highest values and meanings'.[27] It is to this attitude that Goytisolo takes the strongest exception; Mannheim's definition encapsulates, indeed, his quarrel with Western secular society, communism, and Franco's Spain. It is this mentality that he seeks to undermine throughout the fiction. Even in the early novels, attention is drawn to the unjust treatment of the Andalusians and compared with the complacency of the conservative utopian bourgeoisie (to use Mannheim's term). In *Fiestas*, for example, the pitiless, smug attitude of the Catalonians towards the poverty-stricken Andalusian underclass is presented ironically: 'Esta era la triste realidad. Pese a las promesas de los periódicos de acabar con las chabolas y devolver a los sin trabajo a sus covachas de Murcia y Andalucía, aquéllas continuaban proliferando lo mismo que hongos' ('This was the sad truth of it. Despite the promises in the newspaper to do away with the shanty-dwellings and return the unemployed to their hovels in Murcia and Andalusia, the shacks went on multiplying like toadstools').[28] In the later novels, the theme of conservative utopianism expands to include a defence of all the socially oppressed, battling for survival in a community that believes its values to be incontestably perfect. The non-conformists range from the unorthodox writer who must be normalized in *Juan sin tierra* (*JT*, pp. 276–81; *JL*, pp. 244–8), to the dog-fetishist of *Paisajes* (*PB*, pp. 37–9; *LB*, pp. 24–7).

At this point, it is useful to consider the concept of order and chaos, for it would seem that this could underlie the blanket rejection of secular Western values, communism, and Spanish Catholicism, all of which are radically different from one another, yet are treated with equal derision, in contrast to the Muslim world. Mannheim's conservative utopianism will not suffice, for that is an attitude towards a particular society rather than an inherent feature of it.

Perhaps the only characteristic common to all the derided social orders is that they are just that: an order of one kind or another, and this orderliness is invariably emphasized. The Arab world, on the other hand, together with all other favoured societies, is depicted as fundamentally chaotic.[29] Countless examples could be given to demonstrate this treatment; here are just a few:

[Tangier] la geometría delirante de la ciudad . . . : ajena a las leyes de la lógica y del europeo sentido común (the hallucinatory geometry of the city . . . : entirely foreign to both the laws of logic and European common sense)

(*DJ*, p. 70; *CJ*, p. 57)

[Tangier] Eros y Tánatos mezclados (Eros and Thanatos intermingled)

(*Ma*, p. 51; *Mb*, p. 50)

[Turkey] el puente Karaköy y su armonioso, concertado caos (the Karaköy Bridge and its harmonious, carefully attuned chaos)

(*JT*, p. 104; *JL*, pp. 90–1)

[Le Sentier] un caos de pasajes y arcadas (a chaos of pedestrian passages and arcades)

(*PB*, p. 74; *LB*, p. 57)[30]

Contrast with:

[Spain] la rígida inmovilidad de los principios, . . . normas misteriosas que gobiernan la human sociedad jerarquizada en categorías y clases sociales (the rigid immobility of principles, . . . mysterious norms that govern human society arranged hierarchically into categories and social classes)

(*SI*, p. 229; *MI*, p. 190, adapted)

[Western society] esclerosis doctrinal, compartimentación (doctrinal sclerosis, compartmentalization)

(*Ma*, p. 43; *Mb*, p. 40)

[Communism] la ley marcial en Varsovia barre brutalmente . . . la noble aspiración popular (the proclamation of martial law in Warsaw brutally sweeps away . . . the noble aspirations of a people)

(*PB*, p. 143; *LB*, p. 115)

Mitigating features of Spain revolve around chaotic phenomena that have survived the imposition of order, as we saw in chapter 1 with Alvaro's love of the 'dédalo de callejuelas' (*SI*, p. 90; 'labyrinth of narrow streets', *MI*, p. 73) and his description of Barcelona as a 'geometría caótica' (*SI*, p. 422; 'chaotic geometry', *MI*, p. 352), prefiguring his later description of Tangier, quoted above. In *Paisajes*, the protagonist delights in the imported chaos of the Le Sentier quarter of Paris, brought by non-European immigrants. Perhaps this is why the battle of the title is over: because chaos has engulfed order in the West, now that 'Africa empieza en los bulevares' (*PB*, p. 164; 'Africa begins on the boulevards', *LB*, p. 133).

If chaos is the key to Goytisolo's ideal society, then it would seem worthwhile to try to establish exactly what he means by this and what a chaotic society has to offer that an ordered one does not.[31] Both in Tangier and in Le Sentier, the author is at pains to stress that he is not advocating assimilation of one ethnic group into another, the binding together of disparate elements to form an amorphous mass. He uses a chemical image for Tangerine society, ascribing to each type of inhabitant solid, liquid, or gaseous substance:

> abajo, el sólido de los sólidos: costra del mundo, base del edificio social, sobre el cual se pisa, se anda, se sube: ni más ni menos que una piedra: en medio, el hombre líquido: corriendo y serpenteando encima del anterior: en movimiento continuo: a la caza de vacantes y empleos: hoy arroyo, mañana río: y en la cúspide, la ártica región del pensamiento: el hombre-gas, el hombre-globo: asombroso por su grandeza y su aparato y su fama: elevándose olímpicamente hacia alturas sublimes: con fuerza irresistible, como del tapón de una botella de champán: zonas bien demarcadas, reconocibles a simple vista

> (at the very bottom, the most solid of solids: the earth's crust, the base of the social edifice, on which we tread, from which we work our way upward: exactly like a stone: in the middle, man-the-liquid, meandering across the stratum beneath: continuously moving about in search of a job or a vacant post: today a little brook, tomorrow a river: and at the very top, the Arctic realm of thought: man-the-gas, man-the-balloon, a creature of amazing splendor and grandeur and glory: rising to sublime, Olympian heights: with irresistible force, like a champagne cork: these are sharply defined strata, recognizable at a glance)

> (*DJ*, p. 21; *CJ*, p. 12)

Exactly parallel with this, but in keeping with the lighter tone of
*Paisajes*, there is the image of a fancy cake, with many layers of
sponge, fillings and icing:

> Arriba, en la costra o corteza de chocolate, los comerciantes
> judíos .... Debajo de ellos, en la tongada correspondiente a la
> pasta de harina intermedia, portugueses y españoles, amos de las
> porterías o inquilinos de lóbregos y ruinosos apartamentos ....
> Después, en la porción de miel o confitura de fresas, la reciente
> diáspora de orillas del Bósforo .... En la capa inferior – de crema o
> pasta de nueces, según el gusto de los clientes –, los árabes y
> beréberes que excavan las zanjas de obras públicas .... Al fin –
> hemos llegado a la base del pastel –, los afganos, paquistaneses y
> bangladesís, esa masa ... que vende a diario, a bajo precio y sin
> contrato alguno, su fuerza de trabajo.
>
> (*PB*, pp. 20–1)

> (On top, on the chocolate icing or layer, the Jewish
> merchants .... Below them, in the layer corresponding to the
> puff pastry, Portuguese and Spaniards, living in concierges' quar-
> ters or tenants of shabby, gloomy flats .... Next, in the portion
> with honey or strawberry jam, the recent diaspora from the shores
> of the Bosphorus .... In the next layer down – of butter or nut
> cream, depending on the customer's preference – the Arabs and
> Berbers who dig the ditches [in the roads] .... Finally – we have
> now arrived at the bottom of the cake – the Afghans, Pakistanis,
> and Bangladeshis, the ... mass that sells its labor by the day, for
> next to nothing and with no definite contract.)
>
> (*LB*, pp. 11–12)

Both of these images bring out an important point, in addition to the
separateness of each layer; they admit that there is a top and a
bottom, but at the same time, they tacitly reject the idea that there is
any standard by which the upper strata could be adjudged better than
the lower. Just as it would be absurd to maintain that water was
better than stone, for example, or that puff pastry was better than nut
cream, Goytisolo demonstrates that the different strata of a chaotic
society are not evaluated according to their position in the whole.

Thus, Goytisolo's concept of chaos negates the ordering of society
into a hierarchy of 'higher means better', which is to say an
ascending vertical order. It also refuses to conform to an order of

forward movement or progress. These two dimensions of order, as they might be termed, are both rejected outright: 'despréndase del binomio opresor espacio-tiempo' (*JT*, p. 131; 'rid yourself of the oppressive space-time binomial', *JL*, p. 118).[32] The spatial order comes under fire in statements that describe the cosmos as chaos, not order, such as the allusion to 'la caótica y delirante geometría de los astros' (*JT*, p. 42; 'the chaotic and delirious geometry of the stars on high', *JL*, p. 31). This of course overturns the traditional attitude, typified by Fray Luis de León in his poem 'Noche serena':

> el gran concierto
> de aquestos resplandores eternales,
> su movimiento cierto,
> sus pasos desiguales,
> y en proporción concorde tan iguales.

> (the great
> concert of this eternal brilliancy,
> its movement straight
> with steps so oddly free
> yet all in a concordant symmetry)[33]

In his mocking utopia in *Juan sin tierra*, Goytisolo again undermines the vertical hierarchy, as we have seen, by setting the modern concept of equality against it. By suggesting that all animal and vegetable life should be on a par with humanity in a truly egalitarian society, he makes a double-edged criticism; on the surface, he draws attention to the anachronistic attitude, still deeply rooted in the Western mentality, that human beings are superior in value to the rest of creation in some transcendental framework. More subtly, by proposing something as silly as a society that does not see fit to protect itself against poisonous snakes, parasites, bacteria, and so forth, he reasserts the undeniable existence of the phenomenon represented elsewhere by the solids, liquids, and gases, or the fancy cake. Taken together, these points imply that whilst it is pointless to try to rid society of a top and a bottom, with all the states in between, it is wrong to ascribe ascending value to each higher layer.

The temporal hierarchy of progress is attacked just as ruthlessly. The concept of forward movement in time going hand in hand with the betterment of the world gives rise to what is regarded as vacuous worship of novelty for its own sake; and youth, as representative of the next generation—necessarily superior to all previous ones in this schema – acquires the respectability that age and experience carry in societies unseduced by the progress ethos. Sanford sees the worship of youth as deriving from the ideas of explorers and pioneers of the New World: 'The newness of the country, the expectation of some kind of rebirth or beatitude in the near future, and the eternal promise of future blessings associated with the land produced a distinct emphasis on youth in America . . . . The cult of newness . . . contributed to a characteristically American disrespect for tradition and history'.[34] Old age in a progress-oriented society signifies obsolescence; hence, the tongue-in-cheek passages in *Makbara*, where euthanasia and suicide are encouraged: 'evite convertirse en una carga para familiares y amigos! . . . : una, dos, tres docenas de píldoras en un simple vasito de agua y añadir unas gotas de güisqui para mejorar el sabor' (*Ma*, pp. 32–3; 'don't allow yourself to become a burden on your family and friends! . . . : one, two, three dozen pills in a glass of plain tap water, adding a few drops of whiskey to make sure it tastes better', *Mb*, pp. 27–8). Goytisolo's depiction of modern consumer society is, in this sense, that of a dystopian. Like Huxley in *Brave New World*, for example, he suggests that progress worshipped today as bringer of material bliss can turn into a dehumanizing, tyrannical force tomorrow. The so-called test-tube babies that give happiness to childless couples today may become the alpha to delta system of Huxley's tomorrow, one might think, or equally, may dehumanize procreation through the introduction of systematic artificial insemination in Goytisolo's sterile Pittsburgh:

> Inseminación racional y científica . . .
>> un ahorro increíble de dinero, capacidad y energía!
>> para la comunidad
>> para los contrayentes
>> para todos . . .
>> EL TIEMPO ES ORO!
>
>> (*Ma*, pp. 134 and 138)

> rational and scientific insemination . . .
> an unbelievable saving in money, talent, and energy!
> for the community
> for the contracting parties
> for everyone . . .
> TIME IS MONEY!
>
>> (*Mb*, pp. 153 and 159)

By contrast, progress is a completely alien concept to the Tanger-
ines: 'los beneficios de la ínclita sociedad de consumo no se manifiestan aún en estas tierras' (*DJ*, p. 21; 'the marvelous benefits of the
consumer society have not yet reached these parts', *CJ*, p. 12). This is
confirmed when, as tourists in *Makbara*, some Arabs are shown the
technological wonders of Pittsburgh, which leave them 'aturdidos'
(*Ma*, p. 139; 'dazed', *Mb*, p. 160). When people such as these move to
Paris, along with other Eastern immigrants, they take their chaotic
heritage with them. This is seen as a redemptive force, contrary to
the perspective of traditional symbolism, which imbues the order-
figure – a dragon–slayer in many cases – with redemptive powers.
The age-old parallel between non-Christian races and the symbol of
the dragon or monster, a hagiographical commonplace, is exploited
by Goytisolo in *Don Julián*, where the victorious bull (echoing the
Minotaur) gores the toreador and is called 'el Thur arábigo' (*DJ*,
p. 201; 'the Arab Thur', *CJ*, p. 169). Even closer to the traditional
construct, St James the Apostle is depicted in the same novel as the
loser in the battle against the dragon/infidel: 'la sierpe fanbrienta se
apercibe al ataque . . . : dragón vencido, no : maligna vencedora reptante: condensada virtud de ruda vitalidad arábiga' (*DJ*, pp. 144–5;
'the famished serpent prepares to attack . . . : not a conquered dragon:
a sly, creeping, crawling conqueror: the distilled essence of savage
Arab vitality', *CJ*, p. 121). In *Makbara* too, the same connection is
made, again treating the beast in its reptilian form; Arab turbans are
'como sierpes armoniosamente enroscadas' (*Ma*, p. 122; 'like grace-
fully coiled serpents', *Mb*, p. 137) and the story-teller's style is of
'habla suelta, arrancada de la boca con violencia, como quien se saca
una culebra tenazmente adherida a las vísceras' (*Ma*, p. 221; 'a flood
of words, violently jerked out of the mouth, like someone pulling
out by force a serpent stubbornly holding fast to his viscera', *Mb*,
p. 267). In this sense, the effects of mass immigration in Paris as
depicted in *Paisajes* can be read as another reworking of the subverted
hero–dragon motif, for the non–European infidel dragon has defeated
Western civilization, embodied by Paris. And as one would expect
from an apologist for chaos, this 'paulatina deseuropeización de la
ciudad . . . le colma [al protagonista] de regocijo', because, like
Morocco, it has now become a 'territorio denso y cambiante,
irreductible a la lógica y programación' (*PB*, p. 108; 'the gradual
de-Europeanization of the city . . . fills him [the protagonist] with
rejoicing'; now it is a 'dense and ever-changing territory irreducible
to logic and to programming', *LB*, pp. 85–6). In this respect, the

protagonist's preferences coincide with Goytisolo's own; in his essay entitled 'Por que he escogido vivir en París' ('Why I have chosen to live in Paris'), he states:

> Creo en la virtud de la mezcla dinámica, fructuosa de culturas y etnias .... Yo vivo, por ejemplo, en el Sentier, un barrio animado por la presencia de emigrados de una veintena de países .... Las paredes de las casas están llenas de pintadas e inscripciones en árabe que yo descifro con verdadera delectación. Lenta, insidiosamente, París se *tercermundiza* ... [lo que] me cautiva y encanta.
>
> (I believe in the virtue of the dynamic mix, rich in cultures and ethnic types .... I live, for example, in the Sentier, a neighbourhood enlivened by the presence of emigrés from about twenty countries .... The walls of the buildings are painted and inscribed all over in Arabic which I decipher with real delight. Slowly, insidiously, Paris is *thirdworldifying* ... [which] I find captivating and enchanting.)[35]

In other words, with the advent of large-scale immigration, Paris — or at least Le Sentier — takes on the positive value previously assigned to the Arab world. In sum, then, Paris, once it is overrun with non-European immigrants, Morocco, Turkey, and the old quarter of Barcelona are all good places in Goytisolo's texts, because they are seen to be chaotic.

There is another type of good place, though, in the post-*Señas* novels, namely, the underworld. This introduces the concept of hell. In a way, of course, dystopias are one manner of depicting hell, for the effect they seek to produce is indeed hellish, but since the dystopian technique entails creating a hell from the components of a potential heaven, dystopian writers are obliged to depart from the traditional imagery, which tends to employ descriptive opposites rather than distorted perspective. So it is that whilst heaven is imagined to be cool, the traditional image of hell does not reassess coolness so that it becomes something unpleasant, but takes up the opposite and makes hell stiflingly hot, associating it with all kinds of fire and burning.[36] This contrast comes across clearly in the Revelation of Saint John the Divine. Those in heaven will find that 'neither shall the sun light on them, nor any heat' (8.16). This coincides with classical tradition too; in Curtius's discussion of what he calls the 'ideal landscape', as imagined by the poets of classical antiquity, he observes: 'What are the requisites of such a spot? Above all, shade —

of great importance to the man of the South'.[37] The bottomless pit
of hell, on the other hand, emits smoke 'as the smoke of a great
furnace' (9.2), the female temptress 'shall be utterly burned with fire'
(18.8), and in the second death, after the millennium, hell is described as 'the lake which burneth with fire and brimstone' (21.8). So
although dystopia is a type of hellish vision, for the sake of clarity, I
shall not refer to it as such. *Hell*, and its linguistic derivations will be
reserved for the traditional method of using opposites and contrasts
rather than twisted perspective.

Now, order is traditionally associated with good and chaos with
evil, despite the fact that in Creation stories such as the Judaeo-
Christian or ancient Babylonian one, chaos has no negative implications, but is simply the pre-formed state of the cosmos which is to be
surpassed. However, logic suggests that if the deity responsible for
creating order from this chaos – the Almighty in Genesis, Marduk in
the Babylonian myth – is venerated for having done so, order is
naturally aligned with good. Hence, the opposite of order, chaos,
can easily become identified with evil.[38] It is hardly surprising,
therefore, that order is an attribute of heaven and chaos the principle
of hell. Since Goytisolo's fiction plainly sees good in chaos and evil in
order, it follows that many of the traditional features of hell will
seem heavenly there. Indeed, the love of chaos would seem to have
sparked off a re-interpretation of the other aspects of the conventional picture of hell, in the same way that a dystopian text reinterprets
the attributes of a supposed heaven: through shifting perspective. In
what might be termed *anti-dystopian* fashion, Goytisolo distorts the
perspective of what is potentially hellish and thus bestows positive,
heavenly value upon it. Above ground, this is to be found in the love
for the heat of the desert, in the desire to be in contact with filth and
excrement: 'el desierto te invita de nuevo, vasto y tenaz como tu
deseo' ( *JT*, p. 87; 'the desert beckons to you once again, as vast and
stubborn as your desire', *JL*, p. 72); 'la realización del . . . sueño . . . :
arrojar los inútiles zapatos de tacón, hollar descalza la fina ondulación
de las dunas, caminar, caminar, perderse en el desierto' (*Ma*, p. 44;
'the . . . realization of the dream . . . : throwing away your useless
high-heeled shoes, sinking your bare feet into the delicate ripples of
the sand dunes, walking on and on, losing myself in the desert', *Mb*,
p. 42); 'olores densos, emanaciones agrias que voluntariamente
aspiras' (*DJ*, p. 43; 'strong odors, acrid emanations that you eagerly
breathe in', *CJ*, p. 32); 'liberados del anatema que envuelve el horado
nefando y sus viscerales emanaciones impuras' ( *JT*, p. 155; 'freed of

the anathema that surrounds the abominable hole and its impure visceral emanations', *JL*, p. 144).

However, perhaps the most striking application of the anti-dystopian device is in the positive treatment of the underworld. Sewers, mines, even the Paris metro provide havens for the protagonists of the novels, in this most blatant rejection of the key attribute of hell as horrible: its location in the bowels of the earth. To choose to go into the earth for a good place, rather than up to the sky, revalues the bodily nature of man. Instead of yearning to soar heavenward, leaving the base, earthbound body behind, Goytisolo affirms the high value that he places on corporality by voluntarily strengthening his characters' bond with the earth, seeking the ideal place deep inside it. This does not imply, however, that he advocates escaping from the spirit, simply because it would be a neat opposite. Chaos, it is as well to recall, rejects nothing except differentiation itself; to reject the spiritual side of man would be as ordered as to reject the bodily side. On the contrary, life underground is seen to be most conducive to creative imagination and fantasy. Probably the most vivid sexual fantasies take place underground (for example, *Ma*, pp. 154–5; *Mb*, pp. 180–2), together with the amusing, imaginative transformation of the sewers into Pompeii (*Ma*, pp. 95–102; *Mb*, pp. 106–14).

The darkness of the underworld is another descriptive opposite that may be traced back to Saint John's Revelation, in which there is said to be no night in heaven (21.25 and 22.5). In Goytisolo's anti-dystopian perspective, darkness becomes a positive attribute of the underworld. In the mine, there is a reference to 'la dicha a oscuras' (*Ma*, p. 155; 'bliss in the dark', *Mb*, p. 181); in the sewers it is 'tiniebla amena' (*Ma*, p. 99; 'agreeable darkness', *Mb*, p. 109), in contrast to the scathing allusion to 'la crepuscular civilización de las luces' (*Ma*, p. 98; 'the crepuscular civilization of the world of light', *Mb*, p. 108).

Logically enough, if the underworld is refocused so that it becomes paradisiacal instead of hellish, life above ground, seen as heaven on earth by what Mannheim calls its conservative utopian inhabitants, takes on the value of hell. Thus, the protagonist of *Makbara* feels that he has left hell behind him when he goes underground: 'abolido el infierno, el mundo de ellos' (*Ma*, p. 100; 'the inferno, their world, blotted out', *Mb*, p. 111). This attitude is bound to be utterly incomprehensible to the conservative utopians themselves, typified in the personages of Joe Brown and Ben Hughes, the PB Radio broadcasters of *Makbara*, who incredulously record: 'nuestros trogloditas han preferido la tiniebla a la luz, la suciedad a la limpieza, el roedor al humano, una opción difícil de comprender' (*Ma*, p. 147; 'our troglodytes have preferred darkness to light, filth to cleanliness, the rodent to the human, a choice difficult to understand', *Mb*, p. 168), and later in the same programme, 'compatriotas, ... voluntariamente al margen de nuestros principios filosóficos de rendimiento y progreso' (*Ma*, p. 149; 'fellow citizens, who of their own free will have chosen not to embrace our philosophical principles of productivity and progress', *Mb*, p. 172).

These same broadcasters introduce another theme, which forms an important part of the symbolic labyrinth of Goytisolo's underworlds. They point out that the 'troglodytes' are seeking happiness 'lejos del tráfago y frenesí de la vida diaria' (*Ma*, p. 159; 'far from the hustle and bustle of daily life', *Mb*, pp. 187–8), recalling the recurrent desire, notably in Golden Age Spanish literature such as that of Fray Luis de León, to escape from a corrupt world to the peace of a 'vida retirada' (life of withdrawal).[39] The parody of the sentiments expressed in Fray Luis's poem often so called, is clear. Like him, Goytisolo's various troglodytes are disillusioned with the rest of society and, like him, they want to flee to a more peaceful abode where they can be:

a solas, sin testigo,
libre de amor, de celo,
de odio, de esperanzas, de recelo.

(alone, with no talkative
friends, and free of lies,
love, hatred, hopes or fear that might arise.)[40]

Also like Fray Luis, the surroundings of their retreat inspire them with thoughts that transcend their physical environment. For the Golden Age poet, the beauty of nature sparks off contemplation of eternal bliss:

Oh campos verdaderos,
Oh prados con verdad frescos, y amenos,
riquísimos mineros,
oh deleitosos senos
repuestos valles de mil bienes llenos.

(O meadows! O sweet field
of truth, fresh, redolent with pleasure! Springs

from deepest veins revealed!
O swollen hills and rings
of hidden valleys filled with all good things!)[41]

For Goytisolo's personages, however, it is to thoughts of sexual bliss that they turn when released from the tribulations of everyday life (*Ma*, pp. 154–5; *Mb*, pp. 180–2, for example). The twist is an ingenious one. Both the novelist and the poet have seen through the vacuous materialism of the society in which they live; both have sought and found escape through their literary constructs; thus, both depict a dream of ultimate happiness. The difference lies only in the fact that whereas for Fray Luis, 'el apartamiento del mundo no es otra cosa que un atisbo de célicas visiones' ('the withdrawal from the world is nothing but a glimpse of celestial visions'), as one commentator puts it,[42] for Goytisolo's recluses it is, on the contrary, a glimpse of terrestrial visions.[43]

The Paris Metro of *Paisajes* synthesizes the pleasures of the teeming, chaotic Arab market above ground, with the inspiring symbolism of the solitary but equally sublime sewers. In the tunnels of the Metro, there is a 'multitud indiferente' (*PB*, p. 51; an 'indifferent mob', *LB*, p. 37), reminiscent of the 'público indiferente' of the Moroccan market (*Ma*, p. 204; 'indifferent . . . crowd', *Mb*, p. 243). The random decoration of advertisements and graffiti reinforces the chaotic atmosphere, yet at the same time, the mysterious influence of the underground location is retained, so that the effect is as conducive to creativity as that of the sewers of *Makbara*: 'el metro de París . . . es vasto y rico en posibilidades . . . . Examinar el plano del metro es ceder al recuerdo, evasión, desvarío; abrirse a la utopía, la ficción y la fábula' (*PB*, p. 110; 'The Paris métro . . . is vast and rich in possibilities . . . . To examine the map of the métro system is to yield to memory, to escape, to delirium; to accept utopia, fiction, fable', *LB*, p. 87).

Further points of contact exist between Goytisolo's different good places; the cinema auditorium of *Makbara* has much in common with the underworld, for example, both places being warm, dark, and protected from everyday life, which is to say, womb-like. They are also both conducive to sexual fantasy, the cinema providing films for inspiration and the underworld dispensing with this (the very experience of being underground is sufficient, presumably). True to his rejection of order in favour of chaos, Goytisolo has built up a labyrinthine pattern of symbolic associations in the later novels, rendering it impossible to follow paths in an orderly, linear fashion. As we have done here, and as the protagonist does in *Don Julián*, it is often necessary to double back in order to find a new route.[44]

Indeed, Goytisolo's style clearly displays his love of chaos. The novels refuse to progress in a linear direction. *Señas* flits to and fro in time throughout; *Don Julián* is constructed cyclically, so that when the protagonist retires at the end of the book, reversing the morning routine where it opened, the reader realizes that the whole text will be repeated on the morrow, as it no doubt was on the previous day, and so on indefinitely into future and past.[45] In *Juan sin tierra*, *Makbara*, and *Paisajes*, there is a random quality to the order of the sections, giving the reader the impression that they might have been arranged differently without destroying the essence of the texts.

This chaotic structure of the later novels is perhaps the most powerful blow struck at utopianism as a literary genre. By this means, Goytisolo tacitly declares that the methodical form of the utopian novel, clearly and logically describing the ideal society, is itself a threat to freedom. The constraints imposed by literary convention are just as much a threat to joyous creativity and fertility as are the contents of the writing. Hence, he will not compartmentalize his own writing any more than he will defend compartmentalization in society. His stance in the novels refuses to be exclusively utopian or dystopian; he will not allow the literary critics to fit him neatly into either group. He uses both techniques as and when it suits him. He sounds like a faithful utopian in his lack of sentimentality towards what he sees as flawed present society: 'amor a la basura: patria a la basura: dioses y reyes, a la basura ... : ha llegado la hora de limpiar la cizaña' (*DJ*, p. 157; 'love, into the garbage can: love of country, into the garbage can: gods and kings, into the garbage can: ... the time has come to root out the quackgrass', *CJ*, pp. 132–3). On the other hand, he adopts the standard dystopian stance in his depiction of Disneylandia in *Paisajes*, shifting the perspective without altering the details of the vision, so that what might have appeared a beautiful dream, comes out as a ghastly nightmare. Finally, he also employs his own device that I have termed anti-dystopianism, where he alters the perspective of a hell to reveal it as a heaven. Though closely connected with both utopianism and dystopianism, it is neither of these, for like the utopian writers, Goytisolo creates a good place, but like the dystopians, he shifts and distorts perspective in order to achieve this.

More than an *Erewhon*-style *contre-pied*, the defence of filth, sexual perversion, and other things commonly condemned or deliberately ignored, together with the vehement attack on what are usually seen as the best aspects of society, should be taken as a manifestation of what is perhaps the most important guiding principle behind the later novels: the *reivindicación del caos* (vindication of chaos), as one might call it. This emerges most clearly when one considers the butt of Goytisolo's attacks: not the direct opposites of what he defends, not cleanliness nor spirituality themselves, but only their monopoly of approval. Whiteness, for example, is not condemned when it is not rated above other colours; the 'níveo atuendo fesí' of an Arab (*Ma*, p. 47; 'snow-white fesí robes', *Mb*, p. 44) is not weighted negatively. By the same token, cleanliness is fine in a non-hierarchical setting, such as when Arabs are described as having 'cuerpos tersos y limpios' (*Ma*, p. 49; 'clean, firm, smooth bodies', *Mb*, pp. 46–7). Only if beautiful, healthy, sane, chastely spiritual people want to place themselves above the ugly, sick, mad, or fleshly, on some evaluative scale, only when they want to lock them up, banish them, or induce them to commit suicide, only then does Goytisolo turn on them. It is, for example, because the pristine hostesses at the 'Salon du Mariage' of *Makbara* (*Ma*, pp. 75–94; *Mb*, pp. 79–105) are glacial towards the unconventional narrator that they are condemned, not because of their own appearance.

Hence, Goytisolo's ideal society emerges as one where details of the lifestyle – so dear to utopians and dystopians alike – are not of primary importance. It is the underlying principle that makes the Arab world preferable to others: nothing, no one is excluded and nothing, no one is judged better or worse than anything or anyone else, either at a given moment or as a function of time. In other words, chaos – spatial and temporal – is the ideal basis for society, irrespective of physical minutiae, for out of chaos come fertility, creativity, rich sensuousness,[46] as opposed to the insipid procreation, dehumanizing productivity, and vacuous material wealth offered by ordered society.

In the final analysis, it becomes apparent that Goytisolo is as concerned with the intangible, spiritual requirements of man as Fray Luis de León or the most fervent missionary. Indeed, in an essay, he attacks politicians of the left and right because they 'eliminan de su vocabulario toda noción de trascendencia – el misterio insoluble de la creación de la materia, la realidad del dolor, la inevitable tragedia de la vejez y la muerte – o responden con vulgaridades seudocientíficas a las naturales inquietudes e interrogantes que han servido y sirven de base a las manifestaciones del fenómeno religioso' (they 'eliminate from their vocabulary all notion of transcendence – the insoluble mystery of the creation of matter, the reality of pain, the inevitable tragedy of old age and death – or they respond with pseudo-scientific vulgarities to the natural worries and questions which have formed and form the basis of manifestations of the religious phenomenon').[47] The later novels show a preference for hunger over boredom, sickness over narrow-mindedness, poverty over complacency, through the societies they favour in contrast to those they deplore.[48] Where Goytisolo differs only concerns the way of fulfilling man's non-material needs; for the Christian, it is through faith, at the relatively small cost – as the believer sees it – of the pleasures of the flesh; whereas for Goytisolo, it is through physical and mental freedom, at the relatively small cost – in his eyes – of material comforts and acceptance by conventional Western Europeans. It is at the *Zoco Grande* of *Don Julián* that this unexpected proximity between the author and the religious zealot emerges most clearly, for the protagonist delights in the unsavoury atmosphere with what is described as 'fervor catecúmeno' (*DJ*, p. 43; 'the fervor of a catechumen', *CJ*, p. 32).

Goytisolo's mission is as sacred as the utopian's wish to establish a perfect order or the Christian's missionary zeal. Fundamentally, he has much in common with them. The utopian believes that man will find happiness and fulfilment in a rationally perfect society; the Christian believes that the secret lies in following Christ's teachings; Goytisolo believes that it is to be achieved through *la reivindicación del caos*.

# 5
## *Todo es posible en la página:** Metamorphoses

Fluidity of form is an important weapon in Goytisolo's campaign against order, for when something or someone can change into something or someone else, this undermines the order-lover's desire to contain everything in firm categories. It is in keeping with the thrust of the later novels, therefore, that metamorphosis should be a key motif. However, as soon as one attempts to examine the concept, it becomes apparent that it is as hard to pin down as its master, Proteus himself.[1] As far as the etymology of the word is concerned, there is no special component of its meaning that sets it apart from any other type of shape-changing; there is nothing in its composition that requires the transformation to be instantaneous, magical, or even surprising; yet when the word is used casually, this is often what is implied. One might expect metamorphosis to be found only in fanciful mythology or folktale, apart from a few biological curiosities, such as caterpillars turning into butterflies, but if the semantic overtones that have accumulated around the term extraneously are disregarded in order to contemplate the simple notion of changing shape, metamorphoses spring up all around:

> Shape-shifting is a phenomenon arising naturally from our con-
> stantly changing experience of people. Our images of a person
> may change visibly, as the pictures created by our fantasy pass
> swiftly through our minds . . . and as we apprehend fresh aspects
> of this person . . . and observe the elusive and constantly changing
> nature of people's moods . . . . The elusive and constantly

*The title quotation comes from *Juan sin Tierra*, p. 110: 'everything is possible on the written page', *JL*, p. 96.

changing nature of our own moods is also a vitally important factor in this process.[2]

In this critic's view, then, there is no need for a metamorphosis to be visible to all those present. She accepts the individual perspective as sovereign; if a person takes on a new appearance in our eyes simply because we are feeling angry or amorous at the time, for instance, that is as much a metamorphosis for us as individuals, as if that person were literally and physically turned into another creature.

The breadth of such a definition could be seen as controversial, but it is as well to remember that the word is absolutely open etymologically. At all events, from a purely pragmatic point of view, such an all-inclusive interpretation sweeps away numerous – and often insurmountable – problems of classification for the student of Goytisolo; problems that do not add to an understanding of his works, but only sidetrack one into futile minutiae.

The question of subjectivity and objectivity of description exemplifies this, for the later novels tend to be ambiguous in this regard. With the form of first- and second-person discourse in which they are mainly written, not only does the reader have to contend with the usual concept of the text coming wholly from within the author's mind, but also with the additional layer of the narrator's subjective vision, a vision, moreover, that makes no claim to neutrality. Goytisolo's narrators, furthermore, are not always unequivocally distinct from the authorial voice, so that the reader cannot be sure on occasions whether the perspective on some element of the text is the narrator's or the author's, or of both fused together. As a consequence of this ambiguity, it is impossible to limit the definition of metamorphosis in Goytisolo to a transformation depicted as objectively true.

Besides, all metamorphoses in literature are a figment of the imagination; is it valid to call those that are in the author's mind more real or legitimate than those he puts within a character's mind? Is it helpful to categorize metamorphoses according to whether the author has, on the one hand, put the vision into the minds of many of his characters simultaneously and uniformly, thus giving an appearance of objective truth, or whether, on the other hand, he has placed the phenomenon in the mind of just one character, thus giving the appearance of fancy, or a highly figurative mode of expression? I would argue that since all metamorphoses in literature are part of the author's subjective imagination anyway, the question of 'real' versus 'imagined' transformation pertains only to a discussion of style and should not be treated as a significant thematic distinction.

Before considering Goytisolo's approach to metamorphosis in detail, it would seem worthwhile to survey the methods of some other writers who have exploited the theme. This will provide a background of possible approaches against which to consider the introductory comments above and to assess how much Goytisolo follows literary tradition or departs from it.

In fiction generally, an attempt to restrict the definition of metamorphosis to a description of objective truth raises the problem of distinguishing between several types of presentation. The description of a transformation by a character within the story, who is nothing more than a fortuitously placed observer, is one way of giving the reader an impression of objective truth. Such a character conveys the happening, one feels, more or less as anyone present might have done. Thus, in Ovid's *Metamorphoses*, Urania describes the transformation of the Pierides from the standpoint of a mere onlooker: 'As they tried to speak, menacing us with loud cries and wanton gestures, they saw feathers sprouting from their nails and plumage covering their arms . . . . The had become magpies'.[3]

Another type of seemingly objective verification for metamorphosis is to have an omniscient and neutral narrator; in this, as in the disinterested–onlooker case, the reader must accept the events narrated as reliably and accurately recorded. The petrification of Aglauros is but one example of a great many in Ovid's *Metamorphoses* where the omniscient narrative voice creates an impression of trustworthiness and objectivity: 'As Aglauros tried to rise, she found her limbs so sluggish that they could not be moved from a sitting position. She struggled to stand upright, but her knee joints had become rigid, a coldness pervaded her body to her very fingernails, and the blood drained from her pallid veins . . . . She sat, a lifeless statue'.[4]

Whichever of these two methods of depiction is chosen by an author – the testimony of a reliable character within the story, or that of an omniscient narrator – the impression of objectivity may be reinforced by describing the reactions of other bystanders. When there are several additional witnesses to a transformation, all of whose reactions tally with the chronicler's, the reader tends to feel that this is somehow a 'real' metamorphosis. Thus, in Ovid again, the tranformation of Cadmus into a snake is first described by the narrative voice:

As he [Cadmus] was speaking, his body did indeed begin to stretch into the long belly of a snake; his skin hardened, and turned black in colour, and he felt scales forming on it, while blue-green spots appeared to brighten its sombre hue. Then he fell forward on his chest, and his legs, united into one, were gradually thinned away into a smooth pointed tail.[5]

This is then supported by the reaction of Cadmus's wife looking on: '"Cadmus", she cried, "stay, my unhappy Cadmus, rid yourself of this monstrous shape! Cadmus, what is happening? Where are your feet, your hands and shoulders, your fair complexion, your features? – All that is you is vanishing as I speak"'. Finally, in case it might appear that such a principally involved character were in some bewitched state of hallucination or spoke in arcane, figurative language, Ovid gives the testimony of ordinary bystanders: 'All who were there ... were terrified'.[6] Thus, it is clear that Ovid, unlike Goytisolo, is intent upon giving the appearance of objective truth in his descriptions of metamorphoses; indeed, one might say that the spectacularly powerful effect of his work is based largely, if not entirely, on his talent for making the outlandish and impossible seem real.

In Robert Louis Stevenson's *The Strange Case of Dr Jekyll and Mr Hyde*, another celebrated work with metamorphosis as its theme, there is similar insistence on the objective truth of the transformation. Jekyll gives a detailed description of his own metamorphoses at the end of the story, which comes as the explanation for the strange relationship between himself and Hyde, seen for the most part hitherto from the standpoint of the honest and unimaginative Mr Utterson, who takes Hyde for a disreputable friend or possibly a blackmailer of Jekyll. Although Ovid's order is reversed, therefore, to create a mystery, the same technique of involved character's testimony, supported by disinterested onlooker's, is utilized. Jekyll's confession is laden with philosophical debate regarding the radical duality of man:

It was on the moral side, and in my own person, that I learned to recognize the thorough and primitive duality of man; I saw that, of the two natures that contended in the field of my consciousness, even if I could rightly be said to be either, it was only because I was radically both .... It was the curse of mankind that these incongruous faggots were thus bound together – that in the agonized womb of consciousness these polar twins should be continuously struggling.[7]

However, the metaphysical question of the good and evil in human nature, whilst presented as the key to the 'strange case', is not meant to devalue the metamorphosis from prodigy to metaphor. Utterson and others bear witness to the objective truth of Jekyll and Hyde's separate existence, and the former confirms in his declaration that they are one and the same man: 'I had now two characters as well as two appearances, one was wholly evil, and the other was still the old Henry Jekyll, that incongruous compound [of good and evil]'.[8]

Any yet, whether the book in his hand is Ovid or Stevenson, the reader knows that, ultimately, narrators and characters alike are depicted according to the author's whim. Even in Ovid's use of mythological material, where the characters cannot be said to be the author's creation, the selection and ordering of the different stories and the colours in which people and events are painted are uniquely Ovid's. Notwithstanding the realism and credibility that both writers manage to create within their texts (in spite of the unworld-liness of their theme), in the final analysis one can step back and regard the whole as each author's subjective, fantasized metamor-phoses. It is he who makes the characters corroborate the truth of the happening and, after all, they too are a product of his own imagina-tion and individual vision.

Contrasting with this style of portrayal is Hermann Hesse's depic-tion of the Steppenwolf in the novel of that title. He treats the protagonist's wolf persona in purely figurative terms and yet it is no less powerful than a realist portrayal of lycanthropy: 'he *called himself* the Steppenwolf . . . nor could I today hit upon a better description of him. A wolf of the Steppes that had lost its way and strayed into the towns and the life of the herd, a more striking *image* could not be found for his shy loneliness, his savagery, restlessness, his homesick-ness, his homelessness'.[9] Is this *thematically* different from a story in which a man physically changes into a wolf? Surely it is not a question of theme, but of style; therefore, transformation depicted as objective truth is not a useful criterion to use when analysing the concept of metamorphosis itself. If Goytisolo's metamorphoses are ambiguous as to whether they are figurative like Hesse's or intended to be like Stevenson's and Ovid's, this should not make their status as legitimate metamorphoses doubtful, but only pose questions pertaining to style.

These very questions are posed by Homer's *The Odyssey*, in the episode where Circe changes some of Odysseus's companions into pigs, for the poet would seem to be unconcerned about making a clear distinction between subjective and objective depiction of metamorphosis. The presentation of the event is vague and ambiguous, for even though 'to all appearance they were swine: they had pigs' heads and bristles, and they grunted like pigs', this is followed by the confusing statement that 'their minds were as human as they had been before the change'.[10] How human were their minds before the change? They seem to have been behaving like pigs long before they come into contact with Circe, so perhaps Homer is saying that she gave them bodies to match their inner character. The matter is further complicated by what Hermes tells Odysseus, namely, that the men are 'in Circe's house, penned *like* pigs'.[11] They are not really pigs then, as far as Hermes is concerned, but is that because Homer means that Circe only bewitched them into thinking that they had been physically changed into pigs, or because Hermes knows that they are men underneath their physically transformed porcine exterior? Whichever way one may like to take this, the fact remains that Homer's treatment of the metamorphosis does not come down clearly in favour of either the objectively true method of portrayal, as used by Ovid and Stevenson, or the purely subjective hallucinatory vision, like the Steppenwolf's self-image in Hesse's novel.

To return to Goytisolo, one finds that his texts cannot be neatly aligned as wholly in the Ovid/Stevenson mould, any more than in that of Hesse or Homer, since he moves freely between metamorphoses portrayed, on the one hand as wholly within a character's mind, and on the other, as objective truth within the text, with many intermediate stages, so that it is often impossible to establish where a given transformation stands. In *Señas*, the style of which tends more to realism than any of the other later novels, the reader is not asked to believe in the type of metamorphosis depicted as objectively true. The figurative use of transformation here parallels Hesse's style. When, for example, Alvaro buys a children's book of the lives of child martyrs, similar to the one that was read to him when he was a boy, the following metamorphosis takes place: 'Habías examinado el libro, redactado aproximadamente en el mismo lenguaje que el de la señorita Lourdes y el pasado había irrumpido en ti de modo imprevisto, metamorfoseando tu libro en el perdido libro, tu voz en la atiplada voz de la señorita de compañia' (*SI*, p. 21; 'You had examined the book, written in approximately the same language as

Señorita Lourdes's, and the past had erupted in you in an unforeseen way, metamorphosing your book into the lost book, your voice into the flutey voice of the nursemaid', *MI*, p. 15, adapted). There is no doubt that here it is Alvaro's mind that effects the transformation; the same is true when he realizes, much later in the novel, that Dolores and Antonio are flirting with each other: 'El paisaje se transformó. Los objetos cobraron una existencia autónoma, impenetrable. La nada se abrió a tus pies' (*SI*, p. 356; 'the landscape was transformed. Objects took on an autonomous, impenetrable existence. Nothingness opened up at your feet', *MI*, p. 296, adapted).

Indeed, in this first novel of the trilogy, objectively true metamorphosis is shown to be a fraud, bringing painful disillusionment with its inevitable failure. When Alvaro, as a child in *Señas*, tries to become a child martyr himself, like one in his story-book, the physical metamorphosis that he expects will accompany his baptism of blood is what he seems to desire most of all: 'Pensabas más en tu traza que en toda otra cosa, al acecho del instante grandioso en que la coronita ingrávida iba a volar sobre ti, tratando de consolarte con la idea que, después de muerto, tus tirabuzones se volverían rubios' (*SI*, p. 29; 'You were thinking more about your appearance than anything else, waiting for the grandiose instant when the weightless coronet would descend upon you, trying to console yourself with the idea that after you were dead your ringlets would turn blond'. *MI*, p. 22, adapted). When his belief in the reality of such a transformation is shattered, the misery the disappointment causes him suggests that Goytisolo is criticizing the inculcation of ingenuous children with a belief in the truth of impossible miracles, such as magical shape-shifting. Alvarito's reaction is described in emotive language: he is *sollozando* ('sobbing') and thinks about the *irremediable fracaso* ('hopeless failure') with *amargura* ('bitterness'; *SI*, pp. 30–1; *MI*, p. 23, adapted).

The effect on Alvaro in *Señas* of his exile from Spain could have been depicted as an Ovidian-style transformation, but again more like Hesse, Goytisolo clearly makes it no more than a powerful metaphor: 'Lentamente, conforme se rompían las raíces que lo ligaban a la infancia y a la tierra, Alvaro había sentido formarse sobre su piel un duro caparazón de escamas: la conciencia de la inutilidad del exilio y, de modo simultáneo, la imposibilidad del retorno' (*SI*, p. 259; 'Slowly, as the roots that tied him to childhood and the land were broken, Alvaro could feel forming on his skin a scaly crust: the feeling of the uselessness of his exile and, simultaneously, the impossibility of return', *MI*, p. 215).

In *Don Julián*, metamorphoses have become Homeric in their vagueness over the issue of objectivity versus hallucination. This may be attributed in part to the nature of the work's very premise, as Genaro Pérez explains: 'Contrary to the conventional novel, the action in *Don Julián* takes place in the mind of the narrator-protagonist so that self-examination and execution [and metamorphosis?] can be witnessed only by the reader, not the other characters in the novel'.[12] However, despite the lack of corroboration from either an omniscient, reliable narrator, or from other characters within the fiction, it is possible to discern tendencies, so that in a stylistic study of the work, metamorphoses might be classified as more or less objective or hallucinatory in treatment. Tending towards the subjective, hallucinatory end of such a scale, there is, for example, the transformation of the crippled beggar into a graceful ballet-dancer, his limping gait becoming dainty, prancing steps:

> un mendigo que viene hacia ti trabajosamente, abreviando en su lastimera persona todo el humano rigor de las desdichas : el cráneo cubierto de pupas : un ojo tracomoso estrecho como un ojal y el otro adornado con un ojo de muñeca de color turquino : ... piernas desnudas, normal una y encogida la otra, con un pie casi vertical que apoya solamente en el suelo la punta de los dedos descalzos, como si caminara de puntillas : cuando te tiende la mano y le das unas monedas tu gesto te parece en seguida sacrílego : limosna a un rey? : el pordiosero se aleja oscilando como una peonza y su pie contraído tal pezuña de chivo cobra de pronto, al andar, la gracia alada de un Pawlowa o un Nijinsky : perdiéndose en el gentío con su súbita y esbelta hermosura
>
> (*DJ*, p. 44)

> (a beggar ... painfully making his way toward you, summing up in his pitiful person the entire burden of human misery: his bare skull covered with pustules: one eye badly affected by conjunctivitis, as narrow as a buttonhole, and the other with a bright-blue doll's eye ... : bare legs, one of them shorter than the other, with an almost vertical foot, the naked toes of which barely touch the ground, as though he were walking on tiptoe: when he holds out his hand and you drop a few coins in it, your gesture suddenly strikes you as sacrilegious: alms to a king? the beggar goes down

the street, spinning like a top, his rigid foot, like the hoof of a goat, suddenly taking on the winged grace of a Pavlova or a Nijinsky: losing himself in the crowd with his sudden, swift beauty or movement)

(*CJ*, pp. 32–3)

Less obviously subjective are the metamorphoses of the master-weavers and their apprentices into spiders and their prey. Although the spider is more naturally associated with spinning than with weaving in English, the verb *tejer* ('to weave') is used for the making of a cobweb in Spanish, so the spider is more appropriate symbolically than it might seem to the English reader. Furthermore, it is a symbol of devouring chasm, according to Erich Neumann, so suits Goytisolo's purpose better than some other *tejedor* (weaver), such as the silkworm. Neumann adds that the spider represents the female who traps the unwary male, and in this symbolic value Goytisolo rebels against sexual role conventions, as he also does, for example, when he makes his Red Riding Hood into a boy.[13] He would seem to be saying that males can trap unwary males just as much as females can (the spider image) or, in the case of Red Riding Hood, that males can be trapped by males just as much as females can.

The weaver-scene transformation is presented as a subtle progression from straightforward simile, through metaphor and then on to metamorphosis, so that the reader is gently carried forward on the tide of imagery, scarcely aware of the powerful undercurrent of metamorphosis until he is too far out of his depth to start protesting on grounds of implausibility. The simile that comes first may strike him as ingenious and apt; at all events, it does not seem ridiculous: 'niños aprendices que sostienen la urdimbre en medio de la calle, maestros tejedores que traman y traman en sus exiguos talleres como pacientes, laboriosos arácnidos' (*DJ*, p. 63; 'little apprentices holding the loom upright in the middle of the street, master weavers tirelessly threading the shuttle back and forth in their tiny little shops, like patient, busy arachnida', *CJ*, p. 50). Next comes the use of metaphor, with a description of the arachnids that the master-weavers resemble: 'artrópodos terrestres con cuerpo cubierto de quitina, cefalotórax breve, abdomen grande y redondeado: dos orificios respiratorios y seis abultamientos provistos de numerosos tubitos por donde salen los hilos con que fabrican la red' (*DJ*, p. 63; 'terrestrial arthropods, with chitinous shells, rather undeveloped cephalothoraxes, and huge, bulging abdomens: two spiracles and six nipplelike processes with minute orifices which extrude the threads for the trap', *CJ*, p. 50). The details of this anatomical description clearly cannot coincide with the physical appearance of the human weavers and at first it seems to be a whimsical quotation from a biology textbook, triggered in the narrator's mind by his own simile just before. Indeed, memories of biology classes recur throughout *Don Julián* (see, for example, *DJ*, pp. 91–4; *CJ*, pp. 74–7), so this would be in keeping with the thematically unified construction of the novel. No doubt, such a first impression is not mistaken, but rather, reveals only one of the multiple layers of meaning in the description. Additionally, one may liken the repugnance inspired in the narrator when he was a boy in biology classes, with the repugnance the weavers and their apprentices inspire in him now. In this specific sense of the emotional effect on the witness of the scene, the biological revulsion is a vivid metaphor of the socio-anthropological distaste that he now experiences.

Next, and scarcely distinguishable from the foregoing metaphor, the metamorphosis begins to creep insidiously in: the fabric is no longer merely like a cobweb, it has become one. However, the boundary between metaphor and metamorphosis is blurred by there being no subject for the gerund, nor for the subsequent infinitive (two gerunds in the English version). Consequently, the reader does not know whether he is still within the anatomical metaphor, or is now considering the scene before the narrator's eyes in a changed state: 'construyendo la telaraña insidiosa con esmerada destreza : seda seca en el centro y radios, viscosa en la espiral : sin moverse de sus escondrijos laterales, pero al tanto de lo que ocurre fuera gracias a un hipersensible hilillo avisador' (*DJ*, p. 63; 'carefully and swiftly weaving a treacherous web: dry silk for the center and the radiuses, sticky wet silk for the spiral: never moving from their secret hiding places at the edge, but immediately aware of what is happening all along the web, thanks to a slender, supersensitive warning-thread', *CJ*, p. 50). One one level, of course, this really is a continuation of the biological description, but it is simultaneously the first part of the metamorphosis, as emerges when one reads on to find the apprentices caught in the cobweb: 'cuando los niños aprendices tocan la tela se quedan pegados y todos sus esfuerzos por separarse resultan inútiles' (*DJ*, p. 63; 'the moment the apprentices touch the fabric they are caught fast and their every effort to free themselves is useless', *CJ*, p. 50, adapted). In other words, the cloth has really become a sticky cobweb; the whimsical thought-association has been externalized so that it is now affecting the scene in front of the narrator.

The externalization gathers momentum as the weavers now really become spiders:

> el tejedor presencia el forcejeo con la calidoscópica, potenciada visión de sus ocho ojos: podría abalanzarse ya sobre la víctima y rematarla: pero espera: el niño presiente su fin, quiere huir y se enreda, se enreda cada vez más: y él no tiene prisa: su mirada es fría, su resolución implacable: paso a paso se aproxima al desdichado aprendiz: podría salvarlo todavía si se lo propusiera, liberarlo con gesto magnánimo: pero no quiere: suavemente le hunde los quelíceros venenosos en el cuerpo, le inyecta su propio jugo digestivo y va disolviendo y chupando todas las partes blandas
>
> (*DJ*, pp. 63–4)

> (the weaver witnesses the whole desperate struggle through the eight eyes that give him stereoscopic vision: he might readily pounce upon his victim and gobble him up: but he bides his time: the youngster has a premonition that the end is near and tries to escape his fate but merely becomes more hopelessly entangled in the web: the weaver is in no hurry: he has a cold, implacable look in his eye as he slowly creeps up on his unfortunate prey, step by step: he still might spare his victim's life, magnanimously give him his freedom, were he so inclined: but he does not care to do so: instead he delicately inserts his poisonous chelicerae in his little victim's body, injects his own digestive juices into it, dissolving the softest parts of it and slowly sucking them out)
>
> (*CJ*, pp. 50–1)

The fact that the apprentices do not metamorphose heightens the pathos and shock-value of the passage; it also keeps the reader in the realm of the scene before the narrator's eyes, denying him the merciful escape into a flight of fancy triggered by, but no longer descriptive of, the real world. This point is perhaps the climax of the vignette, for from here onwards, the description turns jocular with the birth of baby spiders. However, lurking beneath the playful mood that now dominates, there is an implicit but no less alarming extra metamorphosis. Devoured by their arachnid-masters, the apprentices are reborn as baby spiders, implying that they will become the predators in time and thus perpetuate the horrid 'cannibalism'. Finally, the metamorphoses are dismantled by the narrator's sociological gloss: 'una telaraña que no lo es sino para quienes atrapa e inmoviliza desde niños, ligándolos para siempre a un trabajo duro y mal estipendiado' (*DJ*, p. 64; 'a spider web that isn't one save for those whom it traps and immobilizes from childhood, tying them for the remainder of their lives to hard labor that pays almost nothing', *CJ*, p. 51, adapted).

When, as in this example, Goytisolo does not make a metamorphosis tend too far towards a subjective, hallucinatory vision, he often uses this device of a progression from innocuous simile, in order not to jeopardize the potency of effect on the reader through the latter's incredulity. The powerful impact of transformation could be seriously weakened if the presentation were too bald from the outset, for the reader could then dismiss the whole episode as ludicrous at once. The same technique is used, therefore, in the transfiguration of the *carpetovetónico* in the course of *Don Julián*. First there is the unexceptionable simile: 'sus articulaciones crujen como las piezas mal ajustadas de una armadura' (*DJ*, p. 79; 'his joints creak painfully . . . like ill-fitting sections of a suit of armor', *CJ*, p. 65). Then, what appear to be metaphors follow: 'se acomoda . . . haciendo crujir, por turno, las distintas piezas de su caparazón óseo' (*DJ*, p. 80; '[he] settles down comfortably . . . with each of the various articulations of his bony carapace cracking in turn', *CJ*, p. 66); 'mezcla híbrida de mamífero y guerrero medieval : su cabeza, casco : su frente, visera : su pecho, coraza : sus antebrazos, manoplas : su cintura, escarcela : sus pies, escarpes' (*DJ*, p. 160; 'a cross between a mammal and a medieval warrior: his head a helmet: his forehead a visor: his chest a cuirass: his hands gauntlets: his legs thigh-pieces: his feet sollerets', *CJ*, p. 135). However, when his subsequent downfall is related, the reader realizes that the apparent metaphors concealed a subtle metamorphosis: 'su coraza se agrieta y algunas escamas caen : el tamaño se reduce también : los rasgos abultan menos, las extremidades articuladas se achican : espejismo tuyo? : metamorfosis real' (*DJ*, p. 178; 'cracks appear in his carapace and a fair number of scales fall off of it: it is much smaller now: its facial features diminish in volume and its articulated appendages shrink in size: an optical illusion?: no, a genuine metamorphosis', *CJ*, p. 151). In a sense, one might see an additional metamorphosis in this device, but on a linguistic or stylistic, rather than narrative level. In the case of the *carpetovetónico*, for example, there is the basic metamorphosis of man into monster on the plane of the narrative, but there is also the linguistic or stylistic metamorphosis as the discourse changes from gentle simile into brutal metamorphosis itself.

In *Juan sin tierra*, transformations that tend towards the subjective or hallucinatory are again to be found, though as in *Don Julián*, the style is too complex to suffer absolute division into two distinct groups of subjective and objective, or hallucinatory and real metamorphoses. In the following example, where Vosk, the establishment stereotype of the novel, takes the narrator on one side to criticize his literary style, the reference to the narrator's own childhood suggests a tendency towards the subjective pole, owing to this link with his own individual past: 'la paulatina transformación del lugar y el olor a incienso de su niñez . . . insidiosamente envolverá la cola de pentientes a casi cinco lustros de distancia' (*JT*, p. 273; 'the gradual transformation of the place and the odor of incense of his childhood . . . will insidiously envelop the line of penitents at a distance of nearly twenty-five years away', *JL*, p. 241, adapted). There are also more objective presentations of metamorphosis, as when the Virgin Mary, depicted initially as just resembling the slave-owner's daughter, Fermina, actually becomes her:

> el Ama del Ingenio de Arriba lee lentamente, con el mismo refinado esmero que pone al declamar niña Fermina . . . :
> te leo otro, Papá?
> los que tú quieras, Fermina
>
> (*JT*, p. 34)

> (the Mistress of the Sugar-Plantation on High reads slowly, with the same careful and elegant diction as young Fermina . . . :
> shall I read you another one, Papa?
> however many you like, Fermina)
>
> (*JL*, pp. 23–4, adapted).

Although there are no disinterested bystanders or an omniscient narrator to corroborate this transformation, there is no suggestion of private fantasizing either. And let us note once again how the metamorphosis creeps in unnoticed at first; in this instance, the effect is achieved through the ambiguity of the Virgin's use of *Papá*, for in the context of the passage, which depicts the Virgin's relationship with God the Father as humorously familiar, it seems to be as appropriate a way of addressing Him as one's own physiological father.

In *Juan sin tierra* as in *Don Julián*, Goytisolo also uses the stylistic progression from simile to metaphor verging on and merging with metamorphosis, what I have called stylistic or linguistic metamorphosis: 'lentamente te has despojado de los hábitos y principios que en tu niñez te enseñaron: no cabías en ellos: *como* culebra que muda de piel, los has abandonado al borde del camino y has seguido avanzando: tu cuerpo *ha adquirido* la reptante flexibilidad del ofidio' (*JT*, p. 83, my italics; 'you have slowly cast off the habits and principles that you were taught when you were a child: you no longer fit in them: *like* a serpent that sheds its skin, you have abandoned them on the roadside and gone on: your body *has acquired* the flexibility of a creeping ophidian', *JL*, p. 68, adapted).

In a realist work, the discourse must be presented in such a way as to give the impression that the author is merely a chronicler, recording real events, even if these seem incredible, as in the case of a story of metamorphosis like *Dr Jekyll and Mr Hyde*. The reader must not be reminded that the writer is the creator of everything that appears between the covers of the book, that he is like a god relative to his text. Goytisolo rejects this convention, preferring instead positively to draw attention to his omnipotence over the text, which is to say, his divine status in relation to his writing.[14] In this role, it is fitting that he should wield the power of metamorphosis, for as Maryvonne Perrot puts it in *L'Homme et la Métamorphose*, 'c'est à l'origine, le Dieu qui possède le privilège de la métamorphose' (originally, it is God who possesses the privilege of metamorphosis).[15] And sure enough, when he loudly proclaims his omnipotence in *Juan sin tierra*, this power of metamorphosis is given special emphasis:

YO/TU
pronombres apersonales . . . : odres huecos . . . : de un mero trazo de pluma os hago asumir el dictado de mis voces proteicas cambiantes: . . . mudan las sombras errantes en vuestra imprescindible horma huera, y hábilmente podrás jugar con los signos sin que el lector ingenuo lo advierta: sumergiéndolo en un mundo fluyente

(*JT*, pp. 146–7)

has recorrido de un extremo a otro el ámbito del Islam desde Istanbul a Fez, del país nubio al Sáhara, mudando cameleónicamente de piel gracias al oficioso, complacente llavín de unos pronombres apersonales prevenidos para el uso común de tus voces proteicas, cambiantes

(*JL*, p. 158)

(I/YOU

apersonal pronouns . . . : empty wineskins . . . : with a mere stroke
of the pen I force you to obey the dictates of my protean,
ever-shifting voices: . . . the wandering shades change in your
indispensable hollow mold, and you will be able to play sly games
without the reader's noticing: submerging him in a world in flux)

(*JL*, pp. 132–3)


(you have gone from one end of the Muslim world to the other,
from Istanbul to Fez, from Nubian country to the Sahara, changing skin like a chameleon thanks to the handy, satisfying passkey
of certain apersonal pronouns, ready and waiting for the common
use of your protean, ever-shifting voices)

(*JL*, p. 147)[16]

In classical mythology, many of the gods display their ability to
metamorphose at will; Zeus springs to mind at once with all his
different shapes, assumed in order to effect countless seductions and
rapes: a bull to win Europa, a shower of golden rain for Danaë, a
swan for Leda, to mention but a few of the more spectacular
examples. Indeed, this ability of the gods seems to be taken so much
for granted that when Ovid relates how Mercury fell in love with
Herse, he comments on the god's unusual decision *not* to change his
shape before approaching her.[17]

Goytisolo's narrator-creators use their power of metamorphosis to
become whatever they please, too. In *Don Julián*, for example, the
narrator transforms himself when he enters the Arab café, from an
*emigrado* (*DJ*, p. 20; an 'émigré', *CJ*, p. 11) – one of those whom he
has described as 'juntos sí, pero no revueltos' with the locals (*DJ*,
p. 21; 'lying one atop the other without ever combining', *CJ*, p. 12) –
into an 'árabe, árabe puro' (*DJ*, p. 41; 'an Arab, a pure Arab', *CJ*,
p. 30). This voluntary abandonment of his Spanish roots is linked to
the bingo game taking place in the café by way of a pun on *loto*,
Spanish for both 'lotto' and 'lotus', evoking the lotus-eaters, who,
according to the legend, forget their homeland by so doing.[18]

Now, the gods of classical mythology are not only able to change
their own shape, but also to inflict metamorphosis on others, either
as reward or punishment, or with some other motive, such as when
Jupiter changes Io into a heifer in order to conceal his adultery with
her from his wife.[19] The concept of reward and punishment coming
from these deities can be seen as justification for a metamorphosis

after the event, but there is no clear or predictable system of retribution. As Harold Skulsky puts it in his study of Ovid:

> Divine reward . . . is as much a whim of power as divine punishment . . . . It is a mood rather than a matter of settled principle, and often it is sardonically ambiguous. The beatific deaths of Philemon and Baucis are indistinguishable in the horror of their actual detail, from those of Myrrha and the Heliades – a cancerous and strangling growth of leafy bark in each case.[20]

Goytisolo's narrator-creators also inflict metamorphosis on their creatures and at times the question of reward and punishment is as difficult to disentangle as in Ovid's masterpiece. The *carpetovetónico* (Hispano stereotype) of *Don Julián*, for instance, turned into a strange armoured beast, as we have seen, is clearly condemned by the narrator; yet there is no revulsion in the texts for animals or for bestial resemblances in human beings. On the contrary, animals are seen as decidedly not inferior to humans and, on occasions, even superior:

> desdeñaréis en adelante el escalafón que conduce . . . del cuadrúpedo al ángel . . .
> abandonando para siempre el ilusorio papel de reyes y señores de la Creación por . . . las especies insectiles más ruines
> (*JT*, pp. 155–6)

> (you will henceforth disdain the steep stairway that leads . . . from quadruped to angel . . .
> abandoning forever the illusory role of lords and masters of Creation in favor of . . . the most insidious insect species)
> (*JL*, pp. 144–5)

The key to the apparent paradox could be in the abyss that separates the narrator's values from those of the victim of the metamorphosis, the *carpetovetónico*. For the latter, it is indeed a horrific punishment to be turned into a monster, even if the narrator-creator who imposes the transformation deems monsters superior in many ways to men and especially men like the *carpetovetónico*. In other words, the element of punishment arises from the attitude of the victim. Like the dreaded Room 101 of Orwell's *Nineteen Eighty-Four*, where the mode of torture is decided according to each delinquent's individual phobias,[21] the godlike narrator of *Don Julián* punishes not according to his own standards of horror, but to those of his victims.

Thus, his revenge on the *carpetvetónico*'s daughter, the stereotypical Spanish woman, is to turn her into an erotic go-go dancer (*DJ*, pp. 163–5; *CJ*, pp. 137–9).[22] Again, the narrator's own attitude towards sexuality and eroticism could scarcely be further from prudish, so one might wonder why being turned into a seductive woman from a nun should be a punishment, coming as it does from him. The answer can only be that it is what the girl herself would most dread to see herself become.

The metamorphoses inflicted on Vosk in *Juan sin tierra* are more obviously explicable. Sometimes it is not a question of reward and punishment at all, but of narrative necessity; as the establishment stereotype in a novel set in diverse locations and epochs, he has to assume several different shapes in order to play this role in changing surroundings. Thus, for example, he is the priest on the sugar-cane plantation, but later, when the action moves to modern Western society, he is the psychiatrist intent on 'normalizing' the protagonist. The element of punishment is only introduced with his destruction, at which point the narrator-god seems to take gleeful pleasure in 'rendering transformation', like Ovid, 'as the ordeal of persisting awareness'.[23] First he decides to depict Vosk 'conforme a los cánones de su propia escuela' (*JT*, p. 258; 'in accordance with the canons of his own school', *JL*, p. 228), which is realism. Thus Vosk can joyfully proclaim soon after: 'me he convertido en un personaje de carne y hueso!: ... soy un ser individualizado y tridimensional, de densidad sicológica y acciones transitivas, índice y expresión de una propia e intransferible personalidad: ... he cambiado mucho: he encarnado' (*JT*, pp. 263–4: 'I have turned into a character of flesh and blood! ... I am an individualized, three-dimensional being, with sociological solidity and actions that are entirely self-consistent, the index and the expression of a personality that is my own inalienable property: ... I have changed a great deal: I have taken on weight', *JL*, pp. 233–4). When the narrator then decides to dismantle the realistic portrayal of Vosk, the latter retains a personality with which to suffer the trauma and a voice with which to bewail his lot:

> me está ocurriendo algo atroz ... : estos escritorzuelos ladrones me han despojado poco a poco de mis haberes, elementos y rasgos: he perdido peso, estatura, expressión, atributos, carácter: ... esos desalmados ... , no contentos con haberme arrebatado mis bienes raíces y muebles acaban de privarme asimismo de rostro y figura!:

me miro en el espejo y no veo nada!: ... ahora nadie me reconoce
en la calle ni se interesa por mí ni se molesta en averiguar qué me
ha pasado'

(JT, pp. 288–9)

(something dreadful is happening to me ... : those thieving pen-
ny-a-line scribblers have gradually stripped me of my assets, my
substance, my inalienable possessions: I have lost weight, stature,
expression, attributes, character: ... those soulless creatures ... ,
not content to have robbed me of my real property and my chattel,
have also gone so far as to deprive me of a face and figure!: I look
into the mirror and see nothing at all!: ... today no one recognizes
me on the street or takes any interest in me or bothers to see what
has happened to me)

(JL, pp. 255–6)

The narrator-creator figure in the later novels also uses metamorphosis to reward his creatures, as we have seen in the case of the
crippled beggar of *Don Julián*, who is turned into a graceful ballet-
dancer. And the same concept of the victim's own standards deter-
mining the positive or negative value of the transformation applies
here too, for the narrator sees nothing wrong in being a cripple or a
beggar, as chapter 3 has shown. Presumably, though, the metamorphosis into a lithe dancer would be the realization of the beggar's
greatest dream and has nothing to do with the narrator's own
opinion.

In Goytisolo's fiction, a place, not just a person, may undergo a
transformation, but here, logically enough, it is the narrator's attitude to it that determines its status, as it could not have aspirations or
dreads of its own to take into account. Thus, the Spanish landscape is
to turn green, as we have seen, with the new invasion of the Moors,
representing an improvement in the narrator's eyes (*DJ*, p. 147; *CJ*,
p. 123). And the baths of *Don Julián*, which at first seem undefined
and unreal, as well as having associations with Tartarus, become
Elysium: 'efluvios de vapor que esfuminan las líneas ... : baño de
irrealidad ... : [then, having found a place] vivo, vivo!: no en el
proteico reino de lo blando e informe ... : sin Radamanto, sin Tisí-
fone, sin Cerbero ... : en la llanura de deliciosas praderas y rumoro-
sos bosques, ámbito de los seres felices' (*DJ*, pp. 84–5; 'swirls of
vapor that blur the contours of everything about you ... : a bath of
unreality ... : [then, having found a place] you're alive! still alive!:
not in the protean kingdom of the flaccid and formless ... : with-

out Rhadamanthus, without Tisiphone, without Cerberus: . . . on the broad plain with its delightful meadows and rustling forests, the kingdom of the blessed', *CJ*, pp. 69–70). A feature of this metamorphosis worth noting because it reveals a thematic similarity with certain other transformations in the later novels is the atmospheric shift by means of which the contemporary world turns into the mythological world. From an ordinary street scene, the narrator enters the baths and thereupon the mood changes to reflect the underworld of classical mythology which has now replaced the bustling atmosphere of present-day Tangier; the doorman is Pluto and the narrator is like Virgil's Aeneas entering his realm. At first his impression is hellish; mentally he passes through the region of torment before his change of mood takes him over the psychological boundary – as Aeneas crossed a geographical one – into Elysium. In *Juan sin tierra*, a similar change from contemporary reality to the mythological takes place, this time in the sewers under New York City. The atmospheric metamorphosis is slightly subtler in this case perhaps, since the starting-point is not just everyday reality – the streets of Tangier, the sewers of New York – but a piece of modern myth, namely, the story that crocodiles and alligators roam the city's sewers. Where the metamorphosis of the baths imbued the contemporary world with the atmosphere of classical tradition, this one effects a superimposition of this ambience on the shallowness of modern myth. The Manhattan sewers gradually assume the eerie atmosphere of Tartarus, as the style quietly moves from matter-of-fact, journalistic tones to florid, vivid, adjective-laden description:

> en el subsuelo actual de Manhattan, a lo largo de la laberíntica red de sumideros y túneles que socava el perfil exterior de la isla, una colectividad . . . se ha implantado, vive y tiende a extenderse por las densas tinieblas de su laguna Estigia: cocodrilos, caimanes, lagartos, iguanas infestan en número creciente las nauseabundas cloacas y, adaptándose a las insólitas condiciones del medio, se metamorfosean lentamente en función de su sombría existencia nocturna: nuevas especies anfibias, de voracidad monstruosa, se multiplican con sigilo . . . : reptantes, lucífugas, tortuosas
>
> (*JT*, p. 78)

(in the subsoil of Manhattan today, along the labyrinthine network of sewers and tunnels lying below the surface of the island, a collectivity . . . has installed itself, lives and attempts to propagate itself amid the dense shadows of its stygian lagoon: crocodiles, alligators, lizards, iguanas infest, in increasing numbers, these nauseating cloacae, and adapting itself to the unusual conditions of this environment, this collectivity slowly metamorphoses as a result of its somber nocturnal existence: new amphibious species, possessed of a monstrous voracity, multiply secretly . . . : crawling, writhing, light-shunning)

(*JL*, p. 64, adapted)

A similar atmospheric change is brought off to maximum effect in the section of *Paisajes* entitled 'Lo dijo ya Platón' (*PB*, pp. 119–23; 'As Plato Said', *LB*, pp. 95–8). In this piece, the protagonist, who is being treated as separate from the narrator, and therefore is as impotent as any other fictional character, watches his own identity being changed despite himself, as his surroundings are transformed before his eyes. From a respectable citizen calling at the police station to see to a routine matter, he is turned into a criminal, as the comfortable ante-room in which he is waiting becomes a spartan interrogation-room. Correspondingly, the unctious courtesy of the police alters with the décor, until he is addressed in the brutal and vulgar language barked at a delinquent: 'Y tú, ¿qué coño esperas? ¿Yo? Sí, tú, maricón, ¿no me has oído?: ¡el cinturón, la cartera, el reloj, los zapatos!' (*PB*, p. 121; 'Hey, you, what the hell are you waiting for? Me? Yes you, you fuckin' queer, didn't you hear what I said? Your belt, your wallet, your watch, your shoes!', *LB*, p. 97). The concept of a changing environment metamorphosing the helpless individual who happens to be there runs through the whole of *Paisajes*; the transformation of Le Sentier effected by the influx of non-European immigrants takes place around the impotent natives until the very street signs are altered from French to Arabic, changing the indigenous population into the seemingly illiterate outsiders whom the immigrants once were: 'algunos se apeaban a interrogar humildemente al corro de individuos risueños instalados en la terraza del café: árabes, afganos o paquistaneses que, con naturalidad, casi con desparpajo, respondían a las preguntas de los analfabetos y les indicaban condescendientemente el camino' (*PB*, p. 15; 'a number of drivers jumped from their cars to question the group of smiling individuals comfortably installed on the terrace of the café: Arabs, Afghans, or Pakistanis who, with a self-assurance bordering on insolence, answered the questions of the illiterate and condescendingly pointed out which way to go', *LB*, pp. 6–7). The theme is picked up again in the section entitled 'Sólo para los listos' (*PB*, pp. 83–5; 'For Sharp Customers Only', *LB*, pp. 64–6), when man's position in the universe is seen to be dependent upon uncontrollable forces, in this instance, climate. The narrator-protagonist, if not responsible for climatic change, nor indeed for the immigrant presence in Le Sentier, is delighted; the havoc being wreaked on society 'le colma de regocijo' (*PB*, p. 108; it 'fills him with rejoicing', *LB*, p. 86). Furthermore, he does his share in order to maximize unrest, if not in the real world, in his fantasy-life, which after all is the only place where he can expect to be a god wielding the power of metamorphosis: 'A fin de alimentar una estrategia de tensión y mantener viva la combatividad de los componentes de tu propio bando, difundirás también, en secreto, la propaganda contraria: la de esos comandos de Charles Martel, resueltos a atajar con las armas la taimada invasión de grupos alógenos que amenaza la homogeneidad y tradiciones castizas del vecindario' (*PB*, p. 173; 'In order to maintain the combat readiness of the members of your own group, spread as well, in secret, the propaganda of the other side: that of Charles Martel, determined to stop, by force of arms, the stealthy invasion of allogeneous elements threatening the homogeneity and the venerable traditions of the neighborhood', *LB*, p. 140). Thus, *Paisajes* continues the association between creation and metamorphosis found in the trilogy, even if here, it is the creation of a fantasy rather than a written text that is the focus.

In *Juan sin tierra*, where, unlike *Paisajes*, there is no split between the protagonist in the fiction and the character writing it, nor the blanket parody of the non-creative chronicler-narrator convention, the protagonist who is also the narrator-creator can flaunt his total control, underlining that he determines what is to be within his own text. He chooses, for example, to imagine himself physically trans-figured in order to display his changed character since leaving Spain, but he does not conceal the fact that such a metamorphosis can be realized only within his own imagination: 'el exilio te ha convertido en un ser distinto, que nada tiene que ver con el que conocieron: . . . visitarás tu propia mansión y te ladrarán los perros: . . . *eres el rey de tu propio mundo*' (*JT*, p. 63, my italics; 'exile has turned you into a completely different being, who has nothing to do with the one your fellow countrymen once knew: . . . you will visit your own dwelling and dogs will bark at your heels: . . . *you are the king of your own realm*', *JL*, p. 50). In this novel, where the workings of the narrator's imagi-nation are openly displayed, the reader is shown his hesitation as he contemplates the infinite number of possible shapes into which to transform himself, his creatures, and their surroundings. Thus, when the white sugar of his ancestors' plantation triggers the idea of turning the torrid Cuban scene into a snowscape, he experiments with three possible visions of the little girls of the family: 'las granduquesas niñas acariciando el lomo de un venado o haciendo muñecos de nieve o a horcajadas de un docto y sagaz San Bernardo' (*JT*, p. 39; 'the grand-duchess daughters stroking the back of a stag or making snowmen or sitting astride a wise and discerning Saint Bernard', *JL*, p. 28). The three images flash through the reader's imagination successively, leaving the overall impression not of any particular scene, but of the abstract concept of a stereotypical snow-scape. Far from weakening the effect, this device economically conveys the cliché without sidetracking one into an analysis of any specific version of it. Instead of pausing to consider the significance, say, of the Saint Bernard dog, one realizes at once that the detail is unimportant and grasps the notion of the cliché itself.

The creator's freedom to bestow whatever shape he pleases on himself and his creatures is explicitly linked with the theme of fertility in *Juan sin tierra*:

> tu abortado nacimiento en el seno de la limpia y virtuosa familia . . . : pesadilla renuente y atroz que obstinadamente te acosa . . . a pesar de tus viejos, denodados esfuerzos por liberarte de ella : la cuartilla virgen te brinda de nuevo posibilidades de redención exquisitas . . . : basta un simple trazo de pluma : recrearás sus cuerpos . . . :
> plenitud genésica entre tus manos
>
> (*JT*, pp. 96–7)

> (your aborted birth in the bosom of the pure and virtuous family . . . : a cruel and unwelcome nightmare which stubbornly pursues you . . . despite all your bold, long-standing efforts to free yourself of it: the virgin sheet of paper again offers you splendid possibilities of redemption . . . : a simple stroke of the pen suffices: you will recreate their bodies
> genesic plenitude between your hands)
>
> (*JL*, pp. 79–80)

Such a relationship between metamorphosis and fertility is posited by Perrot too; according to *L'Homme et la Métamorphose*, mythological metamorphoses '*témoignent de l'effort humain pour sauvegarder la fécondité du principe de vie... face au règne de l'inerte qui fige, fixe et cristallise*' (bear witness to the human effort to safeguard the life-principle in the face of the reign of the inert, which congeals, fixes, and crystalizes).[24] Significantly, she draws attention here to the human mentality; it is humans who endow their gods with the power of metamorphosis, for this represents the quintessence of omnipotence to the human psyche with its abode in one basically unchangeable person: '*Ce pouvoir* [de la métamorphose] ... *est vraiment révélateur de toute une somme de désirs... qui témoigne des préocupations... du psychisme tout entier*' (This power [of metamorphosis] really reveals a whole series of desires which bear witness to preoccupations of the psyche as a whole).[25] In short, the dream of metamorphosis reveals mankind's underlying yearning to transcend the human condition itself. In this light, it would seem plausible that the process of literary creation provides one way of quenching this longing; an author's absolute power over the text – proven by exercising the divine privilege of metamorphosis – can make him feel he has transcended human limitations, as is apparent when Goytisolo's narrator revels in his omnipotence on decreeing the metamorphosis of the Spanish landscape in *Don Julián* and even more noticeably perhaps, when he delights in his power over a fictional creature of his making, such as Vosk: '*el rostro del coronel Vosk se enardece a medida que habla y las venas azules de su frente parecen a punto de estallar: estallarán?: por qué no?: todo es posible en la página!*' (*JT*, p. 110; 'Colonel Vosk's face turns beet red as he speaks and the purple veins at his temples appear to be about to burst: will they burst?: why not?: everything is possible on the written page!', *JL*, p. 96).

In addition to the transcendental opportunities offered to the creator of fiction, Goytisolo's later novels also raise questions about other outlets for this deep psychological need. Perrot states that metamorphosis '*se présente également comme la faculté de transformer autrui.... Notre forme moderne d'action psychologique n'est d'ailleurs pas exempte d'un semblable espoir de manipulation de la conscience par une métamorphose intérieur*' (appears equally as the faculty to transform someone else. Our modern form of psychological action is not exempt, furthermore, from a similar hope that we may manipulate consciousness through an inner metamorphosis).[26] The power to brainwash, in other words, gives those that possess it the same satisfaction of feeling like a god as that achieved by the author who can manipulate his literary creatures at his pleasure. This brainwashing type of metamorphosis is dramatized in the *escuela de normalización* of *Juan sin tierra* (*JT*, pp. 276–88; 'the Normalization Institute', *JL*, pp. 244–55), as well as in *Makbara*: 'nuestro sistema es el más justo e idóneo . . . : sólo un esquizofrénico, un caso clínico podría rebajarse y actuar como tú has hecho : paciente, amorosamente nosotros te ayudaremos a recobrarte de tu rebelde e insidiosa enfermedad' (*Ma*, pp. 189–90; 'our system is the most just and most suitable one . . . : only a schizophrenic, a clinical case could lower himself and behave as you have done: we will help you, patiently, lovingly, to recover from your rebellious and insidious illness', *Mb*, pp. 224–5). The benevolent, altruistic implications of patience, love, and help, offered to the brainwash victim here, cloak the speaker's true, sinister motives, one of which is surely to satisfy his own longing for the power to change his victim, which is to say, the power to effect the metamorphosis of another human being's mind.

By the same token, the concept of utopianism could be seen as having its essential psychological source in the same yearning to transcend the human condition. Instead of moulding, shaping, and reshaping fictional characters, as the novelist does, or of re-forming the minds of other individuals, as the brainwasher seeks to do, the utopian seeks the power to transfigure society as a whole. In Pittsburgh, as it is depicted in *Makbara*, the utopians have had and are having their way; the tablets that they have introduced to replace food are just one example of their transformation of society. That they see the innovation in just these terms is explicit in the text: 'Hemos transformado de modo radical la primitiva, tradicional noción de alimento' (*Ma*, p. 125; 'we have radically transformed the primitive, traditional conception of food', *Mb*, p. 141). And at the start of the fifth section of *Juan sin tierra* (the one that is devoted to utopianism and utopians), the narrator sets down the essential psychological satisfaction that utopians derive from constructing their brave new worlds, by emphasizing the fantasy element and the dream of the power to metamorphose: 'trocándose en edenes los desiertos y eriales . . . : ensueños idílicos, ilusiones bucólicas que . . . permitían fantasear' (*JT*, p. 215; 'turning the deserts and uncultivated fields into edens . . . : idyllic dreams, bucolic illusions which . . . gave a chance to fantasize', *JL*, p. 190, adapted).

In *Paisajes*, the very word *utopía* takes on a meaning that would seem to be at least parallel to, if not synonymous with, fantasy. For the protagonist of this novel, to contemplate the map of the Paris metro is 'abrirse a la utopía, la ficción y la fábula' ('to accept utopia, fiction, fable'). The explanation for this has been given at the beginning of the same paragraph: 'el metro de París ... es vasto y rico en posibilidades' (*PB*, p. 110; 'the Paris métro ... is vast and rich in possibilities', *LB*, p. 87). There is no metamorphosis here, but one detects the same type of pleasure that the power of metamorphosis or the creation of a utopia promises, namely, an infinite choice of creative possibilities. However, the numerous different ways of going from one place to another on the underground are in no way hierarchically ordered. One route might be less direct than another, but it cannot be adjudged inferior in any absolute sense. In this respect, metamorphosis can differ significantly from riding the Métro. If a human being becomes a god or a saint, people consider the transformation in a very different light from a metamorphosis into a snake or a stone, for example. This notion of ascent or descent in the cosmic hierarchy is a fundamental property of metamorphosis, both in mythology and modern literature. Kafka's Gregor Samsa in the story called *Metamorphosis* becomes a sort of giant beetle or cockcroach; and it is the appearance of this lowly creature that instils horror in the other characters, not merely the fact that he no longer looks as he did. In other words, they are at least as horrified by his descent in the cosmic hierarchy as by the shock of metamorphosis itself.

Dr Jekyll's metamorphosis into Mr Hyde in Stevenson's story is also a descent, even though the protagonist remains ostensibly within the species of human being. The downward movement is subtler because it is not based on biology, but on the belief in the duality of man. Thus, Hyde's moral inferiority to Jekyll is reflected in his physical inferiority, a correspondence that the protagonist himself and the other characters seem to take for granted, the implication being that a creature with no good in him is a creature with no soul or spirit: Hyde, therefore, will resemble an animal, not a human. Utterson automatically excludes Hyde from the normal human species on the basis of his moral inferiority: 'God bless me, the man seems hardly human! Something troglodytic, shall we say?'. And yet he admits that there is nothing physiologically abnormal about him: 'he gave an impression of deformity without any namable malformation'.[27] In sum, Hyde is classified as lower in the metaphysical hierarchy, because he is devoid of the noble half of human nature (as the dualistic scheme sees it), and this is transferred by all who meet him to the physical scheme, so that he is deemed biologically inferior when, in fact, there is no justification for this.

By comparison with Ovidian and Homeric metamorphoses, Stevenson has made a significant break with tradition and one in which Goytisolo follows him, as we shall see. In classical mythology and traditional tales, metamorphosis will involve a change of species where a point is being made about moving into a new position in the cosmic hierarchy. Transformations that leave the subject within the same species take the metaphysically neutral form merely of a useful ploy. Thus, for example, Ovid describes how Cephalus's appearance is changed, thanks to Aurora, in order to test Procris's fidelity to him.[28] It is the more dramatic metamorphoses that represent a change of position in the order of the universe. So Hercules, for example, rises from man to god, which Ovid's Jupiter says is a 'gift' he has 'deserved'.[29] Numerous examples could be cited of humans changed into beasts or inanimate objects – that is to say, pushed down onto a lower plane of existence ... in punishment for some crime or sin; Byblis, to name but one, becomes a fountain as a result of her incestuous passion for her brother.[30] With *Jekyll and Hyde*, departure from tradition involves a combination of components that are found only separately in mythology and traditional tales. Stevenson's originality lies in his amalgamation of the phenomenon of a man metamorphosing only into a different man, with the concept of descent in the cosmic hierarchy; a hierarchy, moreover, that is based on the moral standards of his culture rather than empirically verifiable biological laws. Hyde's body is but a secondary effect of his metaphysical metamorphosis – what Utterson calls the 'radiance of a foul soul that ... transfigures its clay continent' and 'Satan's signature' on his face[31] – a mere bi-product of his altered character, not the *sine qua non* of transformation.

In Goytisolo's fiction, the same sort of departure from tradition is to be found, although the moral inferiority of Stevenson's Hyde is replaced by social inferiority. This is more a question of emphasis than a clear distinction, however; after all, Hyde's wickedness makes him a social outcast and Goytisolo shows that social prejudice may have its roots in a long-standing stigma of immorality attached to an ethnic group like the Arabs. Vosk, indeed, typifies this belief in Muslim immorality when he rants that the 'clave de su personalidad' ('the key to its national character') is 'el sexo!: en todos lados el sexo!: ni mi esposa ni yo podemos salir a la calle!' (*JT*, p. 109; 'sex! sex wherever you turn!: neither my wife nor I dares go out on the streets!', *JL*, p. 95). Nevertheless, the social hierarchy is in the

spotlight in *Paisajes*; in the '¡Atención morenos!' section (*PB*, pp. 27–
30; 'Watch Your Step, Swarthy-Faces!', *LB*, pp. 17–19), a suntanned white man is taken for black in the poor light of the Metro
and discovers how brutally non-whites are treated by policemen. By
virtue of his tan and the gloom, he is effectively transformed into a
member of a socially inferior ethnic group. Thus Goytisolo manages to create a vivid metamorphosis without recourse to magic,
divine intervention, or science fiction; it is perhaps the unexpectedness of such a depiction of metamorphosis, without fantastical
premises of one kind or another, that gives the tableau its shock-
value. The light, jocular tone sharpens the irony of the piece; the first
few lines are typical of the style of the rest: 'Recién vuelto de sus
maravillosas vacaciones veraniegas no coja usted el metro: lo mismo
si viene de orillas del mar que de la alta montaña: bastará con que el
sol haya atezado suficientemente su rostro para que pueda ser confundido, sin malicia alguna, con el de cualquier meteco' (*PB*, pp. 27–
8; 'Once back from your splendid sunny vacation, don't take the
subway: no matter whether you've basked on the sands of the
seashore or sojourned amid alpine slopes, your face need only have
browned sufficiently for it to be taken, without malice aforethought,
for that of a dark-skinned alien', *LB*, p. 17).

The subject of racial (and thus, social) metamorphosis is treated
more seriously, although not necessarily more effectively, in the
Mendiola trilogy. The narrator of *Juan sin tierra* is determined to
transform himself into an Arab, 'resuelto to imitate their mental
foundation y cameleónicamente take on the Arab skin' (*JT*, p. 98;
'resolved to imitate their mental foundation and take on the Arab
skin like a chameleon', *JL*, p. 81).[32] Like Dr Jekyll, he does not yearn
to ascend metaphysically or socially, but to reinstate the earthly,
carnal part of himself, symbolized by the stereotyped image of the
Arab in the West. This stereotype is explained by Goytisolo in his
essay, 'De *Don Julián* a *Makbara*: una posible lectura orientalista'; the
proximity between his treatment of Islam and Stevenson's depiction
of Hyde is striking:

> El Islam ha representado de cara al mundo cristiano occidental
> un papel autoconcienciador en términos de oposición y contraste:
> el de la alteridad, el del Otro, ese 'adversario íntimo' demasiado
> cercano para resultar totalmente exótico y demasiado tenaz, coher-
> ente y compacto para que pueda ser domesticado, asimilado o
> reducido .... El Islam es ... el negativo de Europa: lo rechazado

por ésta y, a la vez, su tentación .... Los actores y comparsas que cruzan los espacios imaginarios de Tánger, Fez o Marraquech [en mis tres últimas novelas] no son, o no son sólo marroquís 'de carne y hueso' sino sombras o máscaras creadas por una tradición occidental embebida de represiones, temores, deseos, animosidad, prejuicios.

(Vis-a-vis the Western Christian world, Islam has played a role of creating self-awareness in terms of opposition and contrast: the role of otherness, of the Other, that 'inner adversary' too close to be totally exotic and too tenacious, coherent, and compact to be tamed, assimmilated or reduced .... Islam is ... the negative of Europe: what Europe has rejected and at the same time, her temptation .... The actors and extras who cross the imaginary spaces of Tangier, Fez, or Marrakech [in my last three novels] are not, or are not only 'flesh-and-blood' Moroccans, but shadows or masks created by a Western tradition steeped in repression, fears, desires, animosity, prejudice.)[33]

Bearing this quotation in mind, it would not seem too far-fetched to assert that the narrator's urge to metamorphose into an Arab represents just the same type of yearning as Jekyll's in Stevenson's story. In both cases, the protagonist feels an affinity with the very nastiness of his dream: 'olores densos, emanaciones agrias que voluntariamente aspiras con fervor catecúmeno ... : todo lo que sea secreción, podredumbre, carroña será familiar para ti' (DJ, pp. 43–4; 'strong odors, acrid emanations that you eagerly breathe in with all the fervor of a catechumen ... : everything that is secretion, rottenness, carrion will be your chosen realm', CJ, p. 32); 'When I looked upon that ugly idol in the glass, I was conscious of no repugnance, rather a leap of welcome'.[34] Indeed, Goytisolo seems to recognize the common ground between himself and Stevenson, for he actually draws a parallel in Don Julián between one of Julián's deceptive manifestations – a penitent Spaniard on this occasion – and the Jekyll-Hyde construct: 'al doblar la esquina, por la tortuosa calleja del Moro, cofradías y hermandades experimentan una insólita transformación: Doctor Jekyll y Mr. Hyde, sí: pero sin sufrimiento ... : suavemente, sin tropiezo ... : el caballero ... se ha liberado del capirote y luce ahora una nívea turbante sobre su risueña faz de traidor: eres tú, Julián!' (DJ, p. 185; 'as the procession rounds the corner and heads down the narrow winding Calleja del Moro, the fraternal orders and brotherhoods undergo an astonishing transformation: Dr. Jekyll suddenly becomes Mr. Hyde: painlessly, however, . . . : smoothly, with no hitches . . . : the gentleman . . . has cast off his penitent's hood and a snow-white turban now crowns his grinning traitor's face: he is you, Julian!', *CJ*, pp. 156–7).

In this depiction of metamorphosis, as in many others of Goytisolo's, the transformation is an unmasking, a revelation of the true character beneath a disguise. In this respect his approach diverges from Stevenson's, for although Jekyll does reveal a part of his true self when he becomes Hyde, it is nowhere suggested that Hyde is somehow the 'real' Jekyll, who normally wears a disguise of respectability. On the contrary, the fact that the true Jekyll consists of both good and evil is stressed: 'Of the two natures that contended in the field of my consciousness, even if I could rightly be said to be either, it was only because I was radically both'.[35] For Jekyll then, the metamorphosis is only the unmasking of a part of himself, whereas for Goytisolo's protagonist, to become the arch-traitor of Spain – Julián in *Don Julián* – or a real Arab – as in *Juan sin tierra* – is the revelation of the whole, true character, the emancipation of the *pulpa* beneath the *cáscara* (the pulp beneath the shell).

The concept of metamorphosis as the putting on or off of a disguise is well-known in classical mythology, as was observed above, as well as in traditional tales. Both those lucky enough to have the power of voluntary metamorphosis, and those whose transformations are imposed upon them, are often transfigured for purposes of disguise or revelation. The numerous shapes assumed by Jupiter, enabling him to accomplish his sexual exploits are, as we have seen, little more than disguises or stratagems, whilst the metamorphosis that a god inflicts upon a mortal is often like an unmasking in that it reveals the essential nature of the victim, as we saw in one of the widely accepted interpretations of Circe's transformation of Odysseus's men in Homer. In fairy-tales too, there are those who are likewise given the appearance they deserve through enchantment; Cinderella's virtue and beauty are at first concealed by her wretched state among the cinders, but the Fairy Godmother gives her a new appearance matching her inner stature with outer splendour. Then again, there are many characters in folklore like Beast of 'Beauty and the Beast', who have had their horrid aspect thrust upon them by prior evil enchantment and who regain their former and rightful glory when the spell is broken.

Revelatory metamorphoses of this traditional sort are to be found in Goytisolo's fiction too. The *carpetovetónico*'s daughter, for example, is unmasked through metamorphosis in *Don Julián*. Her outer appearance before transformation is one of devout piety, but she is turned into an erotic sex-symbol: 'vestida de monja, reza devotamente . . . : descorre la mórbida cremallera de su hábito: al punto un pijama de seda negra emerge . . . : sucesivamente desabrocha la chaquetilla de su pijama, se despoja del pantalón . . . : ligas floridas, sujetas a las bragas, sostienen las medias de redecilla . . . : cuando el encaje cae, los pechos brotan' (*DJ*, pp. 163–4; 'dressed in a nun's habit, [she] is devoutly reciting her prayers . . . : [she] unzips her soft habit: and immediately black silk pajamas come into view . . . : she first unbuttons the jacket of her pajamas, then slips the pants off . . . : her mesh stockings are held up by flowered garters attached to her panty girdle . . . : when the lace falls, her breasts burst forth', *CJ*, pp. 138–9). That this metamorphosis is revelatory may be inferred from the image of stripping off outer garments. The seductive clothes are underneath the nun's habit, suggesting that they are symbolic of her inner self; the narrator does not, after all, have her taking off the habit and then putting on the erotic garb, from which it would be logical to surmise that both outfits carried equal value as expressions of her personality. Furthermore, it would seem legitimate to class a change of clothing as tantamount to shape-shifting in a Goytisolo text, in the light of what he says on the subject in *Makbara*: 'concepción del vestuario como símbolo, referencia, disfraz: . . . mudar de ropas para mudar de piel' (*Ma*, p. 209; 'the conception of wearing apparel as symbol, reference, disguise: . . . changing one's clothes so as to change one's skin', *Mb*, p. 250). Finally, the girl's natural sexual attributes – her breasts – are also revealed once she removes the nun's habit and with it her pious *cáscara*, so even without the seductive underwear, the removal of her outer garments would reveal the inescapably sexual identity of her *pulpa*.

Her father, the *carpetovetónico* himself, is also depicted as having a false exterior, but in his case, there is nothing behind or beneath it: he has become the mask: 'fundido con su máscara, incrustado en su armadura y en estrecha simbiosis con ella' (*DJ*, p. 160; 'symbiotically fused with his mask, imbedded in his armor', *CJ*, p. 135). When it is destroyed, therefore, he simply dies. In his case, the metamorphosis is, on the one hand, an imagistic technique operating in the reader's imagination; gradually one comes to visualize him as an armoured crustacean. On the other hand, there are the metamorphoses of the mask itself, as it swells to the point of explosion. The revelatory element is two-fold as well; first it is revealed that this ponderous armoured exterior is an appearance befitting such a character and then that the façade concealed nothing but a void stuffed with a little sawdust (*DJ*, p. 181; *CJ*, p. 153).

Whereas the vacuousness of the *carpetovetónico* and the falsity of the daughter's image are treated unsympathetically, if not aggressively, the wearing of a mask in order to accomplish something worthwhile under cover is weighted favourably. The concept arises as early as *Señas*, with Jerónimo, the resistance fighter passing as a farm hand (*SI*, pp. 42–9; *MI*, pp. 32–9). The mask is not explicitly connected with metamorphosis in this instance, for the reader never glimpses Jerónimo's true self nor any transformation in either direction. However, the basic idea of the mask as useful protection is taken up in *Paisajes*, this time with a clear link to the theme of transformation. The disguise here functions on two levels. First, there is the pro-tagonist's behaviour within the story: 'Por encima de todo: pasar inadvertido. Mudar cameleónicamente de piel, adaptarse a los col-ores y matices del barrio. Crear poco a poco las condiciones que aseguren tu invisibilidad y te permitan actuar en un clima propicio' (*PB*, p. 171; 'Above all, don't call attention to yourself. Change skin like a chameleon, adapt yourself to the colors and subtle tones of the neighborhood. Gradually create conditions that will assure your invisability and provide you with a valuable climate for your activi-ties', *LB*, p. 139). The perfect façade, then, is one that can itself be transformed at will, as circumstances dictate. As with the *carpetovetónico* of *Don Julián*, the metamorphosis is not concerned with the stripping off of a mask but with the shifting shapes of the mask itself. Second, there is the level of language and style in which *Paisajes* is written: 'Tras las máscaras y celajes de la escritura, la meta es el desdén: el rechazo orgulloso de la simpatía o admiración ajenas será el requisito indispensable a la alquimia interior operada bajo el disfraz de una crónica burlona y sarcástica, de los lances y aventuras de una autobiografía deliberadamente grotesca' (*PB*, pp. 183–4; 'Beneath its masks and veils the aim of writing is disdain: the proud rejection of the sympathy or admiration of others as the indispensable requisite for the attainment of that inner alchemy practiced beneath the disguise of mocking and sarcastic chronicle, of incidents and adven-tures in a deliberately grotesque autobiography', *LB*, p. 149).

The jocular tone of the novel is some kind of a mask then, and there is an allusion to the alchemists, who worked under cover of turning base metals into gold, but whose real aim was 'to produce a *corpus subtile*, a transfigured and resurrected body'.[36] Treatises on the subject of this delicate operation were coded in highly symbolic language, lest they fell into the wrong hands and the alchemists were accused of heresy. Behind their mask of theologically innocuous scientific work, the alchemists were metaphysicians potentially lethal to Church doctrine, for they were challenging the fundamental principle of the duality of fallen humanity in their search for a unity and perfection that the Church taught could come only with the Millennium.[37] Goytisolo's mention of alchemy therefore suggests, first, that *Paisajes* is couched in language designed to put outsiders off the scent of what the book really signifies; second, that the underlying meaning challenges established values and beliefs; and third, if the implications are taken literally, that the concealed meaning is concerned with some kind of self-purification, perhaps even with a search for escape from duality. Whether this has anything to do with Goytisolo's own purpose in writing *Paisajes*, one can but speculate. However, the attitudes of the narrator-protagonist are accessible and throughout the text one does indeed find him challenging established views and beliefs regarding morality and attacking ethnocentricity and xenophobia. His *opus*, like that of the alchemists, would appear to seek unification too; the key to its relationship with the text of *Paisajes* seems to be contained in the following passage:

Quisieras abarcar en un lapso brevísimo la increíble variedad de credos, cultos, ceremoniales, costumbres, valores, ideas, sentimientos, obsesiones de los hombres y mujeres que te han precedido y te seguirán: entrar en su fuero interno y morada vital, comprender sus aspiraciones y anhelos, comulgar con su fe, sentir sus tristezas y alegrías; componer un libro abierto al conjunto de sus voces y experiencias, construido como un rompecabezas que sólo un lector paciente, con gustos de aventurero y etnólogo, sería capaz de armar.

(*PB*, p. 188)

(You would like to encompass in an extremely brief lapse of time the incredible variety of creeds, cults, ceremonies, customs, values, ideas, sentiments, obsessions of the men and women who have preceded you and will follow you: to plumb their innermost hearts and aspirations, to commune with their faith, to share their joys and sorrows; to compose a book open to all their voices and experiences, constructed like a puzzle that only a patient reader, with a taste for adventure and ethnology, would be capable of putting together.

(*LB*, p. 153)

The search for unity in the form of all-inclusiveness, expressed here in *Paisajes* and fundamental to the alchemical *opus*, is linked to the notion of order and chaos. Chaos and unity could be regarded as parallel concepts, the crucial difference lying not in what they denote, but in the implications associated with each: negative for chaos, positive for unity. Whilst chaos is shunned and even dreaded, to aspire to unity sounds a noble quest. And yet, what is chaos if not the ultimate unity? By definition, chaos is where there is no differentiation; hence, it is the state in which nothing is separated from anything else. Can there be a greater or purer unity than that?

On turning to consider chaos/unity as an ideal in the context of metamorphosis, however, we face a paradox: if one thing is to be changed into another, the process presupposes two fixed and different states, corresponding to its condition before and after transformation. If the aim is to attain a state of chaos/unity, there can be no fixed, final state, for the concept embraces all shapes simultaneously and without differentiation between them. There may be symbols that represent chaos, such as mythological beasts composed of many species, or flying dragons with their elemental combination of earth in their reptilian body, air in their bird's wings, fire in their burning breath, and water in their abode under the sea or in coastal caves. The alchemists used such dragons in their symbolism, together with other illustrations of the idea, but all must remain images and nothing more, a way of picturing something that defies literal visualization.

If I am right in my assertion that Goytisolo's novels hold up chaos as the ideal, the implications as far as the theme of metamorphosis is concerned seem to become complex to the point of self-negation. How can the author bestow the power of metamorphosis on his narrator-protagonists without presupposing fixity before and after they exercise their privilege? No matter how often or how quickly they can metamorphose, there must be stasis at either end of the process and this undermines the notion of the infinite fluidity of chaos. Let us wind back the thread in this labyrinth of symbolism and return to our starting-point of Proteus, 'who has no settled shape', according to Ovid.[38] Unlike the other gods, who are able to assume any number of different shapes at will but who have an enduring true appearance to which they return at the end of each exploit, Proteus is shapeless. He dons different bodies when he pleases, but his true form is formlessness itself, the principle of chaos. It is Proteus whom Goytisolo's characters seek to emulate, not Jupiter, with his superficial guises of convenience. As early as *Señas*, there is a tree image that is developed strikingly in *Don Julián*:

> La nostalgia de España se había desvanecido poco a poco, como si las raíces que te unieran a la tribu se hubiesen secado una tras otra como consecuencia de tu dilatada expatriación y de vuestra indiferencia recíproca. Rama amputada del tronco natal, planta crecida en el aire
>
> (*SI*, p. 341)

> el hombre no es el árbol: ayúdame a vivir sin suelo y sin raíces: móvil, móvil
>
> (*DJ*, pp. 124–5)

> (The nostalgia for Spain had been disappearing little by little, as if the roots that had joined you to the tribe had been drying up, one after the other, as a consequence for your long expatriation and of the reciprocal indifference. An amputated branch of the native trunk, a plant growing in the air)
>
> (*MI*, p. 283)

> (man is not a tree: help me to live without soil or roots: mobile, mobile)
>
> (*CJ*, p. 104, adapted)

From the image of shrivelled roots first, to the rootless 'planta crecida en el aire' (plant growing in the air) of *Señas*, the narrator progresses to a complete rejection of the parallel between man and tree in *Don Julián*. Thus the concept of merely exchanging one shape for another is rejected in favour of fluidity; in the terms of the tree image, the protagonist noticeably does not want to be uprooted in order to be replanted in what he deems more fertile soil, but to be constantly moving, never rooted anywhere. Similarly, the desire to 'confundir mar con tierra' expressed in *Makbara* (*Ma*, p. 205; 'making no distinction between sea and land', *Mb*, p. 245), implies not a wish

to change earth into sea or vice versa, but to have the two elements
mingled together without differentiation.

The ideal of chaos on the level of its manifestation in language
lucidly conveys the concept of eternal flux rather than temporary
fluidity between two static forms:

> vivir literalmente del cuento: de un cuento que es, ni más ni
> menos, el de nunca acabar: ingrávido edificio sonoro en de(con)-
> strucción perpetua: lienzo de Penélope tejido, destejido, día y
> noche: . . .
> lectura en palimpsesto: . . . infinitas posibilidades de juego a partir
> del espacio vacío
>
> (*Ma*, pp. 219 and 222)

> (to live literally by storytelling: a story that, quite simply, is
> never-ending: a weightless edifice of sound in perpetual de(con)-
> struction: a length of fabric woven by Penelope and unwoven
> night and day: . . .
> a palimpsestic reading: . . . infinite possibilities of play opening up
> in the space that is now vacant)
>
> (*Mb*, pp. 265 and 270)[39]

Ultimately, then, Goytisolo posits what might be termed metamorphosis into metamorphosis. From the ordered Western world
that creates the constipated, rigid characters of the *carpetovetónico*'s
ilk, more like an empty coat of armour or crustacean's shell than a
living human being, Goytisolo's later novels depict the liberating
escape from this stasis into infinite flux.[40] The journey and the
destination are *both* metamorphosis. Along the way, as we have seen,
transformations are still interrupted by moments of stasis as, for
example, in the different fixed identities assumed by the protagonist
of *Don Julián*. But all the while, the movement leads on towards a
goal of ceaseless flux, the absolute unity of all form and matter:
chaos.

# 6
## *El impacto lustral de la sangre:** Blood Symbolism

The argument that I have posited in the foregoing pages has traced a path of ever-increasing complexity in the underlying themes of Goytisolo's later novels, from the relatively straightforward dualism, which I have called *esquizofrenia colectiva*, to an attack on hierarchies, and ultimately to a defence of chaos. Blood symbolism is relevant to this progression since exactly the same thematic path is revealed, as if this one topos were a microcosm of the fiction as a whole. Before embarking upon an analysis of Goytisolo's use of blood as a motif, though, the origins of its symbolism need to be considered in more general terms, for it is this heritage of Judaeo-Christian and classical traditions that the author exploits.

According to many scholars, the notion that blood is life is widespread in primitive communities the world over, perhaps arising from the simple, observable fact that loss of blood causes loss of life.[1] Both in Leviticus and Deuteronomy, the concept that blood is life is made explicit: 'For the life of the flesh *is* in the blood' (Leviticus 18.11) and 'The blood is the life' (Deuteronomy 12.23). And in the New Testament, Christ's blood would seem to be equated with his life-essence too, as, for example, in Paul's Epistle to the Colossians, where he writes that 'we have redemption through his [Christ's] blood' (1.14), or again, in Peter's First Epistle: 'ye were not redeemed with corruptible things, *as* silver and gold, . . . ;/But with the precious blood of Christ' (1.17–18).

This same belief emerges clearly in superstitions regarding demoniacal blood-suckers such as vampires. On the one hand, the victim must sicken and eventually die as his or her 'life' is sucked out; on the

---

* The title quotation comes from *Juan sin Tierra*, p. 149; 'the ritual spurt of blood', *Juan the Landless*, p. 134.

other, the blood-sucker sustains himself or herself by drinking blood, thus achieving an albeit ghastly form of immortality, but immortality nevertheless. Whilst drinking divine blood in the Christian communion sustains the soul, the consumption of human blood nourishes the body; indeed, in medieval times a vampire was thought to be a body without a soul.[2] Even this very swift survey should suffice to convey how widespread the conviction is that blood is the essence of life; traditions as diverse as the Jewish dietary prohibition of animal blood, the Christian Holy Communion, and vampire folklore can all be traced back to this fundamental notion. Metaphorical commonplaces in both English and Spanish also testify to the degree to which we take the idea for granted. In English a person may be accused of being a blood-sucker, and in Spanish the expression 'chupar a alguien la sangre' ('to suck somebody's blood') is defined as meaning to exploit or gradually ruin someone. 'No quedar sangre en el cuerpo', literally to have no blood left in one's body, is another Spanish expression; it might be rendered into English as 'to be half-dead with fright'.

Other turns of phrase, however, reflect an altogether different source of blood symbolism, as when a person's temperament is described as sanguine. This of course relates to the ancient theory of the four humours, of which blood is one, corresponding to air in the elemental quaternity and characterized by its hot and moist nature.[3] The logic behind the humoral doctrine can be attributed to the well-established belief in man as microcosm of the universe, which led the thinkers of ancient Greece to seek a quaternity in man parallel to that which they discerned in the world around them.[4] Aristotle's acceptance of the humoral scheme (with certain modifications) as the basis of his physical theory lent the doctrine an authority that accounted for its endurance through the Middle Ages and beyond, even into the eighteenth century.[5] Now, according to Galen (A. D. 130–200), probably the most celebrated and influential of the ancient physicians (excepting Hippocrates himself), physical and mental health was based on the balance of the humours. However, blood provided the means of attaining this balance, because in addition to recognizing it as a humour in its own right, he seems also to have been of the opinion that it was a balanced mixture of the other humours. Herein lies the explanation for blood-letting as a cure-all down the ages. Not only can an excess of blood itself – known as *plethora* – require that some be drained off, but an imbalance in any of the humours can be redressed by blood-letting, combined with

compensatory dietary prescriptions.[6] Lesage's Doctor Sangredo in
*Gil Blas* (almost certainly a caricature of a real French doctor of the
times),[7] exemplifies this philosophy with endless leechings together
with recommendations of the copious intake of water.

It becomes apparent that the blood-is-life concept clashes with the
humoral doctrine of balance, most noticeably perhaps when the
context is blood loss: if blood is life, then all blood loss must be
undesirable and ultimately present a mortal threat, whereas in the
humoral scheme, it may be a salutary purge, bringing health rather
than snatching it away. The presence of these two contrasting
symbolic values produces an ambiguity that Goytisolo exploits to
the full. For instance, the following image is used in *Don Julián*
for Spaniards during the post-Civil War years: 'populorum progressio: gracias al tacto y competencia de vuestros esclarecidos tecnócratas:
próvidos celadores del secular enfermo, condenado aún, después de
previsora sangría, a la inmovilidad y al reposo, a la cura de sueño, a la
hídrica dieta: en vía de recuperación al fin bajo la ubicua potestad de
Tonelete' (*DJ*, p. 26; '*populorum progressio*: thanks to the cleverness
and the competence of your brilliant technocrats, the zealous male
nurses of a patient who had been ill for decades, who despite a
provident bloodletting was under strict orders to remain in bed
around the clock and not move a muscle, to take a sleep cure, to stick
to a diet of plain water: but who is now on the way to recovery
thanks to the ubiquitous power of a certain barrel-shaped genleman',
*CJ*, pp. 16–17).[8] The blood-letting the Spaniards think is good for
them – like Sangredo's patients in *Gil Blas* – is in fact weakening them
and ultimately threatening their lives, because in the narrator's view
blood is life. Seneca is depicted in the same work as aided by Sagredo
himself:

> con su inseparable asesor, el ilustre doctor Sagredo, somete el país
> a una prudente terapéutica de sangrías y purgas que restablece
> lentamente, al cabo de varios lustros, su comprometida salud: los
> carpetos lo comprenden así por aquello de quien bien te quiere te
> hará llorar . . . : la precavida eliminación de glóbulos rojos y un
> régimen diatético severo y radical
>
> (*DJ*, p. 118)

(aided by his inseparable companion and assistant, the illustrious
Dr. Leech, he subjects his country to a carefully administered
series of therapeutic bloodlettings and purges which after several

decades restores its once dangerously threatened health: the Hispanos understand him, since they believe in the proverb that he who loveth chasteneth . . . : the judicious elimination of red cells and a severely limited, strict regimen)

(*CJ*, p. 98)

The Spaniards described here are as easily taken in as the people of Valladolid in *Gil Blas*: 'Les gens dont je prenais le nom [les malades] mouraient presque tous' (The people whose names I took down [the patients] nearly all died); yet, 'il n'y avait point, en ce temps-là, de médecin plus accrédité que le docteur Sangrado' (there was no physician of higher repute at that time than Dr Sangrado).[9]

Chief among those who are erroneously persuaded of the efficacy of blood loss – whether literally, in the form of bloodshed, or figuratively, in the form of balancing the temperament – is the late-nineteenth-century essayist, Angel Ganivet, whom Goytisolo quotes directly, calling him 'un estrellado y bizarro discípulo del doctor Sagredo' (*DJ*, p. 150; 'a valiant disciple of Dr Leech's', *CJ*, p. 126). In *Idearium español*, Ganivet proudly proclaims that 'España sobrepuja a todas las demás naciones juntas, por el número y excelencia de sus sangradores . . . . El supremo doctor español es el doctor Sangredo' ('Spain surpasses all other nations put together, in the number and excellence of its blood-letters . . . . The supreme Spanish doctor is Doctor Sangredo').[10] The following passage from *Don Julián* is taken verbatim from *Idearium*:

jamás en la historia de la humanidad se ha dado ejemplo tan hermoso de estoicismo perseverante como el que ofrece la interminable falange de sangradores impertérritos que durante siglos y siglos se han encargado de aligerar el aparato circulatorio de los carpetos [*españoles* in Ganivet], enviando a muchos a la fosa, es cierto, pero purgando a los demás de sus excesos sanguíneos

(*DJ*, pp. 150–1)[11]

(never in the history of humanity has there been a more perfect example of stoic perseverance than that offered by the endless phalanx of dauntless bloodletters who for century after century have taken it upon themselves to improve the circulation of Hispanos ['Spaniards' in Ganivet], admittedly sending many of them to their graves, but purging the rest of their bloody excesses)

(*CJ*, p. 126)

Even though Ganivet is using the terms *sangrador* ('blood–letter') and *exceso sanguíneo* ('bloody excess') figuratively, Goytisolo's narrator renders them as ridiculous as if they had been meant literally, by playing on the ambiguity in blood symbolism. If Ganivet is referring to an unhealthy imbalance in the Spanish national character, courageously redressed by Spanish leaders down the ages, Goytisolo's narrator means life-essence when he uses blood imagery. At once, the noble rhetoric is transfigured into the senseless ranting of an apologist for carnage (again, whether physical or psychological). The same words take on a new meaning, but without losing their humoral significance in the process: the *sangradores* become vampire-like killers, and the *excesos sanguíneos* become a meaningless contradiction in terms – an excess of life, of vitality? – or, more ominously, they become the deranged justifications of mass murder.

Now, despite the clash between the Biblical and humoral values of blood as a symbol, Christian thinkers have managed to reconcile the two. This is where Goytisolo's use of the motif as microcosm of the overall thrust of the later fiction, as I interpret it, begins, for herein lies the *esquizofrenia* phenomenon. We have seen that the Church follows Old Testament symbolism as far as blood is concerned: Christ's blood is His life-essence and since He is divine, the life offered to those who drink it is eternal and spiritual.[12] Logically enough, in other words, the implicit assumption is that God's blood nourishes that part of man which has the potential to be godlike: the soul. In the Christian frame of reference, then, to fortify the soul, improve its 'health', and even guarantee its longevity, the age-old belief in blood-consumption comes to the fore. However, the inferior status of the body compared with the soul, and their traditional relationship of mutual antagonism, results in the state of *esquizofrenia*, whereby taking care of the body is culpable, whilst tirelessly mortifying it is virtuous.[13] Thus the ancient Greek objective of finding health through equilibrium and harmony of the humours no longer applies, since bodily health is not sought but shunned. Hence, blood loss, whether through deliberate action or as a bi-product of other violent activities, takes on the significance of laudable mortification of the flesh, or sacrifice of bodily well-being in the nobler cause of the spirit. Thus, the penitents of *Don Julián* are admired by spectators for their 'pies descalzos, ateridos, sangrantes!' (*DJ*, p. 183; 'naked, freezing-cold, bleeding feet!', *CJ*, p. 154) and in *Juan sin tierra*, the narrator speaks with the voice of the establishment when he refers to a 'purísimo y bravo joven de la Meseta en el momento en

que se disponía a verter generosamente su sangre en aras de la
perpetuación del reinado de Séneca' (*JT*, p. 163; 'the pure-hearted,
valiant lad from the Meseta as he readied himself to generously shed
his blood for the perpetuation of the kingdom of Seneca', *JL*, p. 150).
These characters are lauded for the lack of importance that they
attach to their bodies, in the interests of spiritual objectives: personal
salvation in *Don Julián*; national, patriotic salvation in *Juan sin tierra*.
In this type of symbolism, blood vividly represents life, though not
the life of the whole person, but that of the contemptible body alone.

Goytisolo makes particularly effective use of the connection between blood and body-life in the dualistic scheme, when he shows
up the inconsistency of a doctrine that commends unnecessary
bloodshed in certain circumstances – as Christian mortification of the
flesh or patriotic self-sacrifice – but laments and condemns it in
others, when non-Christians are the perpetrators. At the same time,
he sheds doubt on the dualistic distinction between pleasure and
pain, showing that far from being a voluntary act of self-imposed
suffering, mortification of the flesh, with its often concomitant
bloodshed, creates an ecstasy scarcely if at all distinguishable from
the sexual variety. The dualism of virtue-vice, pain-pleasure, saint-
sinner is thus dismantled. In *Juan sin tierra*, the supposedly virtuous
Père de Foucauld exclaims ecstatically: 'ah, mourir martyr, . . . cou-
vert de sang et de blessures' (*JT*, p. 151; 'ah, to die a martyr, . . .
covered with blood and wounds', *JL*, p. 138). The narrator helps
him to realize this dream: as Foucauld castigates himself,

> la vista de la sangre que brota enciende también la tuya y . . . le
> arrancarás el látigo de la mano . . .
> me gusta verter vuestra sangre : siempre que se me presenta una
> ocasión, la aprovecho
>
> (*JT*, p. 142)

> (the sight of the blood that gushes forth also inflames your blood
> and . . . you will grab the whip out of this hands . . .
> I like shedding your blood: whenever an occasion presents itself, I
> take advantage of it)
>
> (*JL*, p. 128)

The cruel persecutors of hagiography suddenly take on a new
complexion; in one sense, the reader cannot help but think, were
they not providing a service to people whose wish was to be baptized

by blood, people who wanted to suffer pain and derived satisfaction from it? One recalls Alvarito's bitter disappointment in *Señas*, when the Republican militiamen refuse to play the part that he and Señorita Lourdes have assigned to them as henchmen of the Antichrist, refusing to torture Alvarito and so let him become a martyr as he desires (*SI*, pp. 26–31; *MI*, pp. 19–24). Common sense tells the reader that the Republicans are not to blame for thwarting Alvarito by their mercy; the real cause of his misery and of Foucauld's pleasure from pain in *Juan sin tierra* is the Christian teaching that suffering is virtuous.[14]

Blood as representative of the life of the flesh also plays an important role in the depictions of sex, especially from *Don Julián* onwards. Already in *Señas* though, when Alvaro loses his virginity, he is described in terms of the rush of blood to his face: 'encendidas las mejillas, rojos los pómulos' (*SI*, p. 78; 'your cheeks were burning, the cheekbones red', *MI*, p. 63). Indeed, sex is recurrently associated with a rush of blood; when, for example, a pimp gives his sales patter to an Englishman in Turkey, the fair-skinned tourist's face 'deviene poco a poco del rojo sanguino de sus cabellos' (*JT*, p. 105; 'gradually turns the same blood red color as his hair', *JL*, p. 92, adapted) and the odious Parejita Reproductora would 'ruborizarse mutuamente' if they read uncensored literature (*JT*, p. 183; 'both blush', *JL*, p. 164, adapted), this last, possibly an echo of the nineteenth-century writer, Emilia Pardo Bazán's '¡Cuán hartos estamos de leer elogios de ciertos libros, alabados tan sólo porque nada contienen que a un señorita ruborice!' ('How sick we are of reading eulogies of certain books, praised merely because they contain nothing to make a young lady blush!).[15] In *Don Julián*, Alvarito's nervous anticipation of the sexual activity that awaits him in his adult self's hut sends his blood elsewhere: 'su corazón late más rápido y la sangre abandona su rostro' (*DJ*, p. 217; 'his heart begins to beat faster and the blood drains from his cheeks', *CJ*, p. 184). More directly, 'afluencia sanguínea' ('a sudden flux of blood') is frequently used to mean an erection (*DJ*, pp. 77 and 165; *CJ*, pp. 63 and 139; *JT*, p. 72, 'afflux of blood', *JL*, p. 58, for example) and the same idea is found in *Makbara*, with allusions to 'el flujo tumular de la sangre', 'afluencia sanguina, rígida tumefacción', and 'flujos sanguíneos' (*Ma*, pp. 49, 101, and 208; 'the tumular rush of blood', 'a rush of blood, rigid tumefaction', 'rushes of blood' *Mb*, pp. 47, 113, and 249), all with this meaning, as well as the nauseating euphemism of one of the lecherous correspondents of the *ángel*: 'cuando pienso en una mujer como tú, la sangre confluye donde tú imaginas' (*Ma*, p. 109; 'when I think about a woman like you, my blood rushes to the spot that you can well imagine', *Mb*, p. 121).

Blood is not only associated with the pleasures of the flesh via the male anatomy, though. The *Hija de la Revolución Americana*'s attempts to make herself sexually attractive involve the use of red cosmetics: 'la boca embadurnada de rouge . . . : [los dedos del pie] con diez toques de laca rojiza, como otras tantas cerezas rubicundas, apetitosas' (*DJ*, p. 48; 'her mouth smeared with red lipstick . . . : with ten toenails lacquered a rosy red, like a bunch of ripe, tempting cherries', *CJ*, p. 36, adapted).[16] Menstrual blood too is unequivocally linked with eroticism in *Juan sin tierra*. The black slaves and King Kong wish to consume women's menstrual blood for sexual pleasure and the women concerned find this as erotic an experience as the men do. When, for example, the white slave owner's daughters stain their white skirts with a 'sabrosa hemorragia' ('delicious hemorrhage') of menstrual blood, this is what happens:

> incapaces de soportar el tantalesco suplicio, los negros más guape-
> tones se precipitarán al proscenio : abrazándose a las rodillas
> temblorosas de las aún doncellas pero ya no niñas, levantarán
> ansiosamente sus faldas y aplicarán con avidez los labios sedientos
> al en latín, en latín, suplicará la Virgen Blanca pero aunque
> intentarás complacerla y escribirás sanguinis menstruationis lam-
> bent, te será imposible continuar . . .
> las ex-niñas elevan los ojos al cielo con embeleso y arrobo de
> Madonnas
>
> (*JT*, pp. 45–6)

> (unable to bear this tantalesque torture, the most brazen blacks will
> rush up onto the stage: clinging to the trembling kness of these
> girls who are still virgins but no longer children, they will eagerly
> raise the latter's skirts and greedily place their thirsting lips on
> in Latin, in Latin, the White Virgin will beg but even though you
> will endeavor to please her and write sanguinis menstruationis
> lambent, it will be impossible for you to continue . . .
> the three ex-children lift their eyes heavenward with the rapture
> and ecstasy of Madonnas)
>
> (*JL*, p. 34)

As far as the King Kong episode is concerned, when he holds the damsels in his hand, 'rozará delicadamente sus muslos con el extremo

de su dardo lingual: buscando el exquisito néctar periódico ... :
mientras ellas suspiran y gimen y se derriten interiormente de gozo'
(*JT*, p. 75; '[he will] delicately brush the tip of his lingual dart along
their thighs: seeking out their exquisite periodic nectar ... : as the
damsels moan and sigh and melt inside with pleasure', *JL*, p. 61).
This blood-sex image of menstruation extends the symbolic value of
blood in the erection and blushing images, because it refers specifically to what are traditionally regarded as taboo sexual practices,
rather than simply being a way to describe sex in general. As the
passage quoted concerning the slaves shows, virtue personified in the
Virgen Blanca cannot bear to hear such a wicked act enunciated in
the vernacular;[17] so, coupled with bestiality in the King Kong
episode, the menstrual connection of blood with eroticism presents
a picture of the ultimate in what conventional values class as sinful
sex.

In a variety of ways, then, blood is associated with the body or the
flesh, in the dualistic scheme that I have called *esquizofrenia colectiva*,
but as chapter 2 showed, the validity of 'schizophrenic' distinctions
is rejected in Goytisolo's later novels and blood here plays an
important part too. Just as the ambiguity surrounding the differentiation of saints from sinners is demonstrated by showing the
two groups as virtually indistinguishable, blood as a symbol of
carnality is juxtaposed with blood as a symbol of a spiritual nature,
namely, the concept of lineage. Even more powerfully than in the
blurring of boundaries between pairs of conventionally opposed
principles – saint and sinner, black and white, pure and polluted, to
name but a few – blood symbolism undermines the dualistic pattern
of Western psychology, for the opposites are contained within the
very same word. Only the context determines whether *sangre*
('blood') is to mean corporality or spiritual nobility, whether the
latter pertains to aristocratic descent, race, or nationality.

Blood as spiritual pride in racial purity inevitably leads back to the
issue of *limpieza de sangre* (literally, cleanness of blood and used in
Spanish to mean 'of Spanish Catholic descent, untainted by Moorish
or Jewish blood'), which dominated the Spanish Golden Age. Now,
one of the reasons why Goytisolo attacks the Generation of 1898
writers is their attitude to what he scornfully calls the *intocables*
('untouchables') of that period.[18] Whilst he recognizes the literary
value of the Golden Age writers themselves – his essays of literary
criticism amply demonstrate this[19] – he is dismayed by the awe-
inspired reverence with which modern writers have idolized them.

The insect-squashing episode of *Don Julián* is perhaps most significant for its subsequent effect on the *carpetovetónico*: he simply disintegrates as he beholds his sacred texts effaced by insects (*DJ*, p. 181; *CJ*, p. 153). The values espoused by Golden Age drama are those by which the *carpetovetónico* lives: without them he is nothing. Melveena McKendrick has shown that these values, although depicted through the theatrical convention of the honour code, are in fact an expression of the obsession with *limpieza de sangre* and her comments on the latter are worth quoting at some length:

> Spain's seizures of honour in the sixteenth and seventeenth centuries fed off another form of superiority as well, that of race and creed. The combination is not unique to Spain's Golden Age, of course, but it assumed in that place and at that time a vigour that was grotesque in its short-term effects and tragic in the long term: Spain's subsequent reluctance to adjust to the pressures of social, economic, and intellectual change would seem to owe much, if not by any means all, to the association of learning, commerce, and even manual labour with socially (because racially) unacceptable groups .... The historical indications that honour in seventeenth-century Spain was in practice virtually indistinguishable from social standing and social climbing and that *limpieza de sangre* was a crucial element in both of these make the relationship between honour and *limpieza* an inevitably close one.[20]

Clearly, Goytisolo is aware of the importance of *limpieza de sangre* in the Golden Age, for he refers to the *intocables* as 'estrellas fijas del *impoluto* firmamento hispano: ... prosapia de hoy, de ayer y de mañana, asegurada siglo a siglo por solar y ejecutoria de *limpios* y honrados abuelos' (*DJ*, p. 34, my italics; 'the fixed stars of the *pure* Spanish firmament: ... the lineage of yesterday, today, and tomorrow, a patrimony and titles of nobility handed down for century after century by the most honorable and *pure-bred* forebears', *CJ*, p. 24, adapted).[21]

Why, one might ask, should *limpieza de sangre* be relevant to a contemporary writer? The reason must be that Goytisolo sees it as one historical manifestation of a larger problem that is still very much alive in the world of his novels, and this in turn explains why he creates seemingly anachronistic characters like the *carpetovetónico* of *Don Julián*. A twentieth-century manifestation of the obsession with racial and national superiority is to be found in the pathetic

bragging of the Spanish emigrés of *Señas*: 'tras evocar nostálgi-
camente el queso de Roncales, el lacón con grelos y el chorizo de
Cantimpalo, decretar, con unanimidad insólita entre españoles, que
agua pura y fresca y restauradora como la de Guadarrama no había,
pero que no señores, ninguna otra en el mundo' (*SI*, pp. 251–2; 'after
nostalgically mentioning Roncales cheese, shoulders and turnip
greens, and Cantimpalo sausage, to decree with a unanimity unusual
among Spaniards, that pure, cool, and refreshing water like that of
the Guadarrama, did not exist, no sir, anywhere else in the world ',
*MI*, p. 208). In a non-fictional piece, Goytisolo criticizes the post-
Franco regionalism – and indeed, all manifestations of chauvinism –
for the same reasons:

Hoy, el mismo empeño místico, aseverativo, excluyente, enamor-
ado de lo tenido por propio y desdeñoso de lo ajeno, prolifera en el
mosaico de las naciones, nacionalidades, entes autonómicos y
provincias que cubren el suelo peninsular . . . . El cariño único,
ensimismado y defensivo a lo 'nuestro' – llámese español, francés,
árabe, catalán, *euskera*, gallego o corso – y consiguiente desapego a
lo ajeno no sólo empequeñecen el campo de visión y curiosidad
humanos de un pueblo o comunidad, sino que falsean y anulan su
propio conocimiento.

(Today, the same mystical obsession to assert, to exclude, to be in
love with what is held to be one's own and disdainful of anything
alien, proliferates in the mosaic of nations, nationalities, autonomous regions and provinces which cover the soil of the
Peninsula . . . . The defensive, self-absorbed, single-minded affection for what is 'ours' – call it Spanish, French, Arab, Catalonian,
Basque, Galician, or Corsican – and the consequent disaffection for
what is alien, not only diminishes a people or community's human
curiosity and narrows its field of vision, but it falsifies and negates
its self-knowledge.)[22]

Both in *Don Julián* and *Juan sin tierra*, the concept of good or *limpio*
(clean, pure) blood is explicitly mentioned in its traditional meaning,
though of course heavily weighted with irony. Like the *intocables*,
'don Alvaro Peranzules, más conocido ahora por su seudónimo
de Séneca, nació . . . de familia limpia y de muy buena sangre' (*DJ*,
p. 113; 'Don Alvaro Peranzules, better known today by his pseu-
donym, Seneca, was born . . . of a pure-bred family with the best

of bloodlines', *CJ*, p. 93) and in *Juan sin tierra*, 'todos los médicos
y autoridades científicas concuerdan en que los hombres depravados
e individuos de razas espurias o de infecto origen no tienen la misma
sensibilidad al dolor que las personas rectas y de sangre limpia' (*JT*,
p. 179; 'physicians and scientists universally agree that depraved men
and individuals of mixed blood and tainted origins do not possess the
same sensitivity to pain as upright, pure-blooded persons', *JL*,
p. 161). Ironical tongue-in-cheek then, is one device that Goytisolo
employs to attack *sangre* in its racial, spiritual meaning.

Another arises from the central theme of *Don Julián*, namely, the
reinvasion of Spain by the Moors, whose blood was so execrated in
Golden Age Spain. Not only in the fact of the invasion, which
delights the narrator who leads it, but in the description of the
invading hoards as 'beduinos de pura sangre' (*DJ*, pp. 16 and 196;
'pure-blooded Bedouins', *CJ*, pp. 7 and 165) is the notion of *limpieza
de sangre* subverted. Spaniards are denied their monopoly of purity
by this means, for Goytisolo subtly introduces the notion that an
unblemished lineage need not be synonymous with unadulterated
Spanish Catholic stock, as is traditionally implied by the use of
terms related to purity of blood in Spanish. Tacitly but powerfully,
he challenges conventional usage, giving a positive value to non-
Christian, non-Spanish blood. This revaluation of alien blood is
paralleled by a devaluation of Spanish blood: 'los españoles llevamos
el egocentrismo, la envidia y la mala leche en la sangre' (*SI*, p. 283;
'we Spaniards carry self-centredness, envy, and rancor in our blood',
*MI*, p. 234). The earnest tone of *Señas* is complemented by the
technique of trivialization employed in *Don Julián* to the same end,
when a Spanish television presenter is described as 'atávica voz de la
sangre' (*DJ*, p. 90; 'the atavistic voice of the blood', *CJ*, p. 73). The
message that pride in purity of race, the spiritual value of blood
symbolism, is misplaced, is summed up in an article by Goytisolo:
'No hay así en los grandes autores ni en los períodos más fructuosos
y ricos de una literatura influjos unívocos, ni esencias nacionales, ni
tradiciones exclusivas: sólo poligénesis, bastardeo, mescolanza,
promiscuidad' ('Thus, in neither the great authors nor the richest and
most fruitful periods of a literature, are there single influences, or
national essences, or exclusive traditions: only poligenesis, bastardy,
mixture, promiscuity').[23]

Blood as a weapon in the war on *esquizofrenia colectiva*, then, is
wielded ingeniously; Goytisolo uses it as a double-edged sword,
slicing through the concept of carnality with one blade and through

spirituality with the other. It is the semantic ambiguity of *sangre*, like so many other terms with a place in both carnal and spiritual spheres – *arrobo* and *deliquio* (both meaning ecstasy) are just two – that makes his point for him. *Sangre* is not one word that happens to have two distinct meanings, he seems to be saying, but rather, it is a symptom of the sick Western mentality, riddled with dualism, which interprets it thus and, worse still, evaluates one definition positively – the spiritual – and the other, corporeal one, negatively.

The unity of meaning that Goytisolo wishes to establish for *sangre*, in order to transcend its 'schizophrenic' ambiguity, is achieved powerfully through the theme of poisoning and poisoned blood. Principally in *Don Julián*, but also in the rest of the trilogy, physical blood is depicted as being poisoned in order to adulterate the spiritual *sangre*, either of a character or of a whole community. This forms an unbreakable bond between the two meanings of the word and ultimately posits their fundamental unity. In *Señas*, the concept remains figurative, when the influx of foreign tourists to Spain is described ironically as a blood transfusion: 'la incontenible ola turística, dispensadora de prodigalidades y mercedes, inyectaba sangre nueva y despreocupada en el vetusto país . . . : rica transfusión de dólares que circulaba a través de ferrocarriles, aviones, buques, carreteras; inesperada plaga salvadora' (*SI*, p. 373; 'the uncontainable waves of tourists, bearing prodigality and benefits, injected new and unworried blood into the ancient country . . . : a rich transfusion of dollars that circulated by railroad, airplane, ship, highway; the unexpected but saving plague', *MI*, p. 310). The irony is apparent not only from the use of the word *plaga* ('plague'), but also from the generally negative attitude of the author to the effects of tourism on Spain. The implication is that what some see as a cure for Spain's ills is in fact detrimental to the country; the *sangre nueva* ('new blood') is poisoning rather than healing.

This image in *Señas* is counterbalanced by the blood donation motif in *Don Julián*, for in the latter, the opposite relationship is constructed between the curative powers of blood transfusion and the lethal effects of blood poisoning. The protagonist claims to be poisoning the blood of Spain with rabies, but it seems that this is precisely what the country needs in order to be cured of its 'schizophrenic' obsession with national purity. Furthermore, the interplay between poison and transfusion is extended to the protagonist as donor, for the effect on him of infecting Spain with his rabid blood is psychologically beneficial, almost like the purge of a leeching:

cuando la enfermera anude la correhuela en torno del brazo y
hunda la jeringuilla en una de tus serpenteantes venas azules,
respirarás de alivio y satisfacción
(no estás en Tánger, sino en España, y la sangre que tan mali-
ciosamente ofreces infectará obligadamente tu tribu)
espiroquete no, virus de rabia
... ningún dolor, no: al contrario

(DJ, pp. 131–2)


(when the nurse winds the rubber tubing around your arm and
plunges the hypodermic needle in one of your snaking blue veins,
you will breathe a sigh of relief and satisfaction
(you are not in Tangier but in Spain, and the blood that you have
craftily come to donate is certain to infect your tribe)
not spirochetes: the rabies virus ... not the slightest pain: on the
contrary)

(CJ, pp. 109–10)

In short, *Señas* depicts an apparent transfusion which, however, is
really toxic, whilst *Don Julián* has an apparent injection of poison,
which is really curative. Let us not forget that *rabia* means 'rage' as
well as 'rabies'; the narrator is going to rouse Spain from its state of
tourism-poisoned, numb apathy, reinstate passion – in both senses of
the word – awaken the long-repressed corporality of the nation,
through *sangre* as well as through the reinvasion by the Moors,
symbols of carnality *par excellence*.[24]

On the individual level, snake bites are repeatedly described as if
they were injections in *Don Julián*. This emphasizes the fact that it is
the blood of the victim that the snake poisons, drawing attention
away from damage to the skin which the more usual *picar* or *morder*
(to sting or bite) would bring to mind. It also endows the act with a
clinically methodical tone, making it seem chillingly pre-meditated
and deliberately harmful. With Mrs Putifar in *Don Julián*, the narrator imagines the snake 'instilando sin prisa el veneno' (DJ, p. 67;
'slowly infusing the poison', CJ, p. 54) and when Julián's phallic
snake is to poison the purity of Alvarito, his own child self, the
vocabulary is even more clinical. The serpent is 'presta a ...
inyectar ... el líquido mortífero' (DJ, p. 215; 'ready ... to inject ...
the deadly liquid' CJ, p. 181) and Julián is described as awaiting 'el
momento de herirle [a Alvarito] e inyectar tu ponzoña' (DJ, p. 218;
'the moment to pierce him [Alvarito] and inject your poison', CJ,

p. 184). Finally, when the 'course of treatment' begins to take its toll on the child, 'el veneno sutil que inoculas le infecta y sus heridas supuran' (*DJ*, p. 226; 'the subtle poison that you inject infects him and his wounds ooze pus', *CJ*, p. 191).[25]

The inversion of poisoning and curing by injection or transfusion is again present here as in the blood donation episode, since the protagonist is opposed to purity and therefore it must be beneficial to the child to be imbued with carnality. Moreover, since donor and receiver are in fact one and the same person, the benefits to each are fused: just as much as Alvarito is cured of his innocence, Julián cures himself by purging the memory of his former self. Perhaps this identity of *verdugo* and *víctima* (executioner and victim) is latently present in the blood donation episode too; after all, the protagonist is himself a Spaniard even if a reluctant one, so by infecting the Spanish nation with *rabia*, he could be regarded as infecting himself along with his compatriots.

In the attack on sanguine *esquizofrenia colectiva* then, spiritual blood, traditionally deemed good and pure, is devalued: it is identified with physical – and therefore traditionally base – blood, by the blood-donating motif, and then, utilizing this fusion of spiritual with physical *sangre*, it is poisoned, rendered impure through the infiltration of *rabia* in the blood donation and snake venom in the torture of the child self. On the symbolic level, it is as if the spiritual – and therefore pure – meaning of *sangre* were polluted by Goytisolo's associating it with physical blood as part of taboo-breaking sexual practices: sado-masochism and the drinking of menstrual blood.

When one moves on to consider the role played by blood in the attack on ordered hierarchies, the twin concepts of adulteration and poisoning, which presuppose putting something *into* blood, are no longer in the spotlight. Instead, the ruling concept is contained in the words from *Juan sin tierra*, 'el descenso en la escala animal será para ti una subida' (*JT*, p. 79; 'the descent on the animal scale will be an ascent for you', *JL*, p. 65). What one may expect to find, therefore, is the animal kingdom depicted through blood as superior or at least equal to man. Indeed, this is the idea conveyed by the descriptions of creatures that blithely suck blood *out* of humans as the latter stand helplessly by, pompously asserting their dominion over the rest of Creation. In the *Juan sin tierra* case of the louse, the blood-sucking is quite literal: 'depositando los huevos donde nos agrada y restaurando en seguida las fuerzas merced a la gratuidad y abundancia de vuestra densa, nutritiva sangre, hundiendo simplemente en la epidermis

nuestro labio dispuesto en forma de trompa' ( *JT*, p. 157; 'deposit-
ing our eggs wherever we please and immediately recovering our
strength thanks to the gratuitous abundance of your thick, nutricious
blood, simply burying in your epidermis our proboscis in the form
of a tube', *JL*, pp. 145–6). In the playful utopian vision of the same
work, both the poison donors and the blood-suckers of the animal
kingdom are to be on an equal footing with man: 'ahora chinches,
piojos y demás parásitos viven apaciblemente de nosotros del mismo
modo que nosotros vivimos de los bienes fungibles del suelo:
. . . procuramos la reproducción de toda variedad de reptiles y
en particular de las odiotemidas serpientes' ( *JT*, p. 234; 'bedbugs,
lice, and other parasites now live peaceably off us as we live off the
fungible goods of the soil: . . . we ensure the reproduction of all
varieties of reptiles, particularly of hatedandfeared serpents', *JL*,
p. 206). The implication is that snakes and parasites are no more
venomous or exploitative than humans; in other words, as well as
Goytisolo's utopian blueprint recommending the establishment of
equality throughout Creation, there is a subtler undercurrent that
asserts that it already exists; although man may foolishly believe that
he is superior, he is no better than the lowliest parasite.

In figurative terms (but no less sacrilegiously for that), Antonio
of *Señas* carries the equalization of the ordered hierarchy of the
world a step further, placing God Himself on a level with the inverte-
brates: 'Insensible y cerrado al dolor de los hombres [Dios] se nutría
obscenamente como una sanguijuela, de su plegaria inútil' (*SI*,
p. 208; 'Insensible and shut off from the pain of men [God] was
obscenely nourishing himself like a leech on their useless prayers',
*MI*, p. 173). Another type of superhuman force is also reduced to the
status of blood-sucker in *Paisajes*, as socialist rhetoric is mockingly
echoed: 'Mientras las multinacionales gringas extienden sus tentácu-
los por Latinoamérica y chupan ávidamente la sangre de sus venas
abiertas, nuestro héroe redacta una nueva y más indecente carta a las
gemelitas' (*PB*, p. 143; 'As gringo multinationals extend their tenta-
cles all over Latin America and avidly suck the blood from its open
veins, our hero drafts another even more indecent letter to the little
twins', *LB*, p. 115). In the vehement language of *Don Julián* too, the
emotive force of the blood-sucker is utilized, when the narrator's
curse on the Generation of 1898-style poet includes 'que su grotesco
cuerpo flote y sea pasto de las sanguijuelas' (*DJ*, p. 147; 'may his
grotesque body drift on the waters and become food for leeches', *CJ*,
p. 123). To become the prey of leeches, it seems, is worse, more

degrading, than to be left simply to rot naturally, for it represents a drop in the ordered hierarchy of nature, as Judaeo-Christian tradition understands this. To be fodder for blood-suckers is to be inferior to them, at their mercy; the fact that it is blood that they consume – rather than some other part of the anatomy – makes the idea especially horrifying, as human psychology is still deeply affected by the notion that blood is life. Indeed, it is upon the horror that may be inspired by the thought of having an animal suck one's blood that the priest of *Don Julián* bases the imagery of his sermon:

> nada predispone tanto el organismo a la consunción como el pecado: a la manera de sanguijuela insaciable va chupando la sangre . . . :
> los cachorros de león son mansos hasta ver la sangre: pero al primer mordisco, se transforman, se vuelven feroces: amados hijos, perros hambrientos, lobos sanguinarios se esconden en el fondo de nuestra naturaleza caída: no les deis de comer o clavarán sus colmillos en vuestra carne y beberán vuestra sangre pura, fresca y joven
>
> (*DJ*, pp. 103–4)

> (there is nothing that so predisposes the organism to consumption as sin: like an insatiable leech it sucks your blood . . . :
> lion cubs are gentle creatures until they see blood: but at the very first bite, they are transformed, they become savage beasts: my beloved sons, famished dogs, bloodthirsty wolves lie hidden in the depths of our nature as fallen creatures: don't offer them food, or they will sink their fangs in your flesh and drink your pure, fresh young blood)
>
> (*CJ*, pp. 85–6)

The way in which the priest jumps indiscriminately from one creature to another – leech, then lion-cub, dog, and wolf – but holds fast to the blood-drinking image, highlights an important point: the fact of having one's blood drunk is so powerful that the identity of the drinker pales into insignificance. Thus, the traditional hierarchy within the animal kingdom is negated: a mammal like the wolf is no longer superior to a rudimentary invertebrate like the leech. What they have in common – that they drink blood – overrides their differences and unites them all.

This destruction of hierarchy through the levelling effect of blood consumption in the animal realm is also extended to the human group in the texts, with people who drink blood – figuratively or literally – losing their status as 'reyes y señores' of Creation (*JT*, p. 234; 'lords and masters', *JL*, p. 206) and being incorporated into the undifferentiated class of blood-suckers. In *Señas*, the fisherman Taranto's son talks about a crook who took money from Spaniards trying to emigrate and then gave them the wrong papers, so that they were turned back at the border: 'A un elemento así le llamo yo un chupasangres', he concludes (*SI*, p. 193; 'I call somebody like that a bloodsucker', *MI*, p. 161). In *Juan sin tierra*, the narrator describes blood-drinkers as 'seres' rather than *seres humanos* (human beings), suggesting their kinship with blood-suckers in the animal kingdom: 'seres despiadados, brutales, como aquél descrito por Amiano Marcelino en breves líneas inolvidables, cuando acomete al ejército godo con su puñal desnudo, degüella a un mozo e inmediatamente aplica los labios al cuello y sorbe vorazmente su sangre' (*JT*, p. 144; 'pitiless, brutal creatures, such as the one described by Marcelino Amiano in a few brief, unforgettable lines, when he attacks the army of the Goths with his naked blade, beheads a youngster, and immediately places his lips on the boy's neck and voraciously sucks his blood', *JL*, p. 130).

It may be asserted, therefore, that the theme of consuming blood contributes to what I have called the *reivindicación del caos* (the vindication of chaos), for it breaks down the 'empinada escalera que conduce del hedor al perfume' (*JT*, p. 23; 'the steep stairway that leads from stench to perfume', *JL*, p. 13). Sucking blood is the great equalizer, likening leeches to God Himself and effacing all the rungs in between. One might wonder whether this would not exchange the ordered hierarchy of the cosmos for a simple dualism: bloodsuckers on the one hand and all the rest, on the other. This is not the case, though, for Goytisolo depicts all as predators and all as prey, all *verdugos* and *víctimas* (executioners and victims); even the exploited fishermen of *Señas* are living (however wretchedly) from bloodshed: 'Las moscas bullían ávidamente sobre la sangre cuajada de los atunes y en el aire ... flotaba un aroma ... de muerte .... Durante el rodaje del documental Alvaro había tomado unos planos del Joseles, ... con el rostro manchado por la sangre de los atunes' (*SI*, pp. 192 and 194; 'The flies were buzzing avidly over the caked tuna blood and in the ... air ... there floated a smell of ... death .... During the filming of the documentary, Alvaro had taken some shots of Joseles ... with his face stained with tuna blood', *MI*, pp. 160 and 162). Like the defecation motif of *Juan sin tierra*, blood-drinking equalizes because every man and beast indulges in and is subjected to it, figuratively or literally: 'parásitos viven . . . de nosotros del mismo modo que nosotros vivimos de los bienes fungibles del suelo' (*JT*, p. 234; 'parasites . . . live . . . off us as we live off the fungible goods of the soil', *JL*, p. 206).

The metamorphosis topos is also served by the blood motif. In the simplest and most literal sense, blood alters the sea-water in *Señas* as the catch of tunny-fish is drawn in: 'el agua comenzó a teñirse de rosa' (*SI*, p. 194; 'the water began to take on a . . . rosy stain', *MI*, p. 162). The sunset described just after this echoes the sea's bloody change: 'La tarde había caído perezosa y madura e, inesperadamente, todo era de color rojo' (*SI*, p. 194; 'Evening had fallen lazy and ripe and all of a sudden everything was red', *MI*, p. 162, adapted). The depiction of the sky's colour transformation at sunset as bloodshed is echoed in *Makbara*, now in the more exuberant language of that work: 'sol exangüe a fuerza de desangrarse, violento despilfarro final, orgiástica agonía, antes de tramontar' (*Ma*, p. 113; 'an anemic sun that had bled copiously, one last violent hemorrhage, an orgiastic death-agony, before setting', *Mb*, p. 127).

Hence, blood may trigger off a metamorphosis. The priest's sermon from *Don Julián*, quoted above, draws attention to how the taste of blood changes the character of the lion-cubs. Tampering with blood also effects a transformation, as when the child self is tortured in *Don Julián* and the injection of snake poison into Alvarito's blood changes him irrevocably. In *Juan sin tierra*, it is the flow of menstrual blood that metamorphoses the *niñas* ('little girls') into *doncellas* ('damsels') and, on the linguistic plane, blood is one of the triggers of the preacher's switch from the vernacular into Latin, since he cannot bear to utter 'sanguis menstruationis devorant!' in Spanish (*JT*, p. 32; *JL*, p. 22).[26] Perhaps, indeed, it is on the linguistic level that blood most arrestingly represents a microcosm of the symbolism of the fiction. The notion of Protean evasiveness comes to mind as soon as one endeavours to give the meaning of *sangre* a fixed form. In the doctrine that blood is life, it slips between the fingers as one tries to establish whether it is the life of the soul or that of the body, or both. Whilst it is clear that the divine blood of Holy Communion sustains the soul, one enters a grey area when any other blood is consumed. Is the use of a virgin's or a child's blood (popular remedies in the Middle Ages)[27] supposed to impart health to the body only, or does the metaphysical purity and innocence of the blood somehow benefit the soul too? Is it possible, indeed, for both body and soul to be robust in the Roman Catholic tradition? Surely it is the loss of bodily health that brings spiritual well-being; the martyr's baptism by blood is what guarantees his or her spiritual perfection: 'Le baptême du sang efface la souillure définitivement, et rien désormais ne pourra ternir la beauté de l'âme du martyr', says Hippolyte Delehaye, an expert in the field (Baptism by blood erases blemishes permanently and nothing henceforth will be able to tarnish the beauty of the martyr's soul).[28] Baldly put, the view of the Roman Catholic Church seems to be that the loss of bodily blood-that-is-life creates soul-life.

In the humoral doctrine, blood is just as protean: sometimes a humour in its own right, sometimes the sum of the others and, when the theory is applied in the Christian era, as it was until remarkably recently, the anti-flesh attitude and the concept of physical suffering being good for the soul only complicate matters further. What can the meaning of *plethora* be to a Christian physician, who believes that any blood symbolizes an excess of carnality and the only way to achieve spiritual perfection is ultimately to lose all of it, like the martyrs? To weaken the body by blood-letting could be seen as a form of mortifying the flesh, rather than finding the ideal healthy equilibrium, as the Galenists intended. So the meaning of blood even in the medical context of blood-letting is by no means straightforward; the classical objectives of elemental harmony and balance give way to a desire to punish the body, so that disharmony of the body is sought, in order to improve the soul.

So when the reader of literature such as Goytisolo's comes across a reference to blood, he must ask himself a series of almost inevitably unanswerable questions. Is it to be read as a beneficial substance about which one may confidently assume that the more a character has, the better for him, and the less, the worse? This is the scheme of vampire fiction. Alternatively, is it a sign of vice and fleshliness against which to juxtapose the whiteness of virtue and spirituality? This is the pattern of martyrology.[29] Or again, is blood a symbol of nobility – spiritual or ancestral – of nationality, of race? This range of meaning is typical of Golden Age drama, exemplified by Pedro Crespo in Calderón's *El alcalde de Zalamea*, when he says to his son:

> Dime, por tu vida, ¿hay alguien
> que no sepa que yo soy,
> si bien de limpio linaje,

hombre llano? No por cierto:
pues ¿qué gano yo en comprarle
una ejecutoria al Rey,
si no le compro la sangre?

(I, lines 488–94)

(Tell me, in faith, is there anyone who does not know that though
I am of pure-blooded lineage, I am a commoner? Of course not: so
what would I gain by buying a noble title from the King if I did
not buy the blood from him too?)

Finally, it might be just a poetic turn of phrase that does not bear
painstaking symbolic interpretation, as when *derramar la sangre* ('to
spill blood') is a lyrical synonym for *matar* or *morir* ('to kill' or 'to
die'), depending of course on whether *derramar* is self-referential.

Each and every one of these possible inferences could be drawn
from Goytisolo's use of *sangre* in the later novels. Although I have
tried to categorize his allusions to blood symbolically, the word's
fundamental polivalence remains, its fluid physical nature aptly
matching its semantic status. Like its signified, the signifier *sangre*
takes the shape of the vessel into which it is poured, but its true form,
like that of Proteus, is formlessness itself. It imparts life only when it
flows; solid, coagulated blood is dead blood, so one can expect to
find it linked in this form with all the negatively weighted symbols
of solidity and immobility (chick-peas and ponderous crustaceans,
for example). The end of the La Graya massacre in *Señas* is marked
by images of coagulated blood:

Cuando los periodistas llegan al lugar unas horas después del
tiroteo se divisan todavía cuajarones de sangre en la boca de la
atarjea. En la otra alcantarilla hay un reguero negruzco de varios
metros de longitud. Entre los zarzales una boina nueva, un pañuelo
y varios trozos de paño manchados de rojo revelan los esfuerzos de
las víctimas por restañar la hemorragia.

(*SI*, p. 145)

(When the reporters reach the place, a few hours after the shoot-
ing, pools of coagulated blood can still be seen at the mouth of the
drain. In the other culvert there is a blackish flow, several yards in
length. Among the brambles, a new beret, a handkerchief and

several pieces of cloth that are stained red reveal the efforts of the
victims to staunch the bleeding.)

(*MI*, p. 121, adapted)

The same imagery is used later in *Señas* too, this time to describe the
dead tunny-fish, when the flies buzzing around their coagulated
blood create 'un aroma de vacío y de muerte' (*SI*, p. 192; 'a smell of
emptiness and death', *MI*, p. 160).

Thus, it is living, flowing blood that represents the ideal of
constant flux I have posited as the underlying thrust of the later
novels. The link between this image of fluidity and the notion of
ultimate unity through chaos lies in the semantic polivalence of
*sangre*.

Taken together, the fluidity of the substance itself and of the value
of the signifier make it an arresting image for the concept of formless
flux combined with vitality (if vitality did not come into it, any liquid
would do). Goytisolo wallows in semantic polivalence – which is
to say, a lack of clear differentiation between meanings – just as he
revels in the chaos of the Arab market, the underworld, the random
pattern of the night sky, the old quarter of Barcelona, and order-
free eroticism. This comes out powerfully in the gleeful enthusiasm
of the following disclosure of the narrator's purpose, contained in
the breathless succession of verbs and the brevity and number of
phrases: 'captar al intruso ingenuo, seducirlo, embaucarlo, envolverle
en las mallas de una elusiva construcción verbal, aturdirle del todo,
forzarle a volver sobre sus pasos y, menos seguro ya de su discurso
y la certeza de sus orientaciones, soltarle otra vez al mundo, enseñarle a dudar' (*JT*, p. 136; 'to attract the ingenuous intruder, seduce
him, deceive him, envelop him in the meshes of an elusive verbal
construction, confuse him completely, force him to turn around and
retrace his footsteps, less sure now of his powers of language and his
infallible sense of direction, letting him loose again in the everyday
world, having taught him to doubt', *JL*, p. 122). On the basis of the
evidence that has been examined and has supported the idea that
blood stands as a key symbol of life-imbued fluid formlessness in the
texts, a new reading could be proposed for the important explanation
by the narrator of *Juan sin tierra*, when he says he is 'exorcisando
demonios en lúdica confrontación sangrienta, sin más arma ni brazo
que el discurso desnudo: transmutando la violencia en signo' (*JT*,
p. 147; 'exorcising demons in bloody mock confrontations, with no
other weapon save naked discourse: transmuting violence into a

sign', *JL*, p. 133). The *sangriento* ('bloody') nature of the confronta-
tion could imply the fluidity of language as well as its more obvious
and perhaps superficial semantic value; it could mean that the violence imposed by an order-obsessed culture will be attacked by the
semantic fluidity of the discourse.

Be that as it may, *sangre* is a multi-faceted concept in Goytisolo's
later novels and this enables it to play an important role in each of the
various battles fought in the war on order. In the *esquizofrenia
colectiva* attack, blood ridicules polarity by appearing in both camps,
as it were, as a symbol of fleshliness on the one hand and of spiritual
nobility on the other. In the onslaught against ordered hierarchies,
blood makes a significant contribution by levelling God, man, and
the whole of the animal kingdom, through the blood-sucking motif.
Blood is also a trigger of metamorphosis, both in the physical sense
through the content of the texts and in the linguistic sense when it is
responsible for a change of language in the discourse. Finally, its
semantic fluidity, demonstrated by its exceedingly wide applicability
to differing themes in the novels, makes it a powerful image of the
fundamental ideal which, it has been argued, they express: the
chaos-unity of formless flux.

# Conclusion

The first five chapters of this book have sought to beat a new path through the dense discourse of Goytisolo's later novels and the sixth has concluded the argument by drawing the different threads together in their application to the specific symbol of blood. Other leitmotifs could have been analysed in the same perspective. Saintly characters, for example, are opposed to sinful ones, demonstrating the *esquizofrenia colectiva* principle, but they are also depicted as figuring in the hierarchy of Western values, standing on the highest rung of the metaphysical ladder which Goytisolo gleefully knocks over. They are used in metamorphoses too, when they are transformed into masochists, scarcely if at all distinguishable from sexual perverts. Similarly, the illusory virtuous child is set against the genuine child, sexually aware and fascinated by violence, in the dualistic scheme, but he also merges with the saint in his position at the top of the hierarchical order of metaphysical superiority. The figure may be traced further to the metamorphosis into adulthood as the masking *cáscara* ('shell') is finally sloughed. The same underlying progression could be applied to the figure of the labyrinth in the texts: the winding streets of old Barcelona and Tangier, which become the sewers of *Makbara* and the Paris Metro of *Paisajes*, the wanderings of all the protagonists' minds. These stand as one pole of another dualistic opposition, counterbalanced not only by the geometrical precision of Pedralbes or Pittsburgh, but also, on the linguistic plane, by Goytisolo's rejection of circumlocution where the vocabulary of carnality is concerned. The abundant use of simile and metaphor could be examined to reveal a complex linguistic hierarchy joining the two poles, a hierarchy boldy challenged by Goytisolo's style. Thus, when he deliberately muddles the reader, as in the description of the weavers and their apprentices in *Don Julián*, non-figurative language can no longer be distinguished from imagery, so that the words take on a fluid quality as straight exposition gradually metamorphoses into simile, then metaphor, and finally into the fantastic realm of metamorphosis itself.

Together with teaching us to doubt about concepts, ideals, dreads – virtue, order, filth, for example (*JT*, p. 136; *JL*, p. 122) – Goytisolo forces us to question the whole notion of semantic definition, to ponder the meanings of individual words like *penitencia*, *placer*, *arrobo*, *fecundo*, ('penitence', 'pleasure', 'ecstasy', 'fertile'), forces us also to consider the potential for polivalence arising from unconventional syntax and punctuation: pronouns without deixis, verbs denied subjects, interrogatives deprived of the opening question-mark, absent speech marks, sentences fused through lack of a full stop. Ultimately, these linguistic and typographical departures are inseparable from the thematic ones, as the reader is taken by surprise in both cases for the same reason: it is not what he expects, and what he expects is based on what he has already read, what he thinks he knows about the experience of reading, and what he believes to be reliable pre-conditions. The lack of full stops, paragraph divisions, and speech marks are in this sense no different from the assumptions that defecation, travesties of Christian dogma, and irreverent references to other writers, for example, are unseemly in a novel. The shock-value and/or the refreshing nature of Goytisolo's texts arises, not from a comparison of them with real life, but with other literature, mythology, and doctrinal writings (this last, of course, including the Bible itself).

*   *   *

Although my argument has not concerned itself with the question of chronology in Goytisolo's fictional output since 1966, finally it might be of interest to see how *Makbara* and *Paisajes* develop ideas from the trilogy. With the disappearance of both the Church and Spain from the firing-line, the target of attack broadens, to encompass Western civilization as a whole, so that the flesh-spirit opposition, incarnated in *Don Julián* with the Moor versus the Spaniard, and in *Juan sin tierra* with the sinner as against the saint (both of these pairs appearing embryonically in *Señas*, as we have seen), becomes the radical divergence between East and West in *Makbara* and *Paisajes*. Both of these post-trilogy works could be seen as a realization of their predecessor Mendiola's aspirations, but each on a different level: *Makbara* expresses a personal victory over order, whilst *Paisajes* deals with its defeat in society.

Taking *Makbara* first, one could assert that it celebrates the union of opposites on the individual plane, through the person of the narrator. He is not a Muslim, but an *halaiquí nesraní* (*Ma*, p. 200; 'European halaiquí', *Mb*, p. 239), a Christian accepted in the Muslim world. Furthermore, he takes on the identity of both male and female in his story, recalling – perhaps fortuitously, but nonetheless significantly – the alchemical symbol of the androgyne, the sexual union of opposites. And in the tale of the supremely ethereal being, the *ángel*, who falls in love with the quintessence of carnal man, the Western vision of the Arab, spirit and flesh are at length happily united. All the symbolism of the text points to this: the location of their union, for example, is the sewers of Pittsburgh, not Tangier, thus implying a fusion of carnality – sewers – with the anti-physical society typified by Pittsburgh. The *ángel* is wearing a Pronuptia wedding-dress for the occasion which, beyond the obvious irony intended, brings together the concept of spiritual purity symbolized by the traditional gown, with the carnal aspect of their lovemaking.

The particular sexual activity that is described in *Makbara* is oral, returning the reader to the link established in *Juan sin tierra* between sexual and literary creativity. But where the analogy of the latter was with writing, the semen being likened to ink and the organ to the pen, the image of *Makbara* celebrates spoken literature: in *Juan sin tierra* we have the narrator 'empuñando con fuerza el bolígrafo, obligándole a escurrir su seminal fluido, manteniéndolo erecto sobre la página en blanco: en brusco, sincopado movimiento: plenitud gené-sica entre tus manos' ( *JT*, p. 97; 'tightly clutching the ball-point pen, forcing its seminal fluid out of it, holding it erect above the blank page: with brusque, syncopated movements: a genesic plenitude between your hands', *JL*, p. 80) and in *Makbara*, 'contar, mentir, fabular, verter lo que se guarda en el cerebro y el vientre, el corazón, vagina, testículos: hablar y hablar a borbollones' (*Ma*, p. 221; 'telling tales, inventing lies, making up stories, pouring out what is stored up in the brain and the belly, the heart, vagina, testicles: talking and talking, in a torrent of words', *Mb*, p. 267). This lifts the reader out of the narrative being told and up to the level of the teller in the market-place, just as the *Juan sin tierra* quotation reminded one of the discourse being written down; the emphasis has shifted from the written to the spoken word.

As one might have expected from the narrator's desire in the trilogy to leave his Western heritage behind, the tale of *Makbara* is related by a traditional Eastern *raconteur*, harking back to the reference to Scheherezade in *Don Julián* (*DJ*, p. 13; *CJ*, p. 5). Even in *Señas*, though, telling and hearing, rather than reading, stories, had been given an important place, with Señorita Lourdes's presentation of the lives of child martyrs (*SI*, pp. 21–2; *MI*, pp. 15–17). She did not just read aloud from the book either, but interrupted the text to address Alvarito directly with her own elaborations, rather like the story-teller who recounts a traditional tale but puts a personal stamp on it with his own rhetorical flourishes and variations. Again in *Señas*, Alvaro had told Jerónimo the story of his medallion's magical protection, and Jerónimo had countered subversively with a contrary tale (*SI*, pp. 45–6; *MI*, p. 36). In *Don Julián*, there was 'Little Red Riding Hood' being read aloud (*DJ*, pp. 95–9; *CJ*, pp. 78–81), again interspersed and spiced by extraneous dialogue, but this time coming from the next-door garden, and our attention was drawn to the listening process as the child tuned in now to what the maid was reading aloud, now to what the neighbours were saying, so that the final amalgamated product was indeed a 'nueva versión sicoanalítica con mutilaciones, fetichismo, sangre' (*DJ*, p. 13; 'a new psychoanalytic version complete with mutilations, fetichism, blood', *CJ*, p. 5). And in *Juan sin tierra*, the power of oratory was conveyed through the many sermons included in the text, as well as the jesuitical argumentation, presented as if spoken, by means, for example, of the speaker's anticipation of objections from a listener and the use of direct address: 'y los ajusticiados?, me diréis : acaso no son seres humanos como los demás?'; 'pues, hijitos míos, por qué creéis que os hemos ligado a la estaca sino para redimiros?' (both *JT*, p. 179; 'and the condemned men?, you will ask me: are they not perhaps human beings like the rest of us?'; 'listen, my sons, why do you believe that we have bound you to the stake if not to redeem you?', both *JL*, p. 161). Thus, when *Makbara* is revealed to be a wholly spoken text, the reader who is acquainted with the trilogy will recognize that this is the end of a process rather than a sudden innovation.

The static frame or premise of *Makbara* is also familiar. Just as the Alvaro of *Señas* had sat in a garden with his photographs and mementoes of the past sparking off the action of the novel; just as in *Don Julián*, the protagonist's wide-ranging fantasies were contained within the single physical location of Tangier; and just as in *Juan sin tierra*, the narrator remained bodily in 'la abuhardillada habitación en la que obstinadamente te entregas al experto onanismo de la escritura' (*JT*, p. 209; 'the room with the dormer window in which you stubbornly devote yourself to the expert onanism of writing', *JL*, p. 185); so in *Makbara* there is the similar device of a stationary narrator, from whom a geographically unlimited story can spring forth. However, this apparent sameness in structure conceals a progression: *Señas* and *Don Julián* gave the reader the impression that he was listening in on the narrator's thoughts; in *Juan sin tierra* these thoughts were externalized by presenting them as a written text; *Makbara* depicts a completely uninhibited narrator, willing to proclaim his story in public. The anguished introspection of *Señas* became aggressive introspection first (*Don Julián*), then it emerged from the narrator's mind on to the page (*Juan sin tierra*) and finally, with *Makbara*, it comes out of doors (out of a *cáscara* of sorts?) and the narrator presents his story in person.[1]

Lastly, *Paisajes* is a narrative that, for the first time since Goytisolo's early fiction, has a single location, not just as a frame or premise, but in the simple sense that the entire content of the text is set in one place: Paris. The reason that this reduction in complexity is now possible is that there is no longer any need to transport the reader from East to West in order to juxtapose the two worlds, for they have fused through the immigrant presence in Le Sentier. This could be seen as the culmination – perhaps the resolution – of a process first discernible in *Señas* (and earlier still), where the author showed an interest in the meeting of cultures, with Spaniards in France and tourists of various nationalities in Spain. In *Don Julián*, it was the Moorish presence in Spain and the vestiges of the Spanish colonial presence in North Africa, together with the American tourists there in the novel's present, that captured the protagonist's imagination; in *Juan sin tierra*, there were the white colonials in Cuba, foreshadowing the Soviet presence there, suggested by the narrator's vision of the slave-owning family as Russian royalty. In *Makbara*, there were North African tourists in Pittsburgh and the 'monstruo del más acá venido' in Paris (*Ma*, p. 13; 'monster from inner space', *Mb*, p. 1, adapted). But with *Paisajes*, this recurrent theme of foreigner versus local, of outsider versus insider, is transcended, for here the immigrants have taken over their new environment to such an extent that the contrast has melted away: the Parisians no longer feel at home and the immigrants no longer feel like foreigners: on the one hand, 'El Sentier ya no es el mismo que antes; ahora los nativos se sienten ovejas en corral ajeno' (*PB*, p. 124; 'Le Sentier isn't the same as it used to be; the natives feel like orphans turned out of house and home', *LB*, p. 100) and on the other, 'los modestos ilotas de la difunta expansión económica han traído con ellos los elementos e ingredientes necesarios a la irreversible contaminación de la urbe: aromas, colores, gestos' (*PB*, pp. 108–9; 'the humble helots of the now-spent economic expansion brought with them the elements and ingredients necessary for the irreversible contamination: . . . smells, colors, gestures', *LB*, p. 86).

With this fusion of East and West in a single and, for the first time, neutral place or no-man's-land, the problem of *esquizofrenia colectiva* is negated; East and West have met in Le Sentier and even black and white have merged in the image of the suntanned Metro passenger, an emblem perhaps of the union of opposites on a socio-ethnic level. The fact that he is beaten up by the police, who mistake him for an immigrant, only shows how their racial discrimination is now laughably meaningless; indeed, this is reflected in the humorous tone of the piece (*PB*, pp. 27–30; *LB*, pp. 17–19).

The victory over *esquizofrenia colectiva* in *Paisajes* has a domino effect on the subsequent phase of my argument, as once the two poles disappear – be they East and West, black and white, or any of the others that I have discussed – the complex hierarchy of graded values that spans the gulf between them loses its meaning too. Once blackness merges with whiteness, fine differences in shades of grey are no longer significant. So it is that in *Paisajes*, those who still cling to the ideals of a perfect society being ordered according to spiritual values – the Disneylandia thugs – are now a fanatical, violent minority or, in the case of the Albania utopians, a harmless clique of dreamers, and those who wish to retain a superior status to the immigrants are nothing but a group of café bores and bogus activists, a far cry from the ominous figures of authority with massive popular support depicted in the trilogy. There the community leaders – priests, doctors, intellectuals (not to mention Figurón/Séneca/Tonelete (the Figurehead/Seneca/Barrel – shaped gentleman) himself in *Don Julián*) – are all on the side of order, whereas in *Paisajes* they have become a powerless old guard, swamped by the forces of chaos. Western society has undergone the long-sought metamorphosis at the hands of the non-European immigrant population.

Thus, with *esquizofrenia colectiva* and ordered hierarchy dismantled, the battle of the title is indeed over and the yearning to break out of rigidity, so powerful throughout the trilogy, is now satisfied.

Perhaps this is why the language and presentation of the text no longer need to challenge the reader with their unrelenting fluidity. The literary and linguistic freedom fight is also over, now that the walls of Le Sentier are decorated with Arabic graffiti as well as French, harking back to the ending of *Juan sin tierra*; the aggressively expressed wish of the trilogy has become the everyday reality of *Paisajes*.

*   *   *

Although he is indisputably an innovative and unconventional modern writer, I have attempted to show that Goytisolo's very originality is at least partly due to the use he makes of traditional imagery and topoi. Far from detracting from it, the exploitation of the reader's preconceptions, based on the latter's sometimes virtually subliminal knowledge of literary, mythological, and religious tradition, renders Goytisolo's novels sometimes shocking, sometimes offensive and distasteful, but always challenging, always refreshing and exciting.

More important than the numerous allusions to specific characters or stories from mythology and Christian tradition, it is the abstract notions underlying the particular personages and narratives that, in the reading I have proposed, provide the basic thrust of the texts: duality, the cosmic and social order, chaos and fluidity of form, the union of opposites. It is around these antique patterns that Goytisolo constructs the symbolic and ideological architecture of the texts – whether consciously or unwittingly – and in this broad sense, he pays brilliant homage to the traditions of the Church and classical antiquity. Beneath the torrential diatribe there is a much more powerful counter-current that implicitly acknowledges their priceless artistic value. And in the swirling waters stirred by the opposing streams in the discourse, Goytisolo realizes his ideal: ceaseless flux, chaos, unity.

# Afterword

Goytisolo's most recent work of fiction is *Las virtudes del pájaro solitario*, published in 1988. It constitutes a new move in the evolution of his literature, but at the same time it develops many of the preoccupations that were present in the trilogy, *Makbara*, and *Paisajes después de la batalla*, both thematic and stylistic. Like *Makbara*, the narrator's gender is fluid; like *Paisajes*, a fragmented narrative revolves around the notion of an apocalyptic catastrophe, not fully understood by the narrative voice. And as *Don Julián* conducted a dialogue with other writers, but especially Góngora, *Juan sin tierra* especially with Cervantes, and *Makbara* especially with the Arcipreste de Hita, so Goytisolo informs us that San Juan de la Cruz's *Cántico espiritual* 'vertebra la estructura de la novela' (*VPS*, p. 171; St John of the Cross's *Spiritual Canticle* 'forms the backbone of the novel's structure'). As with its predecessors, though, the text stands up dazzlingly on its own too, teeming with perplexing images, challenging the reader to question preconceptions both about literature and present-day socio-cultural values.

I shall limit myself here to considering the text in the light of the arguments posited in this study. There is, firstly, an interesting development of the *esquizofrenia colectiva* phenomenon in its *cáscara/pulpa* manifestation. It would seem that the concept has expanded beyond an individual to a collective sphere. *Don Julián*'s armoured *carpetovetónico* and his daughter concealing a sensual identity beneath a nun's habit; the narrator's child-self hiding his sexuality under a shell of innocent piety; *Juan sin tierra*'s colonial women and their vain attempts to contain their carnality within a shell of white skin and garments: all these manifestations of the topos (and the rest) were confined to individuals, no matter how paradigmatic it was implied that such individuals were. In *Virtudes*, the focus widens to encompass a whole scene *en bloc*. A group of characters is repeatedly to be found chatting on a sunny hotel terrace, a tray of drinks before them and a pretty sea view in the background, but 'todo era fachada y lo sabíamos, el líquido se eternizaba en los vasos, nadie retiraba la bandeja ni reponía los cubitos de hielo, ningún camarero se asomaba a inspeccionar la terraza' (*VPS*, p. 20; 'it was all a façade and we knew it, the liquid remained eternally in the glasses, nobody took away the tray or replaced the ice-cubes, no waiter appeared to check on the terrace'). The scenery is equally artificial, but nobody understands why, or at least, nobody wants to admit to understanding: 'cómo era posible que el sol se prolongara indefinidamente su incendio, las nubes no mudaran su lisonjera rubicundez y un ave perfilada con inocente esbeltez se cerniera por espacio de horas sin mover siquiera las alas?' (*VPS*, p. 20; 'How was it possible that the sun should prolong its fire indefinitely, the clouds not alter their soothing chubbiness and a bird in innocently slender outline, hover for hours without even moving its wings?') The characters feel safer living in this stage-set and studiously avoiding all but the most banal conversation, existing, as it were, at the *cáscara* level of lifeless trivia and artificiality.

But as in the trilogy, the *pulpa* inevitably seeps through. They hear 'discursos *filtrados* a través de talares y bambalinas, consejos elementales, consejos ... difundidos *en sordina* por altavoces' (*VPS*, p. 20, my italics; 'speeches offstage *filtered* through wings and flies, elementary advice, *muffled* advice ... broadcast from loudspeakers'). Instead of focusing on each individual as made up of a *cáscara* and a *pulpa*, the collective situation is a shell in which the characters seek refuge together; but it is as permeable as the *niñas*' white skirts in *Juan sin tierra*, as liable to crack and crumble as the *carpetovetónico*'s armour in *Don Julián*, as superficial as his daughter's nun's habit.

Although it is tempting to assert that the image is not parallel because the *pulpa* of the real world is depicted as outside the artificial shell in *Virtudes*, rather than inside, as in the trilogy, this is less clear-cut than it might at first seem. Exteriority and interiority melted together in the trilogy in this regard, with Alvarito's adult, sexual persona—his *pulpa*—presented in *Don Julián* as another person outside himself. In *Virtudes* too, there is a fusion of exterior and interior: 'lo que occuría fuera parecía responder como un eco a la devastación interior que nos asolaba' (*VPS*, p. 20; 'what was happening outside seemed to answer echo-like to the internal devastation which was destroying us').

Later in the text, the motif returns to the individual frame of
reference, with an allusion to the classical and Christian image of the
body as the soul's prison; however, since the soul in *Virtudes* is no
longer the cruel torturer of natural corporality, but rather a provider
of sensual pleasure through the mystical experience, the prison
becomes a temple: 'mil muertes llevaba ya tragadas para salir de la
cárcel del cuerpo' ('a thousand deaths had I already devoured to leave
the prison of the body'), gives way in the following paragraph, to an
attack on those Christians who only 'buscaban la presencia del
Amado en un templo de cantos y no la hallaban en su fuero interno,
en la sustancia de sus templos vivos! (*VPS*, p. 81; 'they sought the
Beloved's presence in a temple of chanting and they did not find it in
their inner depths, in the substance of their living temples!').

This positive value of soul-life develops a change in direction
already detectable in *Makbara*, where religious faith acted as a *compensación necesaria* for the hardship of everyday reality; the discussion
of this shift away from bitter opposition to religion in the trilogy
applies to *Virtudes*, but with one important added feature. No longer
is Christianity unequivocally opposed to Islam, the former being
treated as invariably damaging and the latter as potentially life-
enhancing. Now the common imagery of mysticism draws the two
together, creating a harmonious relationship, as the quotations that
open the work demonstrate:

'En la interior bodega
de mi Amado bebí'
      San Juan de la Cruz, *Cántico espiritual*
'un vino que nos embriagó
antes de la creación de la viña'
    Ibn Al Farid, *Al Jamriya*


(In the inner wine-cellar
of my Beloved I drank[1]
a wine that intoxicated us
before the creation of the vine)

For the first time in Goytisolo's literature, *Virtudes* accepts an element of Christianity as positive: Christian mysticism. However, it
is stressed that the mystical experience transcends the dogma of one
religion or another: 'las nociones y símbolos de apretura y anchura,
subida al monte, fuente interior, lámparas de fuego o pájaro solitario
sobre los que unos y otros trabajamos no obedecen muy pro-

bablemente a lecturas furtivas del santo sino a vivencias convergentes en un deliquio y suspensión ajenos al cuerpo de las doctrinas' (*VPS*, p. 88; 'the notions and symbols of tightness and looseness, going up to the mountain [or forest], inner fountain, lamps of fire or solitary bird on which we both work, are very probably not attributable to furtive readings of the saint, but to converging experiences of an ecstasy and suspended state alien to the corpus of doctrines').

Rather than a total overturning of the anti-Christian stance of its predecessors then, *Virtudes* can be seen as consistent with their underlying message as I have interpreted it, indeed as a reinforcement and confirmation of my reading. On the one hand, it supports the contention that the life of the spirit is not condemned or devalued *per se* in Goytisolo's fiction, but rather, it is attacked only if it demands that the body should be treated as an inferior component of man, causing unnecessary suffering. Once the spirit can improve life and does not reject the body but rejoice in it, as the mystical tradition does with its sensual imagery and symbolism, then Goytisolo clearly is in favour. It is to his credit that he is willing to recognize this element of Christianity and in so doing to demolish claims by critics and commentators that he shows groundless prejudice against the Church and in favour of Islam.

In short, *Virtudes* focuses on a variety of Christianity that does not make a damaging division of bad body from good soul, but on a mode that has no truck with the despised *esquizofrenia colectiva*.

Although canonized and venerated now, San Juan de la Cruz was, of course, a pariah in his own lifetime, imprisoned and subjected to brutal treatment. As such, Goytisolo's interest in him continues his lifelong preoccupation with society's underdogs, dating right back to his concern for Andalusians in the early fiction and *Señas*, to North Africans and the sexually heterodox in the trilogy, *Makbara*, and *Paisajes*. Hence, despite the unexpectedness of finding a respectful, positive treatment of a Christian saint in Goytisolo – one recalls the very different treatment reserved for Saint Simeon Stylite in *Juan sin tierra*, for example, and for virtuous Christians in general, the Père de Foucauld in *Juan sin tierra*, or the evangelist thumped by the protagonist of *Makbara* – San Juan fits in with the stance adopted throughout his literary career: he is favouring a pariah who, moreover, blended the corporal and spiritual sides of man through his poetry by expressing the mystical union as a profoundly erotic and sensual experience. Even more akin to Goytisolo, San Juan does not balk at gender ambiguity, taking the feminine role in the mystical encounter, as in the Song of Songs, but also moving fluidly between male

and female voices, as well as transcending conventions of the mascu-
line role in lovemaking when, for example, he describes the Amado
as 'giving his breast' to the Amada (verse 27).

What of the concept of order and chaos? Does this text continue
the attack on order and revaluation of chaos that was such a powerful
driving force before? On one level, the opposition between order and
chaos, the former unequivocally associated with the execrated establishment and the latter with freedom and fecundity, melts away in
*Virtudes*, as one might have expected given that the battle was already
over in *Paisajes*. In a depiction of an *auto-da-fé* in *Virtudes*, for
example, we find a breathless succession of short phrases, the style
reserved for chaotic environments in the preceding works:
'sahumerios, plegarias, charanga de cornetas y tambores, cantos
apagados por el griterío de la multitud . . . el gentío se arracimaba en
torno a las jaulas' (*VPS*, pp. 97–8; 'clouds of incense, prayers, din of
cornets and drums, chanting drowned by the clamour of the
multitude . . . the crowd clustered around the cages'). And the victims inside the cages, with whom our sympathies lie, are seeking an
'equilibrio etéreo' (*VPS*, p. 98; an 'ethereal equilibrium'), surely a
type of order amidst the chaotic, hostile throng, Moreover, the
former pleasure found in a descent to the underworld and in particular to the sewers, with their infernal associations with chaos, is also
gone in *Virtudes*. Now it is a harrowing experience:

> había perecido ahogado, sumido en la espiral del remolino, atraído
> al vórtice del abismo por la fuerza torrencial de las aguas?
> una neta sensación de asfixia y la conciencia de haber luchado en
> vano contra la irresistible succión que le tragaba abonaban la tesis
> de la caída, sorbido por la vorágine evacuatoria de las acometidas
> camino de la red de alcantarillado
> alguien, arriba, había accionado simplemente una palanca, impul-
> sando la tromba de agua y su descenso a las entrañas envuelto en
> las volutas del torbellino? como esas cucarachas moscas u hor-
> migas aposentadas en la taza del excusado que examinamos
> brevemente, con oscura satisfacción, antes de desencadenar el
> mecanismo exterminador de su existencia parasitaria, había sido
> contemplado a su vez por el omnímodo e ignoto ejecutor de otra
> sentencia igualmente azarosa e inapelable?
> quién, cómo, por qué?
> ninguna respuesta o explicación, sólo el recuerdo de su sofoco,
> inmersión, busca desesperada de aire
>
> (*VPS*, p. 133)

(drowned, plunged into the whirling spiral, drawn to the vortex of
the abyss by the torrential force of the waters?
a clear sensation of choking and awareness of having struggled in
vain against the irresistible suction which was swallowing him,
supported the thesis of the fall, sucked down by the flushing
maelstrom of the attacks on the way to the sewer system
somebody up there has simply pulled a lever, setting off a whirling
downrush of water and his ['her' and 'their' also possible] descent
to the bowels enveloped in the swirls of the typhoon like those
cockroaches flies or ants residing in the lavatory bowl that we
examine briefly, with obscure satisfaction, before unleashing the
mechanism to exterminate their parasitic existence, contemplated
in his ['her', 'their'] turn by the all-embracing and unknown
executor of another equally random and unappealable sentence
who, how, why?
no answer or explanation, only the memory of his ['her', 'their']
suffocation, immersion, desperate search for air)

On the other hand, whilst this stance reverses the approach
discussed in chapter 4 on a thematic level, Goytisolo's use of language in his latest novel powerfully restates the case for chaos as a
mode of writing. *Virtudes* exploits the potential of Goytisolo's self-
emancipation from the rules of grammar and presentation, as the
passage just quoted demonstrates. The omission of the opening
question mark required by Spanish, coupled with the lack of any
indication through word order that a given phrase is interrogative,
for example, causes the reader at first to mistake questions for
statements, here as in the trilogy and *Makbara*. Hence, the narrator's
doubts are actively transferred as the reader grows accustomed to
this practice and starts every new phrase wondering whether it will
turn out to be a question. In other words, the insecurity of the
narrative voice is matched by reader insecurity, reminiscent of the
aim expressed in *Juan sin tierra* of teaching the reader to doubt. And
surely, such literary insecurity is antithetical to order, which by its
nature entails predictability. So even if chaos no longer needs to be
exalted in the thematic content of the text, the victory of chaos
continues to be enjoyed in the style of *Virtudes*.

Another way of undermining the reader's confidence in his understanding of the text, to be found in this new novel, was also used
before, most prominently from *Juan sin tierra* through to *Paisajes*.
This is the technique of having object pronouns without any clear
deixis, one example of which appears in the passage quoted above

('la irresistible succión que *le* tragaba', 'the irresistible suction which was swallowing *him*'). Added to this is a further element, namely, the mystery surrounding the identity or identities of the narrator or narrators. Not only do these change without warning in *Virtudes*, as they did in the trilogy and *Makbara*, but also there is often no clue as to who each one is. Sometimes, as in the drowning passage quoted, there is not even any indication as to whether the discourse is in the first or third person. In the trilogy and *Makbara*, either the content or the register of unattributed passages indicated, if not always the precise individual speaking, at least a rough categorization, such as 'a voice of the establishment', 'of the Church', 'of the mass media'. But in *Virtudes*, the narrator's identity often remains totally impenetrable and susceptible, therefore, to multiple readings.

One way of approaching this is to recall the storyteller figure of *Makbara*, who speaks with all the voices of his characters and imagine an unstated person of similar function behind the text of *Virtudes*. However, the fact that such a person does not appear in the text makes the idea rather presumptious and seems to me to over-simplify the presentation. It would be more faithful to the work to take the voices and their obscurities at face value, unsettling as this may be for a reader accustomed to texts whose mysteries can be cracked through careful study. In a way, this can be regarded as the outcome of Goytisolo's aspirations to a state of ultimate fluidity; gone are the spectacular metamorphoses from one fixed narrator-identity to another and instead we have only total freedom of movement of the narrative voice because it has no identity from which to depart or metamorphose. We read, for example, at the beginning of the last sub-section of chapter 5:

habla, dijo
era el doctor?, un simple carcelero?, acaso el maldiciente prior de los Calzados? el Nuncio Apostólico en persona?, algún comisario o verdugo a órdenes del Tostado?

(VPS, p. 163)

(speak, he/she/it said
Was he/she/it/I the doctor?, a simple jailer?, perhaps the evil-tongued prior of the Calced?, the Papal Nuncio in person?, some superintendent or executioner at the orders of the Tanned One?)

As the alternatives I have given in the translation demonstrate – and they are not exhaustive – the Spanish leaves all the subjects and objects open; the series of suggestions offered by the narrator remain multiply equivocal because they may refer to possible identities of the person commanded to speak, the person issuing the command, and/or the person recording all this. Thus, *Virtudes* forges ahead of Goytisolo's previous fiction in finding a mode of language that extends the idea of formlessness into new realms.

And yet, he manages not to alienate the reader by means of a startlingly simple device. Instead of adopting the patronizing, teacherly approach of *Juan sin tierra*'s 'enseñarle a dudar' ('to teach him to doubt') towards the reader, he comes over to our side, as it were, confessing his own puzzlement at the obscurities of the text. The series of interrogatives quoted above are not the teasing questions of an omniscient narrator, but the sympathetic gropings of a narrative voice as bewildered as we are. This impression is reinforced by the fact that *era*, like 'was' in English, is both the third- and first-person form of the verb: the narrator is asking not only who the characters are, but also who he is himself.

The reader can, if he needs to find a logical explanation, see the whole text of *Virtudes* as a hallucinatory dream-sequence, clinging to the opening sub-section of chapter 2: 'las pesadillas, cuitas, anacronías, cambio abrupto de temas y personajes, ubicación ambigua de los paisajes, mutación de voces, vaguedad y fragmentos de tramas oníricas ... /había sido todo efecto de los fármacos' (*VPS*, p. 47; 'the nightmares, anxieties, anachronies, sudden changes of subject and characters, ambiguous locations of scenery, mutations of voices, vagueness and fragments of dreamlike plots ... /it had all been the effect of the drugs'). But the text later challenges us implicitly to dispense with such rationalization, when a discussion of the wealth of commentary on San Juan's *Cántico*, cries out to be applied to Goytisolo's own literature. And here would seem to lie the reaffirmation of the message of the previous novels, attacking the rigidity of order and its constraining, limiting effects, and preferring the freedom of fluid, unordered meaning. If any more evidence were needed, here surely, the case for chaos rests:

> era posible descifrar las oscuridades del texto, hallar una clave explicativa unívoca, desentrañar su sentido oculto mediante el recurso a la alegoría, circunscribir sus ambigüedades lingüísticas, establecer una rigurosa crítica filológica, buscar una significación estrictamente literal, acudir a interpretaciones éticas y anagógicas, enderezar su sintaxis maleable, esclarecer los presuntos dislates, paliar su señera y abrupta radicalidad, estructurar, disponer, aco-

tar, reducir, esforzarse en atrapar su inmensidad y liquidez, capturar la sutileza del viento con una red, inmovilizar sus inasibles fluctuaciones y cambios oníricos, reproducir el acendrado esplendor del incendio místico mediante la acumulación de glosas, lecturas, fichas, notas académicas y apostillas, observaciones plúmbeas, gravosas ordenaciones sintácticas, exégesis filtradoras, páginas y páginas de prosa redundante y amazacotada?
no sería mejor anegarse de una vez en la infinitud del poema, aceptar la impenetrabilidad de sus misterios y opacidades, liberar tu propio lenguaje de grillos racionales, abandonarlo al campo magnético de sus imantaciones secretas, favorecer la onda de su expansión, admitir pluralidad y simultaneidad de sentidos, depurar la incandescencia verbal, la llama y dulce cautiverio de su amor vivo?

(VPS, p. 59)

(the possibility of deciphering the text's obscurities, of finding a univocal explanatory key, of disembowelling its occult sense by recourse to allegory, circumscribing its linguistic ambiguities, establishing a rigorous philological criticism, seeking a strictly literal signification, calling on ethical and anagogical interpretations, straightening out its malleable syntax, clarifying the presumed aberrations, palliating its outstanding and abrupt radicality, structuring, disposing, fencing in, reducing, trying to trap its immensity and liquidity, capturing the subtlety of the wind in a net, immobilizing its ungraspable fluctuations and dreamlike changes, reproducing the pure splendour of the mystic fire by means of the accumulation of glosses, readings, card indices, academic notes and jottings, leaden observations, tedious syntactic ordering, filtering exegeses, pages and pages of redundant, clogged prose?
would it not be better to immerse oneself once and for all in the poem's infinitude, to accept the impenetrability of its mysteries and opacities, to liberate your own language from rational shackles, to abandon it to the magnetic field of its secret pulls, to be carried along on the growing wave, to admit plurality and simultaneity of sense, to distil the verbal incandescence, the flame and sweet searing of its living love?)

# Notes

## Introduction

1. For details of publishers, see 'Editions and Abbreviations'.
2. Juan Goytisolo, *Reivindicación del conde don Julián*, edited by Linda Gould Levine, with an appendix by José Manuel Martín, Letras Hispánicas (Madrid, 1985).
3. Carlos-Peregrín Otero, 'Lengua y cultura en *Juan sin tierra*', in *Juan sin tierra*, edited by Octavio Paz and others, Espiral/Revista 2 (Madrid, 1977), pp. 125–49 (p. 132).
   Genaro J. Pérez, *Formalist Elements in the Novels of Juan Goytisolo*, Studia Humanitatis (Potomac, Maryland, 1979), pp. 117–18.
   See also Abigail E. Lee, 'Sterne's Legacy to Juan Goytisolo: A Shandyian Reading of *Juan sin tierra*', *Modern Language Review*, 84 (April 1989), 351–7.
4. Pérez, pp. 136–7, 145–6, 164, and 192–3.
5. Severo Sarduy, 'La desterritorialización', in *Juan Goytisolo*, edited by Gonzalo Sobejano and others, Espiral/Fundamentos (Madrid, 1975), pp. 175–83 (p. 180).
   Guillermo Cabrera Infante, 'El fin como principio', in *Juan sin tierra*, edited by Paz, pp. 225–9 (p. 228).
6. Sarduy, p. 181.
   Michael Ugarte, *Trilogy of Treason: An Intertextual Study of Juan Goytisolo* (Columbia, Missouri and London, 1982), pp. 123 and 119–20.
7. Pérez, pp. 185–6.
   Linda Gould Levine, *La destrucción creadora*, Confrontaciones: Los Críticos (Mexico City, 1976), p. 253.
   'Presentación crítica de J. M. Blanco White', in *Obra inglesa de D. José María Blanco White*, translated and edited by Juan Goytisolo, Biblioteca Breve, third edition (Barcelona, 1982), pp. 1–98.
8. Claudia Schaefer-Rodríguez, *Juan Goytisolo: del 'realismo crítico' a la utopía*, Ensayos (Madrid, 1984), p. 104.
9. Gould Levine, *Destrucción creadora*, p. 170.
   Jesús Lázaro, *La novelística de Juan Goytisolo* (Madrid, 1984), pp. 147 and 150.
10. Jerome Bernstein, 'Cuerpo, lenguaje y divinidad en *Juan sin tierra*', in *Juan sin tierra*, edited by Paz, pp. 151–69 (pp. 154 and 164).
11. Schaefer-Rodríguez, p. 69.
    Lázaro, p. 152.
12. Juan Goytisolo, *Coto vedado* Biblioteca Breve (Barcelona, 1985).
    Juan Goytisolo, *En los reinos de Taifa*, Biblioteca Breve, second edition (Barcelona, 1986).
    An English translation of *Coto vedado* is about to be published in Berkeley, California by North Point Press and very soon in Lon-

don by Quartet Books.

13. Juan Goytisolo, 'Por qué he escogido vivir en París', in *Voces: Juan Goytisolo*, edited by Pere Gimferrer (Barcelona, 1981). pp. 9–11 (p. 10).

14. George Orwell, *Nineteen Eighty-Four: A Novel*, Penguin Modern Classics (Harmondsworth, Middlesex, 1954), pp. 7, 34–5, and 241–2.

15. Juan Goytisolo, 'Hemos vivido una ocupación', in *Libertad, libertad, libertad*, Colección Ibérica (Barcelona, 1978), pp. 20–9 (p. 21).

16. In *Obras completas*, Biblioteca de Autores Modernos, 2 vols (Madrid, 1977), II, 721–803.

17. *En los reinos de Taifa*, p. 163.

18. Interview with Jacques de Decker in the Belgian newspaper, *Le Soir* (31 December 1985) and 'Abandonemos de una vez el amoroso cultivo de nuestras señas de identidad', *El país* (10 April 1984), respectively.

19. 'Regreso al origen', interview with Miguel Riera, *Quimera* 73 (January 1988), 36–40 (pp. 37 and 38).

20. Interview with José A. Hernández, *Modern Language Notes*, 91/2 (1976), 337–55 (p. 340).

21. Karl Ruthven, *Myth*, The Critical Idiom, 31 (London, 1976).

22. Mircea Eliade, *Myth and Reality*, World Perspectives, 21 (London, 1964), pp. 8 and 198–200.

23. Eliade, *Myth and Reality*, p. 5.

24. I follow John J. White's usage here, as he establishes it in *Mythology and the Modern Novel: A Study of Prefigurative Techniques* (Princeton, New Jersey, 1971), p. 7, but with a certain shift in emphasis necessitated by the nature of Goytisolo's fiction; essentially, this entails a greater concentration on patterns in mythology and less analysis of individual characters and plots.

25. Carl Gustav Jung, *Psychology and Religion*, The Terry Lectures (New Haven, Connecticut, 1938), pp. 63–4.

26. Jane Harrison, *Epilegomena to the Study of Greek Religion* (Cambridge, 1921), p. 32.

# Chapter 1

1. Interview with José A. Hernández (1975), p. 341.

2. The Spanish title puns on the double meaning of *duelo*, so that the title could be translated literally as both 'duel' and 'mourning' in paradise.

3. Juan Goytisolo, *Juegos de manos* (1954), Destinolibro, 39, (Barcelona, 1977), p. 146.
Juan Goytisolo, *The Young Assassins*, translated by John Rust (London, 1960), p. 139.

4. *Juegos de manos*, p. 150 (quotation) and p. 255 (realization that former self is dead); *The Young Assassins*, pp. 143 and 247, respectively.

5. Juan Goytisolo, *Duelo en el Paraíso*, Destinolibro, 63, third edition (Barcelona, 1985), p. 173.

6. *Duelo en el Paraíso*, p. 164.

7. *Duelo en el Paraíso*, p. 273.

8. *Campos de Níjar* in Juan Goytisolo, *Obras completas*, Biblioteca de Autores Modernos, 2 vols (Madrid, 1977), II, 341–427.
*La Chanca* in *Obras completas*, II, 609–716.

9. Juan Goytisolo, 'La Chanca, veinte años después', in *Voces*, edited by Gimferrer, pp. 12–14 (p. 12).

10. Emir Rodríguez Monegal, *El arte de narrar: diálogos* (conversations with various authors), Prisma (Caracas, 1968) pp. 165–98 (pp. 178–9).

11. Interview with José A. Hernández, p. 341.

12. Geo Widengren, *Mani and Manichaeism*, translated by Charles Kessler and revised by the author, History of Religion (London, 1965), pp. 43–4.

13. In the first edition of *SI*, Alvaro looks at himself in a mirror and feels alienated from his ageing outer appearance; the gulf between *cáscara* and *pulpa* ('shell' and 'pulp') is already preoccupying him on an age-related basis. However, the thrust of the anguish this causes is reversed; in the first edition of *SI*, he regrets the loss of his youthful exterior, whereas from *DJ* onwards, he is only too keen to expunge all vestiges of his early persona. Juan Goytisolo, *Señas de identidad*, Novelistas Contemporáneos (Mexico City, 1966), p. 453.

## Chapter 2

1. Commentary on part of Lenten Sermon 10 on the Psalm 'He Who Dwells', in Etienne Gilson, *The Mystical Theology of Saint Bernard*, translated by A. H. C. Downes (London, 1940), p. 231.
2. See Introduction for use of *Christian* meaning 'Roman Catholic'.
3. Juan Goytisolo, 'Remedios de la concupiscencia según Fray Tierno', in *Libertad, libertad, libertad*, pp. 95–108 (pp. 95–6).
4. Examples may be found in Revelation 3.4–5 (white); Romans 13.12 (black); Jeremiah 2.22 (stains).
5. Robert C. Spires, 'From Neorealism and the New Novel to the Self-Referential Novel: Juan Goytisolo's *Juan sin tierra*', *Anales de la narrativa española contemporánea*, 5 (1980), 73–82 (p. 80).
6. *Plato's Phaedo*, translated with introduction and commentary by R. Hackforth (Cambridge, 1955), pp. 36, 38.
   Plato's approach and Pauline interpretation of it will be discussed more fully below.
7. *Plato's Phaedo*, pp. 46, 47, 83, 92.
8. Geoffrey Parrinder, *Sex in the World's Religions* (London, 1980), pp. 206–7.

9. Blaise Pascal, *Pensées*, Brunschvicg text (Paris, 1976), p. 69.
10. Juan Goytisolo, 'Quevedo: la obsesión excremental', in *Disidencias*, Biblioteca Breve (Barcelona, 1977), pp. 117–35 (p. 124).
11. This echoes the psychological problem of Freud's Wolf Man. See the *Pelican Freud Library*, edited by A. Richards, 9, translated by J. Strachey (Harmondsworth, Middx, 1979), pp. 298–9 and for an illuminating discussion of the case, Peter Stallybrass and Allon White, *The Politics and Poetics of Transgression* (London, 1986) pp. 165–7.
12. Manuel García Morente, *Idea de la hispanidad*, expanded third edition (Madrid, 1947), pp. 63, 21–22, 74, respectively.
13. García Morente, p. 86.
14. See Abigail Lee Six, 'Breaking Rules, Making History: A Postmodern Reading of Historiography in Juan Goytisolo's Fiction', in forthcoming *Yearbook of Postmodern Studies: History and Postmodern Writing* (Leiden, 1990).
15. García Morente, p. 63.
16. St Thomas Aquinas, *Summa Theologiae*, edition and translation led by Michael Cardinal Browne and Aniceto Fernández, 61 vols (London, 1964–81), XXVIII (1966), translated and edited by Thomas Gilby, 1a, 2ae., Qu.95, Art.1, point 3 (p. 101).
17. Manuel García Morente, p. 114. The interchangeability of *cristiano* and *católico* in the quotation is noteworthy (see Introduction).
18. See Goytisolo's essay, 'Supervivencias tribales en el medio intelectual español' (*Disidencias*, pp. 137–49), in which García Morente is cited amongst others as a writer familiar to schoolchildren and students of Goytisolo's generation.
19. Angel Ganivet, *Idearium español*,

third reprinting (Madrid, 1915), pp. 7–8. The significance of the allusion to Sagredo will be discussed in chapter 6.

20. Alain René Lesage, *Histoire de Gil Blas de Santillane* (1715–35), edited by Maurice Bardon, 2 vols (Paris, 1955), first published 1715–35. This will be discussed fully in chapter 6.

21. Miguel de Cervantes Saavedra, *El ingenioso hidalgo don Quijote de la Mancha*, edited by John Jay Allen, Letras Hispánicas, 2 vols (Madrid, 1977), II, ch. 47, p. 372.
*The Adventures of Don Quixote*, translated by J. M. Cohen, Penguin Classics (London, 1950), p. 765. Although the translations of the two texts are not identical, notice how much closer the Spanish texts are.

22. Manuel García Morente, pp. 215–17.

23. Juan Goytisolo, 'De "Don Julián" a "Makbara": una posible lectura orientalista', in *Crónicas sarracinas* (Barcelona, 1982), pp. 27–46 (p. 29).

24. As above.

25. Juan Goytisolo, *El país*, 10 April 1984, 11.

26. Schaefer-Rodríguez, pp. 58, 61, 69.

27. 'De "Don Julián" a "Makbara"...', p. 31.

28. Juan Goytisolo, 'Vicisitudes del mudejarismo: Juan Ruiz, Cervantes, Galdós', in *Crónicas sarracinas*, pp. 47–71 (p. 71).

29. Carl Gustav Jung, *Modern Man in Search of a Soul*, translated by W. S. Dell and Cary F. Baynes (London, 1933), pp. 236, 40, 144, respectively.

30. For a fuller discussion of this utopian vision in *JT*, and of the author's approach to the ideal society in general, see chapter 4.

31. 'Quevedo: la obsesión excremental', in *Disidencias*, p. 124.

32. This is Linda Gould Levine's opinion too; see her '*Juan sin tierra*: Goytisolo se retrata', in *Juan sin tierra*, edited by Paz, p. 43.

33. 'Quevedo: la obsesión excremental', in *Disidencias*, pp. 118–19.

34. *Modern Language Notes*, p. 345.

35. Juan-Eduardo Cirlot, *Diccionario de símbolos tradicionales* (Barcelona, 1958), p. 293.

36. Cirlot, p. 293.

37. Annie Perrin and Françoise Zmantar, 'El mito del laberinto', in *Voces*, pp. 33–54 (p. 33).

38. For a more detailed analysis of this passage, see Lee Six, 'Breaking Rules, Making History'.

39. Genaro Pérez, p. 135.

## Chapter 3

1. Sir James George Frazer, *The Golden Bough: A Study in Magic and Religion*, third edition, 13 vols (London, 1980), Part II: *Taboo and the Perils of the Soul*.
Mary Douglas, *Purity and Danger: An Analysis of Concepts of Pollution and Taboo* (London, 1966), pp. 68–69.

2. Duncan B. Forester, *Caste and Christianity: Attitudes and Policies on Caste of Anglo-Saxon Protestant Missions in India* (London, 1980), p. 16.

3. Michael Adams, *Single-minded: A Tract on Chastity, mainly in the Context of Celibacy* (Dublin, 1979), p. 43.

4. Schaefer-Rodríguez, p. 48.

5. Miguel de Unamuno, *Abel Sánchez: una historia de pasión* (1917), in *Obras completas*, edited by Manuel García Blanco, 9 vols (Madrid, 1967), II, pp. 683–759 (pp. 689 and 747). The translations are my own.

6. Hermann Hesse, *Steppenwolf* (1927), translated by Basil Creighton, revised by Walter Sorell (London, 1974), p. 94.

7. In *Juan sin tierra*, edited by Paz, pp. 95–105 (p. 97).

8. Juan Goytisolo, 'Presentación crítica de J. M. Blanco White', p. 97.

9. Robert A. Baron and Donn Byrne, *Social Psychology: Understanding Human Interaction*, second edition (Boston, Massachusetts, 1978), p. 260.
Gresham M. Sykes and David Matza, 'Techniques of Neutralization: A Theory of Delinquency', *American Sociological Review*, 22 (December, 1957), 667–9, quoted in Howard S. Becker, *Outsiders: Studies in the Sociology of Deviance* (London, 1963), p. 29.

10. Gould Levine, *Destrucción creadora*, p. 21.

11. Charles A. Kiesler and Sara B. Kiesler, *Conformity* (Reading, Massachusetts, 1970), p. 3.

12. In *Crónicas sarracinas*, p. 71.

13. In *Voces*, pp. 15–22 (p. 18).

14. Leslie T. Wilkins, *Social Deviance: Social Policy, Action and Research* (London, 1964), p. 71.

15. Attacks on Goytisolo in the press during the 1960s are documented by Gould Levine (*Destrucción creadora*, pp. 26–9 and accompanying notes). Accusations of betrayal of literary conventions are also parodied in *JT* throughout section VI (*JT*, pp. 237–305; *JL*, pp. 209–58).

16. *Formalist Elements . . .*, p. 127.

17. Hyam Maccoby, *The Sacred Executioner: Human Sacrifice and the Legacy of Guilt* (London, 1982), p. 126.

18. *Flor nueva de romances viejos*, edited by R. Menéndez Pidal, expanded second edition (Madrid, 1933); Romance segundo, pp. 55–6 (p. 56); Romance cuarto, pp. 57–8.

19. *Flor nueva*, pp. 63–6 (p. 66).

20. Maccoby, p. 128.

21. Gould Levine's observations on the *verdugo-víctima* in *SI* in the context of its relationship with the earlier novels are most instructive. See *Destrucción creadora*, p. 19.

22. Perrin and Zmantar's description of Jerónimo as 'un hombre sin identidad, sin ataduras, que desaparece sin dejar huellas' ('a man with no identity, no ties, who disappears without trace') could also be applied to the protagonist of *PB*, further illuminating their similarities (*Voces*, p. 39).

23. In *Libertad, libertad, libertad*, pp. 30–48 (p. 43); Goytisolo's italics.

24. Stallybrass and White indicate this connection between dualism and hierarchy too: 'Although there are all sorts of subtle degrees and gradations in a culture it is striking that the extremes of high and low have a special and often powerful symbolic charge . . . This does not necessarily militate against subtlety since "above" and "below" may be inscribed within a minutely discriminatory system of classification' (p. 3).

## Chapter 4

1. Northrop Frye, 'Varieties of Literary Utopias', in *Utopias and Utopian Thought*, edited by Frank E. Manuel (Boston, Massachusetts, 1971), pp. 25–49 (p. 31).

2. Alexandre Cioranescu, *L'Avenir du passé: Utopie et littérature*, Les Essais, 171 (Paris, 1972), p. 44.

3. Samuel Butler, *Erewhon* (1872), edited by Peter Mudford, Penguin English Library (Harmondsworth, Middlesex, 1970), p. 102.

4. Cioranescu, p. 237.

5. Butler, p. 121.

6. Schaefer-Rodríguez, p. 90.

7. Frye, in Manuel, ed., p. 27.

8. Jonathan Swift, *Gulliver's Travels* (1726), edited by Peter Dixon and John Chalker, Penguin Classics (Harmondsworth, Middlesex, 1985), pp. 265–346.

9. Other examples include the assertion that Jesus and Mary could not have performed bodily functions (*JT*, pp. 20–2; *JL*, pp. 11–13) and

the apologetics for the *auto-da-fé* (*JT*, pp. 173–82; *JL*, pp. 156–63).

10. More and Bellamy reduce work to a minimum; Morris makes work pleasurable. See Thomas More, *Utopia*, translated and edited by Paul Turner, Penguin Classics (Harmondsworth, Middlesex, 1965), pp. 75–6; Edward Bellamy, *Looking Backward* (1888), edited by Cecilia Tichi, The Penguin American Library (Harmondsworth, Middlesex, 1982), p. 70; William Morris, *News from Nowhere; or, an Epoch of Rest, being some chapters from a utopian romance* (1890), Routledge English Texts (London, 1970), p. 71. The dystopian vision of work as tedium is typified by Orwell; see *Nineteen Eighty-Four*, p. 38.

11. See Hesiod, *Works and Days*, translated and introduced by Dorothy Wender, Penguin Classics (Harmondsworth, Middlesex, 1973), p. 62.

12. Soubhi El-Saleh, *La Vie Future selon le Coran*, Etudes Musulmanes, 13 (Paris, 1971), p. 34.

13. Cioranescu, p. 56.

14. Cioranescu, p. 53.

15. More, p. 132.

16. Genaro Pérez lists the desire to return to the womb as a motif of *SI* (Pérez, p. 126). Thus, with hindsight provided by the post-*Señas* novels, the experience of going to the cinema while Dolores is having an abortion acquires a significance of which Alvaro himself is unconscious at the time.

17. Frye also proclaims this need to include corporality in utopias: 'New utopias would have to be . . . rooted in the body as well as in the mind . . . . Modern utopias will have to pay some attention to the lawless and violent lusts of the dreamer' (Manuel, ed., p. 27).

18. Genaro Pérez links this concept to the Latin heading in *JT*, 'FINIS CORONAT OPUS' (*JT*, p. 179; *JL*, p. 161), which, he explains, can mean 'the end sanctifies the means'; he points out that 'in this section, the priest Vosk tells the slaves they must accept their miserable condition in life as a means to gain eternal salvation' (Pérez, p. 192). In fact, this section contains the apologetics for the *auto-da-fé* – 'la [purificación] del alma del reo condenado a la pira dura escasamente diez minutos: y qué importa este lapso irrisorio frente a la gloria inmortal que os ofrece el Eterno!' (*JT*, p. 181; '[the purification] of the soul of the criminal sentenced to the stake lasts scarcely ten minutes: and what does this ridiculous lapse matter compared to the immortal glory offered you by the Eternal!', *JL*, pp. 162–3) – but the underlying message is parallel.

19. In *Disidencias*, pp. 121–2.

20. *The Koran Interpreted*, translation of Koran by Arthur J. Arberry (London, 1964).

21. F. Martínez de la Rosa, '¡Buenos seamos!', in *Prosa y verso: libro de lectura para parvulitos*, edited by Antonio Alvarez Pérez (Valladolid, 1962), pp. 56–7. The disembodied eye is also used with similar frightening implications by Federico García Lorca in the scenery of his play *El público* (edited by Rafael Martínez Nadal, Biblioteca Breve (Barcelona, 1978), p. 151).

22. Reinhard Kuhn, *Corruption in Paradise: The Child in Western Literature* (Hanover, New Hampshire, 1982), pp. 40–1 and 66.

23. *The Paradise of Dante Alighieri*, edited and translated by Arthur John Butler (London, 1885), 27.127–29. (This passage discussed in Kuhn, pp. 110–11.)

24. A parallel may be discerned in the relationship between the protagon-

ist of *PB* and his wife. The police threaten him with telling his wife about his exploits: '¿qué diría tu mujer si se enterara?' (*PB*, p. 122; 'what would your wife say if she found out?', *LB*, p. 98). Indeed, the protagonist is shown to be greatly distressed when she happens upon one of his obscene letters ('Consecuencias de un portazo intempestivo', *PB*, pp. 156–62; 'Il faut qu'une porte soit ouverte ou fermée', *LB*, pp. 126–31).

25.  Hythloday is the name of More's narrator in *Utopia*, who fell in love with the country when he happened upon it on his travels.

26.  More, p. 34; Butler, p. 39.

27.  Karl Mannheim, *Ideology and Utopia: An Introduction to the Sociology of Knowledge* (London, 1960), p. 210.

28.  In *Obras completas*, I, pp. 621–843 (p. 785).

29.  Gould Levine discusses the concepts of order and chaos in *Destrucción creadora*, pp. 132–41, but she concentrates on the structure and style of *DJ*, rather than on the nature of order and chaos themselves.

30.  In the first edition of *SI*, which has a section on Alvaro's stay in Cuba, a place he loves, Havana is described as having a 'ritmo caótico' (p. 417; 'chaotic rhythm').

31.  Schaefer-Rodríguez asserts that 'el aislamiento absoluto que sienten Mendiola y Goytisolo les conduce a la adopción de una actitude subjetiva de defensa (moral y artística) individual para sobrevivir al caos social' (p. 6; 'the absolute isolation felt by Mendiola and Goytisolo leads them to adopt a subjective attitude of individual defence (moral and artistic) in order to survive the social chaos'). I would argue, on the contrary, that they deliberately adopt a chaotic stance in an attempt to challenge and combat order-ridden societies.

However, Schaefer-Rodríguez seems ambivalent on this subject of order and chaos, for later on, she concedes: 'la satisfacción de la destrucción permanente, el caos y el desorden [son] como esencias ontológicas de la utopía de Mendiola' (p. 65; 'the satisfaction of permanent destruction, chaos and disorder [are] like ontological essences of Mendiola's utopia').

32.  'En *Juan sin tierra* el orden lógico y el temporal son sistemáticamente destruidos' ('In *Juan sin tierra*, logical and temporal order are systematically destroyed'), said Goytisolo in an interview with Julio Ortega (1974), transcribed in *Juan Goytisolo*, edited by Sobejano, pp. 121–36 (p. 127).

33.  *The Original Poems of Fray Luis de León*, edited by Edward Sarmiento, Spanish Texts (Manchester, 1953), pp. 18–20 (p. 19).
     *The Unknown Light: The Poems of Fray Luis de León*, edited and translated by Willis Barnstone (New York, 1979), pp. 58–63 (p. 61).

34.  Charles L. Sanford, *The Quest for Paradise: Europe and the American Moral Imagination* (Urbana, Illinois, 1961), pp. 112–13.

35.  In *Voces*, pp. 9–11 (p. 11).

36.  Dante's unusual depiction of the abode of the most wicked in hell as ice-cold, although unconventional, still conforms to the basic principle of opposition rather than distortion. The coolness of heaven should be understood as the pleasantness of a temperate climate, so that extremes of both heat and cold stand in opposition to it. The dystopian technique would entail a vision of temperate climate which would make this seem undesirable.

37.  Ernst Robert Curtius, *European Literature and the Latin Middle Ages*, translated by Willard R. Trask (London and Henley, 1979), p. 186.

38. For the Ancient Babylonian cosmogony, see Alexander Heidel, *The Babylonian Genesis: The Story of the Creation* (Chicago, 1942).

39. The association of the rural life with virtue and the city with vice may be traced back to the Bible. See Sanford pp. 29–31.

40. *The Original Poems*, pp. 6–8 (p. 7); *The Unknown Light*, pp. 52–7 (p. 55).

41. *The Original Poems*, pp. 18–20 (p. 20; *The Unknown Light*, pp. 58–63 (p. 63).

42. Karl Vossler, *La poesía de la soledad en España*, translated by Ramón Gómez de la Serna y Espina, Estudios Literarios (Buenos Aires, 1946), p. 184.

43. Whatever opinion Goytisolo may hold about the religious faith with which such Golden Age poetry is suffused, his recognition of the literary merits of the period is undiminished. The mockery to be found incorporated above all into the text of *DJ* is aimed 'menos a los clásicos que a la perspectiva de los mismos a través del prisma mezquino y reductor del 98', as Goytisolo said in the Julio Ortega interview (in *Juan Goytisolo*, edited by Sobejano, p. 125; 'less at the classics than at the perspective on them afforded by the small-minded, reductive prism of the Generation of 98' [a group of turn-of-the-century writers unctiously reverential towards their Golden Age forebears]).

44. The protagonist passes the door of D. Alvaro Peranzules on p. 41 and then again on p. 51. On p. 50, he finds himself in a 'callejón sin salida que te obliga volver sobre tus pasos' (*CJ*, pp. 30 and 38; 'a blind alley that forces you to retrace your steps', p. 38).

45. Gould Levine is of the opinion that this novel is structured around the Classical unities (*Destrucción creadora*, pp. 132–3). Nevertheless, it departs from this ordering principle by its circularity. The classical works, after all, hinge upon immense and irreversible events taking place within the framwork of the unities, so that even if time, place, and action are strictly limited, the narrative does move inexorably forward form the beginning to the end of the piece.

Genaro Pérez convincingly links the cyclical, ritualistic structure of *DJ* with certain mythological figures mentioned in the text: 'The purpose of the myth of Sisyphus in *Don Julián* parallels that of Prometheus .... Both myths stress the protagonist's involvement in a daily ritual .... The allusions to the phoenix ... reinforce the motif of recurrence provided by the myths of Prometheus and Sisyphus' (pp. 169–70). Gould Levine also makes this point, but more briefly (*Destrucción creadora*, p. 250).

46. For a vivid expression of this, see *PB*, p. 165; *LB*, pp. 133–4.

47. 'Proceso a la izquierda', in *Libertad, libertad, libertad*, pp. 49–79 (p. 78).

48. This is at least what the fiction conveys. However, the matter is presented in a more balanced light in an essay: 'He vivido en un dilema insoluble: el que opone la visión estética y hedonista del mundo a un enfoque exclusivamente moral. Mi indignación ante las condiciones de pobreza y desamparo en que viven los hombres a quienes más cercano me siento chocan de frente con la seducción íntima de un paisaje desnudo y áspero, de una serie de virtudes primitivas inexorablemente barridas por el progreso e industrialización' ('La Chanca, veinte años después', in *Voces*, pp. 12–13; 'I have lived in the trap of an insoluble dilemma: the aesthetic and hedonistic vision of the world as opposed to an exclusively moral

focus. My indignation at the conditions of poverty and lack of shelter in which the men to whom I feel closest live, clashes head on with the deep-seated seduction of bare, harsh scenery, of a series of primitive virtues inexorably swept away by progress and industrialization').

## Chapter 5

1. 'An ancient sea-god, one of the "Old Men of the Sea"; he is occasionally described as a son of Poseidon, but was probably a more ancient deity. He herded the flocks of seals and sea-creatures for Poseidon, and possessed the gift of prophecy, but was unwilling to disclose what he knew and tried to escape questioners by assuming a variety of shapes, including fire and water and the forms of wild beasts.'
Michael Grant and John Hazel, *Who's Who in Classical Mythology*, Teach Yourself (London, 1979), p. 295.

2. Anne Wilson, *Traditional Romance and Tale: How Stories Mean* (Ipswich, 1976), p. 88.

3. *The 'Metamorphoses' of Ovid*, translated by Mary M. Innes, Penguin Classics (Harmondsworth, Middlesex, 1983), p. 133.

4. Ovid, p. 72.

5. This and the lament of Cadmus's wife, quoted below, in Ovid, p. 109.

6. Ovid, p. 110.

7. Robert Louis Stevenson, *The Strange Case of Dr Jekyll and Mr Hyde* (1886), edited by Jenni Calder, Penguin English Library (Harmondsworth, Middlesex, 1983), p. 82.

8. Stevenson, p. 85.

9. Hesse, p. 22 (my italics).

10. Homer, *The Odyssey*, translated by E. V. Rieu, Penguin Classics, 51 (Harmondsworth, Middlesex, 1967), p. 162.

11. Homer, p. 163 (my italics).

12. Pérez, p. 149.

13. Erich Neumann, *The Origins and History of Consciousness*, translated by R. F. C. Hull, Bollingen, 42, second printing, with corrections and amended bibliography (New York, 1964), p. 87.

14. Genaro Pérez sees this as a technique taken by Goytisolo from Russian Formalism, and using the terminology of this school of criticism, calls it 'laying bare' (pp. 13 and 108). Spires calls it 'self-conscious narration', observing that 'with its focus on the very process of writing, [this] serves to free language from external reality by converting cultural codes; the point of reference switches from external reality to the coming-into-being of the novel as reality' ('From Neorealism and the New Novel . . .', p. 77).

15. Maryvonne Perrot, *L'Homme et la Métamorphose*, Publications de l'Université de Dijon, 56 (Paris, 1979), p. 10.

16. Gould Levine regards the voice of the narrator-creator who is speaking here as that of Goytisolo himself ('*Juan sin tierra*: Goytisolo se retrata', in *Juan sin tierra*, pp. 27–47 (pp. 35–6)). Except inasmuch as all voices in all texts are those of the author, this would seem a little presumptuous. I would favour the views of Otero and Cabrera Infante. Otero says of *Juan sin tierra*, that 'si se lee como una obra de ficción, como parece natural, una consecuencia importante es que el tú-yo del texto no puede ser el autor, por muchas que sean las "señas de identidad" que tengan en común . . . . El tú-yo del texto no puede ser más que un ente de ficción, un ente mimético (en

sentido aristotélico)' ('Lengua y cultura ...', in *Juan sin tierra*, edited by Paz, p. 136; 'if it is read as a work of fiction, as seems natural, an important consequence is that the you-I of the text cannot be the author, however many "marks of identity" they may have in common .... The you-I of the text can be no more than a fictional entity, a mimetic entity (in the Aristotelian sense)'). Cabrera Infante observes, with reference to the ending of *JT* when the narrator bids farewell to the Spanish language, that 'muchos lectores han creído que el autor hace promesa de no escribir más en español y éste tiene que reiterar que quien hace esa declaración no es él sino el personaje' ('El fin como principio', in *Juan sin tierra*, edited by Paz, p. 227; 'many readers have thought that the author makes a promise not to write in Spanish any more and he has to reiterate that the one who makes that declaration is not he but the personage'). Goytisolo himself says about *Juan sin tierra* that 'a veces se cae en la ingenuidad de convertir al autor en el narrador; lo que yo quise hacer con esta novela fue terminar la trilogía del personaje Mendiola' ('Juan Goytisolo: La creación literaria como liberación', interview by Milagros Sánchez Arnosi, *Insula*, 426 (May, 1982), 4; 'people are sometimes ingenuous enough to turn the author into the narrator; what I wanted to do in this novel was to finish the trilogy of the Mendiola character').

17. Ovid, p. 69.
18. A similar point is made by Genaro Pérez (p. 171). However, I would take issue with his assertion that 'in contrast to the lotus-eaters of ancient Greece, the narrator does not forget his national origin', for although it may be only a fleeting achievement, he does declare himself a pure Arab at this point. The only possible reading that would justify Pérez's claim would be for 'árabe, árabe puro' to apply to the café and its atmosphere only, and not to the narrator himself. This seems an excessively restrictive interpretation.
19. Ovid, p. 45.
20. Harold Skulsky, *Metamorphosis: The Mind in Exile* (Cambridge, Massachusetts, 1981), p. 48. Metamorphosis of Philemon and Baucis: Ovid, p. 198. Myrrha: p. 238. Heliades: p. 59.
21. Orwell, pp. 227–8.
22. This scene will be discussed in more depth below.
23. Skulsky, p. 28.
24. Perrot, p. 39, Perrot's italics.
25. Perrot, p. 25.
26. Perrot, p. 43.
27. Stevenson, p. 40 (both quotations).
28. Ovid, pp. 174–5.
29. Ovid, p. 210.
30. Ovid, pp. 215–21. However, the matter is complex and contradictory in Ovid, as discussed above.
31. Stevenson, p. 40.
32. Although this is a quotation from Lawrence's *Seven Pillars of Wisdom*, Goytisolo could have cited it in Spanish. The fact that he places these English phrases in the middle of a Spanish sentence suggests that some additional point, aside from the fact that this is a quotation, should be drawn. The language change could indicate the protagonist's eagerness to abandon his Spanish identity in becoming an Arab. Perhaps he moves into English rather than Arabic, only in order that the reader may have a good chance of understanding; English here would then stand for 'foreign' rather than carry any specifically national overtones.
33. In *Crónicas sarracinas*, pp. 29–31.
34. Stevenson, p. 84.

35. Stevenson, p. 82.
36. Carl Gustav Jung, *Psychology and Alchemy*, translated by R. F. C. Hull, second edition (London, 1968), p. 427.
37. As well as Jung's work, cited in note 36, the following provide background on alchemy and its practitioners:
    Neil Powell, *Alchemy, the Ancient Science*, The Supernatural (London, 1976), pp. 6–39 (simplified survey);
    Titus Burckhardt, *Alchemy: Science of the Cosmos, Science of the Soul*, translated by William Stoddart (London, 1967) (comprehensive).
38. Ovid, p. 50.
39. My view coincides here with Ugarte's: 'from the beginning of the trilogy to the end [and beyond, I would add], one of the most frequent and significant features is the author-protagonist's state of flux, a never-ending division, duplication, and permutation of identities' (p. 147).
40. Julián Ríos expresses the message of *JT* as follows: 'Que todo circule, se derroche, que fluyan las palabras y el semen, y que el vientre se mueva' ('Everything should circulate, spill, words and semen should flow, and the bowels should move'), which could surely be applied to all the later novels (Interview in *Juan sin tierra*, edited by Paz, pp. 9–25 (p. 13)).

## Chapter 6

1. H. Clay Trumbull, *The Blood Covenant: A Primitive Rite and its Bearings on Scripture* (London, 1887), pp. 5 and 38.
   E. and M. A. Radford, *Encyclopedia of Superstitions*, edited and revised by Christina Hole (London, 1961), pp. 57–8.
   Theodore Gaster, *Myth, Legend, and Custom in the Old Testament: A Comparative Study with Chapters from Sir James G. Frazer's 'Folklore in the Old Testament'* (London, 1969), pp. 65–9.
   Gabriel Ronay, *The Dracula Myth* (London, 1972), p. 109.
   Reay Tannahill, *Flesh and Blood: A History of the Cannibal Complex* (London 1975), pp. 6–8.
2. Ronay, p. 10.
3. The exact number and identity of the four humours was controversial, however. As we shall see, the great ancient physician, Galen, for example, sometimes counted blood as a humour in its own right, sometimes as a mixture of the other humours. For a detailed discussion of differing theories, see Rudolph E. Siegel, *Galen's System of Physiology and Medicine: An Analysis of his Doctrines and Observations on Bloodflow, Respiration, Humours and Internal Diseases* (Basel and New York, 1968), pp. 216–41. The best known scheme does count blood, though, giving the other three as phlegm (moist and cold, corresponding to water), black bile (cold and dry, corresponding to earth), and yellow bile (dry and hot, corresponding to fire).
4. Although Democritus (*c.* 460–370 B.C.) is usually accepted as the first Greek to apply the actual word *microcosm* to man, the idea can be traced far further back. See W. K. C. Guthrie, *A History of Greek Philosophy*, 2 vols (Cambridge, 1962), II: *The Pre-Socratic Tradition from Parmenides to Democritus*, pp. 471–2. It is also one of the tenets of alchemy. See Burckhardt, pp. 34–6.
5. Eduard Zeller, *Outlines of the History of Greek Philosophy*, translated by L. R. Palmer, thirteenth edition, revised by Wilhelm Nestle (London, 1931), p. 59. Confirmed by Guthrie, II, p. 143, fn. 1.

6. Fielding H. Garrison, *An Introduction to the History of Medicine, with Medical Chronology, Suggestions for Study and Bibliographical Data*, revised and enlarged fourth edition (London, 1929), p. 298.

7. Katharine Whitman Carson, *Aspects of Contemporary Society in 'Gil Blas'*, Studies on Voltaire and the Eighteenth Century, 110 (Banbury, Oxfordshire, 1973), p. 138. See also Garrison, p. 419.

8. Tonelete, the 'barrel-shaped gentleman' in the translation (from Spanish *tonel* = 'barrel') is General Franco, but with an echo of the famous bullfighter known as Manolete, linking up with all the sarcasm heaped on the ideology and symbolism of the bullfight, which in turn is associated with the Seneca figure, another image for both Franco and the ideal toreador.

9. Lesage, I, p. 81 (Book 2, Ch. 3). The variations in spelling of the doctor's name seem puzzling. The French text has *Sangrado*, Ganivet calls him *Sangredo*, and Goytisolo uses *Sagredo*. The latter's omission of the *n* is perhaps deliberate, though, for it adds a nuance of *sagrado* ('sacred'), linking the name to the attack on the Church as well as to the destruction of *la España sagrada*.

10. Ganivet, p. 7.

11. Ganivet, pp. 7–8.

12. The issue of transubstantiation is not relevant to the present argument, as the concept of drinking Christ's blood remains constant, whether one believes the communion wine really undergoes transformation into blood or is a symbol of it.

13. See above, chapter 2. Examples of this conflict between body and soul are to be found in Saint Bernard of Clairvaux, pp. 249–50. By way of further illustration, see Norman Cohn, *The Pursuit of the Millen-nium: Revolutionary Millenarians and Mystical Anarchists of the Middle Ages*, revised and expanded edition (London, 1970), on the behaviour of self-flagellant groups (p. 133).

14. Mircea Eliade also recognizes the significance of this, although he differs from Goytisolo in regarding it as positive: 'Le grand mérite du christianisme ... a été de valoriser la souffrance: de transformer la douleur d'état négatif en expérience à contenu spirituel "positif"' (*Le Mythe de l'Eternel Retour: Archétypes et Répétition*, Les Essais, 34, second edition (Paris, 1949), p. 141).

15. Emilia Pardo Bazán, *La cuestión palpitante* (1883), edited by Carmen Bravo-Villasante, Biblioteca Anaya, 74, second edition (Salamanca, 1970), p. 151.

16. 'En conexiones tan estrechas como la de la sangre y el color rojo, es evidente que ambos elementos exprésanse mutuamente' (Cirlot, p. 370; 'In connections as close as blood and the colour red, each element clearly expresses the other'). According to Genaro Pérez, she represents 'aggressive and vindictive sexuality' (p. 177), which would fit in with the use of red, implying blood's associations with both violence and sexuality.

17. This is stressed more heavily than it appears out of context, for it echoes the preacher's earlier use of Latin for the same reason: on p. 32 of *JT*, he tells the Virgen Blanca, 'sanguis menstruationis devorant!'.

18. Untouchability here is not the kind that arises from fear of pollution by a pariah, of course, but the taboos of the sacred, analogous to those attached to priests and kings in primitive societies. However, anthropologists observe that the polar opposition that we may feel between these two types of untouchability is not shared by

primitive peoples. See Frazer, for example, *The Golden Bough*, II: *Taboo and the Perils of the Soul*, p. 224.

19. 'Estebanillo Gómez, hombre de buen amor', in *El furgón de cola* (1967), Biblioteca Breve (Barcelona, 1976), pp. 95–120 (in which he alludes respectfully to Cervantes and *Lazarillo* as well as to *Estebanillo Gómez*).
'La España de Fernando de Rojas', in *Disidencias*, pp. 13–35.
'Quevedo: la obsesión excremental', in *Disidencias*, pp. 117–35.
'Cara y cruz del moro en nuestra literatura', in *Crónicas sarracinas*, pp. 7–25 (in which he calls Calderón 'nuestro gran dramaturgo', 'our great dramatist' (p. 14)).

20. Melveena McKendrick, 'Honour/ Vengeance in the Spanish "Comedia": A Case of Mimetic Transference?', *Modern Language Review*, 79 (April 1984), 313–35 (pp. 318–19, 322).

21. See also Goytisolo's comments on the survival of the preoccupation with *limpieza* during the lifetime of Blanco White (1775–1841) ('Presentación Crítica', pp. 74–6).

22. 'Abandonemos de una vez . . .', *El país*.

23. 'Abandonemos de una vez . . .', *El país*.

24. 'Obras occidentales sobre Oriente Próximo y el Maghreb . . . [dan a] los fantasmas o imágenes sexuales . . . un papel primordial . . . .
Las "fantasías orientales" están pobladas de harenes, esclavas, mancebos, princesas, velos, danzas eróticas, sexualidad desbordante' (Goytisolo, 'De "Don Julián" a "Makbara" . . .', in *Crónicas sarracinas*, p. 32; 'Occidental works on the Near East and the Maghreb . . . [give] sexual phantasms or images . . . a major role . . . "Oriental fantasies" are

peopled by harems, slave-girls, young boys, princesses, veils, erotic dances, overflowing sexuality').

25. It is worth noting that one of the definitions of *inocular* is 'comunicar a alguien cosas tales como vicios o ideas nocivas' (María Moliner, *Diccionario de uso del español*, Biblioteca Románica Hispánica: Diccionarios, 5, 2 vols (Madrid, 1981); 'to communicate things like vices or harmful ideas to someone').
In discussion the significance of 'the ritual shedding of the child's blood' (p. 180), Genaro Pérez seems to have confused injection of poison into the child's blood with the spilling of blood, even though his eventual death is a bloodless hanging.

26. 'Latin is a parodic signifier for social mores which deny the animalistic dimension of human existence.' Robert C. Spires, 'Latrines, Whirlpools and Voids: The Metafictional Mode of *Juan sin tierra*', *Hispanic Review*, 48 (1980), 151–69 (p. 160).

27. Ronay, p. 10 and Trumbull, p. 124.

28. Hippolyte Delehaye, *Les Origines du culte des martyrs* (Brussels, 1912), p. 5.

29. 'The emperor or judge is generally presented as . . . thirsting for blood.' Hippolyte Delehaye, *The Legends of the Saints*, translated by Donald Attwater (London, 1962), p. 69.
In contrast, martyrs are ubiquitously associated with whiteness; according to *The Golden Legend*, Saint Agnes, for example, is given 'a tunic of dazzling whiteness' by an angel, to replace the clothes that have been torn from her, and eight days after her martyrdom, she appears 'with a lamb whiter than snow'. Jacobus de Voragine, *The Golden Legend*,

translated by Granger Ryan and Helmut Ripperger (New York, 1948), pp. 111–12.

## Conclusion

1. It is significant with respect to the rejection of differentiation in Goytisolo's fiction that the public place where the storyteller plies his trade is the market, for as Stallybrass and White observe: 'At the market centre of the polis we discover a commingling of categories usually kept separate and opposed: centre and periphery, inside and outside, stranger and local, commerce and festivity, high and low' (p. 27).

## Afterword

1. This is my literal translation; for a poetic, freer rendering of the *Cántico*, see St John of the Cross, *Poems*, translated by Roy Campbell, Penguin Classics (Harmondsworth, Middlesex, 1960), pp. 30–43 (the lines quoted, p. 37).

# Bibliography

The bibliography is divided into three sections: first, texts by Goytisolo, followed by interviews; second, criticism of his work; third, all other material. Works listed that have not have been cited explicitly are included because they have provided me with useful background and are recommended further reading. Each section is arranged in alphabetical order.

## 1. Texts by Goytisolo

'Abandonemos de una vez el amoroso cultivo de nuestras señas de identidad', *El país*, 10 April 1984, pp. 11–12

*Coto vedado*, Biblioteca Breve (Barcelona, 1985)

*Count Julian*, translated by Helen Lane (London, 1989)

*Crónicas sarracinas* (Barcelona, 1982)

*Disidencias*, Biblioteca Breve (Barcelona, 1977)

*Duelo en el Paraíso*, Destinolibro, 63, third edition (Barcelona, 1985)

*El furgón de cola*, Biblioteca Breve (Barcelona, 1976)

*En los reinos de Taifa*, Biblioteca Breve, second edition (Barcelona, 1986)

*Juan sin tierra*, Biblioteca Breve, third edition (Barcelona, 1982)

*Juan the Landless*, translated by Helen R. Lane (New York, 1977)

*Juegos de manos*, Destinolibro, 39 (Barcelona, 1977)

*Landscapes After the Battle*, translated by Helen Lane (London, 1987)

*Libertad, libertad, libertad*, Colección Ibérica, 8 (Barcelona, 1978)

*Makbara*, Biblioteca Breve, fourth edition (Barcelona, 1983)

*Makbara*, translated by Helen R. Lane (New York, 1981)

*Marks of Identity*, translated by Gregory Rabassa (London, 1988)

'Novela, crítica y creación', *Revista Iberoamericana*, 47 (July–December 1981), 23–31

*Obras completas*, Biblioteca de Autores Modernos, 2 vols (Madrid, 1977) [contains early works only]

*Paisajes después de la batalla*, Visio Tundali/ Contemporáneos (Barcelona, 1982)

'Por qué he escogido vivir en París', in *Voces: Juan Goytisolo*, ed. by Pere Gimferrer (Barcelona, 1981), pp. 9–11

'Presentación crítica de J. M. Blanco White', in *Obra inglesa de D. José María Blanco White*, translated and ed. by Juan Goytisolo, Biblioteca Breve, third edition (Barcelona, 1982), pp. 1–98

*Reivindicación del conde don Julián*, Biblioteca Breve, second edition (Barcelona, 1982)

*Reivindicación del conde don Julián*, ed. by Linda Gould Levine, with an appendix by José Manuel Martín, Letras Hispánicas (Madrid, 1985)

*Señas de identidad*, Novelistas Contemporáneos (Mexico City, 1966)

*Señas de identidad*, Biblioteca Universal Formentor (Barcelona, 1980)

*Las virtudes del pájaro solitario*, Biblioteca Breve (Barcelona, 1988)

*The Young Assassins* [*Juegos de manos*], translated by John Rust (London, 1960)

## Interviews

de Decker, Jacques, *Le Soir*, 31 December 1985

Harguindey, Angel S., 'Juan Goytisolo: El ritmo de las cigüeñas', *El país semanal*, 13 January 1985, 10–17

Hernández, José A., *Modern Language Notes*, 91/2 (March, 1976), 337–55

Riera, Miguel, 'Regreso al origen', *Quimera*, 73 (January 1988), 36–40

Rodríguez Monegal, Emir, *El arte de narrar: diálogos*, Prisma (Caracas, 1968)

Sánchez Arnosi, Milagros, 'Juan Goytisolo: La creación literaria como liberación', *Insula*, 37/426 (May, 1982), 4

## 2.   Criticism of Goytisolo

Buckley, Ramón, *Problemas formales en la novela española contemporánea*, second edition (Barcelona, 1973)

Gimferrer, Pere, ed., *Voces: Juan Goytisolo* (Barcelona, 1981)

Gould Levine, Linda, *Juan Goytisolo: La destrucción creadora*, Confrontaciones: Los Críticos (Mexico City, 1976)

Gould Levine, Linda, '*Makbara*: Entre la espada y la pared–¿política marxista o política sexual?', *Revista Iberoamericana*, 47 (July–December 1981), 97–106

Lázaro, Jesús, *La novelística de Juan Goytisolo* (Madrid, 1984)

Lee, Abigail E., '*La paradigmática historia de Caperucita y el lobo feroz*: Juan Goytisolo's use of Little Red Riding Hood' in *Reivindicación del conde don Julián*', *Bulletin of Hispanic Studies*, 65 (April 1988), 141–51

Lee, Abigail E., 'Sterne's Legacy to Juan Goytisolo: A Shandyian Reading of *Juan sin tierra*', *Modern Language Review*, 84 (April, 1989), 351–7

Lee Six, Abigail, 'Breaking Rules, Making History: A Postmodern Reading of Historiography in Juan Goytisolo's Fiction', forthcoming in the *Yearbook of Postmodern Studies: History and Postmodern Writing* (Leiden, 1990)

Navajas, Gonzalo, *La novela de Juan Goytisolo*, Temas, 15 (Madrid, 1979)

Paz, Octavio and others, eds, *Juan sin tierra*, Espiral/Revista 2 (Madrid, 1977)

Pérez, Genaro, *Formalist Elements in the Novels of Juan Goytisolo*, Studia Humanitatis (Potomac, Maryland, 1979)

Romero, Hector R., '*Juan sin tierra*: Análisis de un texto literario', *Anales de la Novela de Posguerra*, 1 (1976), 85–107

Sanz, Santos, *Lectura de Juan Goytisolo*, Ambito Literario (Barcelona, 1977)

Schaefer-Rodríguez, Claudia, *Juan Goytisolo: Del 'realismo crítico' a la utopía*, Ensayos (Madrid, 1984)

Sobejano, Gonzalo and others, eds, *Juan Goytisolo*, Espiral/Fundamentos (Madrid, 1975)

Spires, Robert C., 'From Neorealism and the New Novel to the Self-Referential Novel: Juan Goytisolo's *Juan sin tierra*', *Anales de la Narrativa Española Contemporánea*, 5 (1980), 73–82

Spires, Robert C., 'Latrines, Whirlpools and Voids: The Metafictional Mode of *Juan sin tierra*', *Hispanic Review*, 48 (1980), 151–69

Ugarte, Michael, *Trilogy of Treason: An Intertextual Study of Juan Goytisolo* (London, 1982)

## 3.   Other Material

Adams, Michael, *Single-minded: A Tract on Chastity, mainly in the Context of Celibacy* (Dublin, 1979)

Alvarez Pérez, Antonio, ed. *Prosa y verso: libro de lectura para parvulitos* (Valladolid, 1962)

Aquinas, Saint Thomas, *Summa Theologiae*, edition and translation led by Michael Cardinal Browne and Aniceto Fernández, 61 vols (London 1964–81), 28, translated and ed. by Thomas Gilby (1966)

Atkinson, William C., *A History of Spain and Portugal*, Pelican History of the World, A464 (Harmondsworth, Middlesex, 1960)

Baron, Robert A. and Donn Byrne, *Social Psychology: Understanding Human Interaction*, second edition (Boston, Massachusetts, 1978)

Becker, Howard S., *Outsiders: Studies in the Sociology of Deviance* (London, 1963)

Bellamy, Edward *Looking Backward: 2000–1887* (1888), Penguin American Library (Harmondsworth, Middlesex, 1982)

Bernard of Clairvaux, Saint, *Sermons on Conversion*, translated by Marie-Bernard Saïd Osb (Kalamazoo, Michigan, 1981)

The Bible, King James Authorized Version

Bouglé, C., *Essais sur le Régime des Castes* (Paris, 1908)

Braunthal, Alfred, *Salvation and the Perfect Society: The Eternal Quest* (Amherst, Massachusetts, 1979)

Burckhardt, Titus, *Alchemy: Science of the Cosmos, Science of the Soul*, translated by William Stoddart (London, 1967)

Butler, Samuel, *Erewhon* (1872), ed. by Peter Mudford, Penguin English

Library (Harmondsworth, Middlesex, 1970)

Campbell, Joseph, *The Hero with a Thousand Faces*, Bollingen, 17 (Princeton, New Jersey, 1968)

Carranza de Miranda, Bartolomé, *Comentarios sobre el Catechismo christiano* (1543), Biblioteca de Autores Cristianos, 2 vols (Madrid, 1972)

Cela, Camilo José, *El gallego y su cuadrilla y otros apuntes carpetovetónicos* (1955), Destinolibro, 27 (Barcelona, 1976)

Cervantes Saavedra, Miguel de, *El ingenioso hidalgo don Quijote de la Mancha*, ed. by John Jay Allen, Letras Hispánicas, 2 vols (Madrid, 1977)

Cervantes Saavedra, Miguel de, *The Adventures of Don Quixote*, translated by J. M. Cohen, Penguin Classics (London, 1950)

*Chambers Twentieth Century Dictionary*, ed. by A. M. MacDonald, revised edition with supplement (Edinburgh, 1977)

Cioranescu, Alexandre, *L'Avenir du passé: Utopie et littérature*, Les Essais, 171 (Paris, 1972)

Cirlot, Juan-Eduardo, *Diccionario de símbolos tradicionales* (Barcelona, 1958)

Cohn, Norman, *The Pursuit of the Millennium: Revolutionary Millenarians and Mystical Anarchists of the Middle Ages*, revised and expanded edition (London, 1970)

Curtius, Ernst Robert, *European Literature and the Latin Middle Ages*, translated by Willard R. Trask (London and Henley, 1979)

*The Paradise of Dante Alighieri*, ed. and translated by Arthur John Butler (London, 1885)

Delehaye, Hippolyte, *The Legends of the Saints*, translated by Donald Attwater (London, 1962)

Delehaye, Hippolyte, *Les Origines du culte des martyrs* (Brussels, 1912)

*Dictionnaire de Théologie Catholique*, ed. by A. Vacant, E. Mangenot, and E. Amann, third edition, 15 vols (Paris, 1923)

Douglas, Mary, *Purity and Danger: An Analysis of Concepts of Pollution and Taboo* (London, 1966)

Eisler, Robert, *Man into Wolf: An Anthropological Interpretation of Sadism, Masochism, and Lycanthropy* (London, 1951)

Eliade Mircea, *Myth and Reality*, World Perspectives, 21 (London, 1964)

Eliade, Mircea, *Le Mythe de l'Eternel Retour: Archétypes et Répétition*, Les Essais, 34, second edition (Paris, 1949)

Forrester, Duncan B., *Caste and Christianity: Attitudes and Policies on Caste of Anglo-Saxon Protestant Missions in India*, (London, 1980)

Frazer, Sir James George, *The Golden Bough: A study in Magic and Religion*, third edition, 13 vols (London, 1980)

Freud, Sigmund, *The Pelican Freud Library*, ed. by A. Richards, 9, translated by J. Strachey (Harmondsworth, Middlesex, 1979)

Frye, Northrop, *The Anatomy of Criticism: Four Essays* (Princeton, New Jersey, 1973)

*Funk and Wagnall's Standard Dictionary of Folklore, Mythology, and Legend*, ed.

by Maria Leach (London, 1975)

Ganivet, Angel, *Idearium español*, third reprinting (Madrid, 1915)

García Lorca, Federico, *El público y comedia sin título: dos obras teatrales póstumas*, edited by Rafael Martínez Nadal and Marie Laffranque, Biblioteca Breve (Barcelona, 1978)

García Morente, Manuel, *Idea de la hispanidad*, expanded third edition (Madrid, 1947)

Garrison, Fielding H., *An Introduction to the History of Medicine, with Medical Chronology, Suggestions for Study and Bibliographical Data*, revised and enlarged fourth edition (London, 1929)

Gaster, Theodor H., *Myth, Legend, and Custom in the Old Testament: A Comparative Study with Chapters from Sir James G. Frazer's 'Folklore in the Old Testament'*, (London, 1969)

Gilson, Etienne, *The Mystical Theology of Saint Bernard*, translated by A. H. C. Downes (London, 1940)

Grant, Michael and John Hazel, *Who's Who in Classical Mythology*, Teach Yourself (London, 1979)

Guthrie, W. K. C., *A History of Greek Philosophy*, 2 vols (Cambridge, 1962)

Harrison, Jane, *Epilegomena to the Study of Greek Religion* (Cambridge, 1921)

Heidel, Alexander, *The Babylonian Genesis: The Story of the Creation* (Chicago, 1942)

Hertzler, Joyce Oramel, *The History of Utopian Thought* (New York, 1923)

Hesiod, *Works and Days*, translated and ed. by Dorothy Wender, Penguin Classics (Harmondsworth, Middlesex, 1973)

Hesse, Hermann, *Steppenwolf* (1927), translated by Basil Creighton, revised by Walter Sorell (London, 1974)

Hole, Christina, *Saints in Folklore* (London, 1966)

Homer, *The Odyssey*, translated by E. V. Rieu, Penguin Classics, 51 (Harmondsworth, Middlesex, 1967)

Huxley, Aldous, *Brave New World* (1932) (London, 1971)

John of the Cross, Saint, *Poems*, translated by Roy Campbell, Penguin Classics (Harmondsworth, Middlesex, 1960)

Juan de la Cruz, San, *Poesía*, edited by Domingo Ynduráin, Letras Hispánicas, third edition (Madrid, 1987)

Jung, Carl Gustav, *Modern Man in Search of a Soul*, translated by W. S. Dell and Cary F. Baynes (London, 1933)

Jung, Carl Gustav, *Psychology and Alchemy*, translated by R. F. C. Hull, second edition (London, 1968)

Jung, Carl Gustav, *Psychology and Religion*, Terry Lectures (New Haven, Connecticut, 1938)

Jung, Carl Gustav and C. Kerényi, *Introduction to a Science of Mythology: The Myth of the Divine Child*, translated by R. F. C. Hull (London, 1951)

Kafka, Franz, *Metamorphosis and Other Stories*, translated by Willa and Edwin Muir, Penguin Modern Classics (Harmondsworth, Middlesex,

1984) (*Metamorphosis* first published 1916)

Kiesler, Charles A. and Sara B. Kiesler, *Conformity* (Reading, Massachusetts, 1970)

*The Koran Interpreted*, translation of Koran by Arthur J. Arberry (London, 1964)

Kuhn, Reinhard, *Corruption in Paradise: The Child in Western Literature* (Hanover, New Hampshire, 1982)

Labanyi, Jo, 'Myth and Literature: An Antidote to Alienation, or Political Mystification?', *Spanish Studies*, 4 (1982), 15–29

Larra, Mariano José de, *Obras completas de Fígaro*, fourth edition, 2 vols (Paris, 1874)

Lawrence, T. E., *Seven Pillars of Wisdom: A Triumph*, new edition and format with amendments (London, 1973)

*The Original Poems of Fray Luis de León*, ed. by Edward Sarmiento, Spanish Texts (Manchester, 1953)

*The Unknown Light: The Poems of Fray Luis de León*, edited and translated by Willis Barnstone (New York, 1979)

Lesage, Alain René, *Histoire de Gil Blas de Santillane* (1715–35), ed. by Maurice Bardon, 2 vols (Paris, 1955)

Lewis, C. S., *The Discarded Image: An Introduction to Medieval and Renaissance Literature* (Cambridge, 1964)

Lewis, C. S., *An Experiment in Criticism* (Cambridge, 1965)

Maccoby, Hyam, *The Sacred Executioner: Human Sacrifice and the Legacy of Guilt* (London, 1982)

Mannheim, Karl, *Ideology and Utopia: An Introduction to the Sociology of Knowledge* (London, 1960)

Manuel, Frank E., ed., *Utopias and Utopian Thought* (Boston, Massachusetts, 1971)

McKendrick, Melveena, 'Honour/Vengeance in the Spanish "Comedia": A Case of Mimetic Transference?', *Modern Language Review*, 79 (April 1984), 313–35

Menéndez Pidal, R., ed., *Flor nueva de romances viejos*, expanded second edition (Madrid, 1933)

More, Saint Thomas, *Utopia* (1516), translated and ed. by Paul Turner, Penguin Classics (Harmondsworth, Middlesex, 1965)

Morford, P. O. and Robert J. Lenardon, *Classical Mythology*, second edition (London, 1977)

Morris, William, *News from Nowhere; or, An Epoch of Rest, being some chapters from a utopian romance* (1890), Routledge English Texts (London, 1970)

Murray, Henry A., ed., *Myth and Mythmaking* (Boston, Massachusetts, 1969)

Neumann, Erich, *The Origins and History of Consciousness*, translated by R. F. C. Hull, Bollingen, 42, second printing with corrections and amended bibliography (New York, 1964)

Opie, Iona and Peter, *The Classic Fairy Tales* (London, 1974)

Orwell, George, *Nineteen Eighty-Four: A Novel* (1949), Penguin Modern Classics (Harmondsworth, Middlesex, 1954)

*The 'Metamorphoses' of Ovid*, translated by Mary M. Innes, Penguin Classics (Harmondsworth, Middlesex, 1983)

Pardo Bazán, Emilia, *La cuestión palpitante*, ed. by Carmen Bravo Villa-sante, Anaya, 74, second edition (Salamanca, 1970)

Parrinder, Geoffrey, *Sex in the World's Religions* (London, 1980)

Pascal, Blaise, *Pensées*, Brunschvicg text (Paris, 1976)

Perrault, *Contes*, Classiques Garnier (Paris, 1967)

Perrot, Maryvonne, *L'Homme et la Métamorphose*, Publications de l'Université de Dijon, 56 (Paris, 1979)

*Plato's 'Phaedo'*, translated with introduction and commentary by R. Hackforth (Cambridge, 1955)

Plato, *The Republic*, translated by H. D. P. Lee, Penguin Classics (Harmondsworth, Middlesex, 1955)

Powell, Neil, *Alchemy: The Ancient Science*, The Supernatural (London, 1976)

Radford, E. and M. A. , *Encyclopedia of Superstitions*, ed. by Christina Hole (London, 1961)

Roberts, Robert, *The Social Laws of the Qoran, considered and compared with those of Hebrew and other ancient codes*, new edition (London, 1971)

Ronay, Gabriel, *The Dracula Myth* (London, 1972)

Ruthven, K. K. , *Myth*, the Critical Idiom, 31 (London, 1976)

El-Saleh, Soubhi, *La Vie future selon le Coran*, Etudes Musulmanes, 13 (Paris, 1971)

Sanford, Charles L., *The Quest for Paradise: Europe and the American Moral Imagination* (Urbana, Illinois, 1961)

Schoonenberg, Piet, *Man and Sin: A Theological View*, translated by Joseph Donceel (London, 1965)

Sebeok, Thomas A., ed., *Myth: A Symposium*, Bibliographical and Special Series of American Folklore Society (Bloomington, Indiana, 1958)

Siegel, Rudolph E., *Galen's System of Physiology and Medicine: An Analysis of his Doctrines and Observations on Bloodflow, Respiration, Humours and Internal Diseases* (Basel and New York, 1968)

Skulsky, Harold, *Metamorphosis: The Mind in Exile* (Cambridge, Massachusetts, 1981)

Stallybrass, Peter and Allon White, *The Politics and Poetics of Transgression* (London, 1986)

Stevenson, Robert Louis, *The Strange Case of Dr Jekyll and Mr Hyde and Other Stories*, ed. by Jenni Calder, Penguin English Library (Harmondsworth, Middlesex, 1979) (*Jekyll and Hyde* first published 1886)

Swift, Jonathan, *Gulliver's Travels* (1726), ed. by Peter Dixon and John Chalker, Penguin Classics (Harmondsworth, Middlesex, 1985)

Tannahill, Reay, *Flesh and Blood: A History of the Cannibal Complex* (London, 1975)

Trumbull, H. Clay, *The Blood Covenant: A Primitive Rite and its Bearings on Scripture* (London, 1887)

Tuveson, Ernest Lee, *Millenium and Utopia: A Study in the Background of the Idea of Progress*, Harper Torchbooks (New York, 1964)

Unamuno, Miguel de, *Abel Sánchez: una historia de pasión* (1917), in *Obras completas*, ed. by Manuel García Blanco, 9 vols (Madrid, 1967), II, pp. 683–759

Vickery, John B., ed., *Myth and Literature: Contemporary Theory and Practice* (Lincoln, Nebraska, 1966)

*The Aeneid of Virgil*, translated by C. Day Lewis (London, 1952)

Voragine, Jacobus de, *The Golden Legend*, translated by Granger Ryan and Helmut Ripperger (New York, 1948)

Vossler, Karl, *La poesía de la soledad en España*, translated by Ramón Gómez de la Serna y Espina, Estudios Literarios (Buenos Aires, 1946)

Walsh, Chad, *From Utopia to Nightmare* (London, 1962)

White, John J., *Mythology in the Modern Novel: A Study of Prefigurative Techniques* (Princeton, New Jersey, 1971)

Whitman Carson, Katharine, *Aspects of Contemporary Society in 'Gil Blas'*, Studies on Voltaire and the Eighteenth Century, 110 (Banbury, Oxfordshire, 1973)

Widengren, Geo, *Mani and Manichaeism*, translated by Charles Kessler, revised by the author, History of Religion (London, 1965)

Wilde, Oscar, *The Picture of Dorian Gray* (1891), Penguin Modern Classics (Harmondsworth, Middlesex, 1979)

Wilkins, Leslie T., *Social Deviance: Social Policy, Action, and Research* (London, 1964)

Williams, Watkin, *Saint Bernard of Clairvaux* (Manchester, 1953)

Wilson, Anne, *Traditional Romance and Tale: How Stories Mean* (Ipswich, 1976)

Zeller, Eduard, *Outlines of the History of Greek Philosophy*, translated by L. R. Palmer, thirteenth edition, revised by Wilhelm Nestle (London, 1931)

Zipes, Jack, *Fairy Tales and the Art of Subversion: The Classical Genre for Children and the Process of Civilization* (London, 1983)

# Index

Goytisolo's texts are abbreviated by their Spanish titles only (see p. viii for key). Other works cited are listed under the author's name.